This book is a gift to

_____

From

_____

Date

_____

MORE THAN
CONQUERORS

We are more than conquerors through
Christ who loved us. Rom. 8:37

CHRISTIAN ART
PUBLISHERS

Originally published by Christelike Uitgewersmaatskappy
under the title *Meer as oorwinnaars*

© 2009

English edition
© 2009 Christian Art Publishers
PO Box 1599, Vereeniging, 1930, RSA

First edition 2009

Translated by Mandy Steele

Cover designed by Christian Art Publishers

Images used under license from Shutterstock.com

Scripture quotations are taken from the *Holy Bible*,
New International Version® NIV®.
Copyright © 1973, 1978, 1984 by International Bible Society.
Used by permission of Zondervan Publishing House.
All rights reserved.

Set in 12 on 15 pt Palatino LT Std
by Christian Art Publishers

Printed in China

ISBN 978-1-77036-183-6

11   12   13   14   15   16   17   18   19   20   –   13   12   11   10   9   8   7   6   5   4

Dedication:

To my wife, Louise, who has
lovingly shared 55 years of her life with me.

Introduction

We live in challenging times. Broken marriages, violence, horrific crimes and the adverse economic climate have a destructive influence on all areas of society.

The average person is not left untouched by this disturbing state of affairs. Many people fear the future, and the rising cost of living and meager salaries compound this fear.

In contrast to this chaos is an eternal God who cares and who is waiting to complete His work of salvation. He wants to strengthen your spiritual life with everlasting qualities: love that triumphs over hate; hope that unlocks the future; and faith that forms the foundation for your daily life. Like three unending rivers of grace, faith, hope and love flow into each other. Their origin is in God. They refresh our souls and shape us into the people God intended us to be.

Faith and hope are great, but love is greater still. Faith without love is cold and unfeeling; hope without love is worthless. But love is the fire that ignites faith and the light that turns hope into certainty.

Even in uncertain times it is possible to live a balanced and fearless life through the power of Christ; to be confident in the certainty that you can overcome all situations, and to affirm that the Holy Spirit fills your life with faith, hope and love through God's grace:

"In all these things we are more than conquerors through Christ who loved us." Romans 8:37

Soli Deo Gloria.

Solly Ozrovech

Faith is being sure of what we hope for and certain of what we do not see. This is what the ancients were commended for.
~ HEBREWS 11:1

Almighty God, our heavenly Father through Christ Jesus,
in Your mercy forgive our finite grasp of eternity,
the doubts and suspicions that lead us to question Your heart.
We have so little faith: we pray for more.
We tend to believe in each other, in banks, in trains and airplanes,
even in the strangers who drive our taxis!
Forgive our double-mindedness, O Lord,
because we believe in people we don't even know,
and yet we are so reluctant to have faith in You, Almighty God.
We bring so much suffering upon ourselves through our unbelief!
Give us faith to sow in the bank of Your love,
so we can reap the dividends You desire us to have!
We want to believe, Lord, just like all the giants of faith:
Abraham, Moses, Daniel, Noah, Barak, Deborah, David
and the whole gallery of heroes in Hebrews 11.
We often fall short in our spiritual lives, Lord Jesus,
and so we pray: please help our unbelief!
Make us firm in our faith, grounded on the Rock of Ages!
Thank You for the extraordinary faith of ordinary people,
manifested daily.
Grant our generation an abundance of heroes of the faith!
In the name of Jesus, Restorer of our faith, and for His sake,

Amen.

Never, never pin your whole faith on
any human being: not if he is the
best and wisest in the whole world.
There are lots of nice things you
can do with sand; but do not
try building a house on it.
~ C. S. LEWIS

Faith Is the Answer

Read
Gen. 4:17-26

At that time men began to call on the name of the LORD.
(Gen. 4:26)

Is faith a natural phenomenon or is it something one can acquire? Do humans have a religious 'instinct', or is it something they learn through their culture? Is religion a normal human activity or merely just a crutch for the weak?

Whatever the correct answer to these questions might be, there has never been a time in history when people did not have a relationship with God. Adam and Eve enjoyed God's company in the Garden of Eden. Their sons, Cain and Abel, brought offerings to God. In our text for today people began to call on the name of God. They only responded when God took the first step. People's worship was secondary to God's claim on their lives.

> God has made for us two kinds of eyes: those of flesh and those of faith.
>
> ~ JOHN CHRYSOSTOM

People also called on the name of the Lord because they needed someone to make sense of the bewildering and unsettling historical journey they had embarked upon. Everything seemed to be beyond their strength; too overwhelming and drenched in mystery for their simple minds to fathom.

They were also completely unable to decide on a code of behavior in order to regulate and control society. They needed rules to live by; guidelines and standards for human relationships. By calling on God they found a Source strong enough to give them both direction and help.

We too can find God – not by searching for Him, but by answering His call. We can do this through the guidance and strength of Jesus Christ.

Holy God, grant me enough faith to be able to answer Your call. Amen.

Faith Is Walking with God

Enoch walked with God; then he was no more, because God took him away. (Gen. 5:24)

At a memorial service, many favorable tributes are usually offered. The dearly departed's career and achievements are noted, his or her service to various societies and sports bodies, and family situation will be recounted. Much will be said about the love and care the departed had for others. Seldom, if ever, will attention be drawn to the deceased's wealth, even if he or she has gathered a fortune.

Enoch was known for only one thing—he lived in close proximity to God. "He walked with God." Sadly, the same thing cannot be said of many others, even those who are mentioned in the Bible. When you are close to someone, it means that you are on good terms with that person. You will not take a stroll with an enemy. Enoch was on good terms with God and therefore he was one of God's friends. This also meant that he could keep company with God without having to hide anything. Therefore he was not afraid.

> If the blind put their hand in God's, they find their way more surely than those who see but have not faith or purpose.
> ~ HELEN KELLER

Enoch did not have anything to hide from God. For this to be true he must have led a blameless life. He made time to walk with God and was never too busy to pray. His priorities were set in such a way that God was at the center of his life.

When your life's journey comes to an end, many things will be said about you: your achievements will be emphasized; your good qualities will be pointed out; incidents will be related to illustrate what kind of person you were. Things that were important to you will probably be left out, and other things will be mentioned that you would rather have left unsaid. Will it be possible to honestly say that you walked with God? That you were a true believer?

Thank You, Father, that through Your mercy we can draw close to You. Amen.

Read Gen. 6:5-16	Noah was a righteous man, blameless among the people of his time, and he walked with God. (Gen. 6:9)

The quality of your life is largely dependent on the company you keep. The vast majority of people, unless they are particularly strong-willed or stubborn, are influenced to a greater or lesser extent by the people they associate with. Children usually follow the example of their parents and many teachers have been instrumental in shaping the lives of their learners. Friends and business associates can also exert a strong influence on one's approach to life.

Psychologists often attribute certain types of behavior to the influence of a particular person one has frequent contact with – particularly someone with a dominant personality. The consequences of such an influence can be far-reaching – negative as well as positive – if they are allowed to take complete control over someone's life.

> Faith goes up the stairs that love has made and looks out the window which hope has opened.
>
> ~ CHARLES H. SPURGEON

However, there is one influence that can bring only good to your life, and that is the influence of the Holy Spirit when you accept Christ as your role model and mentor.

Because Jesus is the personification of God's love, it goes without saying that in Him we are able to find everything that is good, praiseworthy, true, honorable, righteous, pure, virtuous and lovely. Let your life be influenced by the living Christ; model your life and aspirations on Him. Then your life will reflect those qualities that can only come from God.

Forsaking all else, Lord Jesus, I open my life to the influence of the Holy Spirit. Amen.

> Noah was a righteous man, blameless among the people of his time, and he walked with God. (Gen. 6:9)

Read
Gen. 6:5-16

A generation or so ago there was a popular song called *I'll Walk with God from This Day On*. The song suggests that walking with God is a conscious decision you make and a choice that you exercise.

Noah chose to walk with God at a time when no one else did. This decision led him to the realization of the important task that God wanted Noah to carry out as an integral part of His plan of salvation. Noah's change of direction brought him strength at a time when weakness reigned. It enabled him to live righteously in a world where people had given themselves over to violence and evil. It also brought him the companionship of humanity's greatest friend: God Himself!

> Pure and simple, faith not lived every day is not faith, it is a façade.
> ~ ANONYMOUS

You also have the choice of walking with God or living life on your own. If you choose to walk with Christ, you will discover a noble purpose that God has set aside just for you to fulfill. Christ will raise you up beyond your own self-interest and personal needs in a way that will make sense of your entire existence and fill your life with meaning. If you decide to follow Jesus, He will provide you with spiritual strength and resources that you cannot attain in your own strength. He will, however, also put you up against the violence and evil in the world around you. If your desire is to remain true and faithful, life will not always be easy for you. But He will travel the road with you and fill your life with hope, joy and love. His love will be all-important to you and you will long to share it with your fellow man.

If you make the all-important decision to walk with God and with Jesus Christ, you will never walk alone.

Grant that I may always walk with You by faith, dear Lord. *Amen.*

Are You Prepared?

Now the earth was corrupt in God's sight. So God said to Noah, "I am going to put an end to all people. So make yourself an ark of cypress wood." (Gen. 6:11, 13-14)

Many people call on Jesus Christ whenever they are in need of help or comfort and then just carry on pretending to be disciples. For some people this is as far as faith goes. Faith can become a permanent crutch, a source of comfort and a refuge to flee to when the pressures of life threaten to overwhelm us.

For Noah, however, faith was so much more. To him it meant being prepared to respond to God's call to action and sacrifice, while the people around him were spending all their time pursuing pleasure. Because Noah's desire was to walk with God, God sought him out and spoke to him. This made Noah very aware of the dynamics, issues and conflicts of the world he lived in.

Faith is never identical with piety.

~ KARL BARTH

Faith encompasses so much more than simply being involved in "Christian things". It is bigger than merely going to church, reading the Bible and singing Christian songs and hymns. Faith is being aware of the dynamics of God. Faith understands God's mission in this world. Faith is the willingness to build an ark when God warns you that the floodwaters are coming; even if you have never built a boat in your life before. Faith means being alert: waiting and watching.

At other times it is an immediate response to God's command. Often it means being labeled a fool by the people around you. But faith always means being prepared to be there for God. Are you ready?

Never let me stop watching and praying, O Savior. Amen.

The Lord had said to Abram, "Leave your country, your people and your father's household and go to the land I will show you." (Gen. 12:1)

Read
Gen. 12:1-9

Most people like safe and familiar surroundings. We are comfortable with what we know and afraid of what we do not know. We are particularly loyal to our own town, city, province and country. We feel that we belong. We fit in.

Abraham, as he was later called, came from Ur of the Chaldeans. Ur was the center of a flourishing civilization. It would have made sense for him to remain there in safety and prosperity. But God intervened. In His plan for the salvation of humanity, God chose one man out of all the peoples and nations of the earth. God commanded Abraham to leave behind everything that was dear to him, everything that was familiar and safe, and start a new life that one day would bring hope and faith to the whole of humanity. Abraham obeyed God.

> Never be afraid to trust an unknown future to a known God.
> ~ CORRIE TEN BOOM

Sometimes God expects you to leave behind the things that you cherish the most, and it is very difficult to let go. But Jesus walked an unknown road with God; and so did the disciples, and Paul, and many others. Are you willing to take the step of faith that requires you to move forward? It might not be about where you live. It could be in the realm of your thoughts, in your ideas about God; the services and duties He expects of you; or perhaps it's the way you worship Him, or the way you manage your money. It could be your recollection of the failures of the past; condemnation you have had to bear; bad habits you have acquired; or broken relationships that need healing.

You could be just one step away from a completely new way of life. Faith and obedience can get you there.

Loving Father, help me to be willing to move forward into the future with You. *Amen.*

Read
Gen. 12:1-9

"Leave your country, your people and your father's household and go to the land I will show you." (Gen. 12:1)

It is human and absolutely natural to fear the unknown. It is so much simpler and less demanding for us to remain where we are. It is easy to live and work in familiar surroundings and with people we know and love. The rut can run deep but it is always the route we prefer.

God intervened in Abraham's life and sent him out into the unknown. "By faith Abraham went, even though he did not know where he was going" (Heb. 11:8). Abraham followed God because he trusted Him. He did not know what was going to happen on the road ahead, but he had faith in the God who sent him on his journey. He trusted in God so much that he was prepared to risk his own life, the lives of his family, and his future.

> The wise man must remember that while he is a descendant of the past, he is a parent of the future.
> ~ HERBERT SPENCER

When Jesus Christ answered to the call of God and resisted the voice of temptation in the wilderness, He also found Himself in unfamiliar surroundings. Disciples, apostles, missionaries and Christian leaders have felt themselves compelled to embark upon new, unknown, and even dangerous roads, into a largely unknown future.

Are you willing to entrust your future to God, or do you only want to cling to the familiar and the safe? God may decide to call you to a new life, a new hope, even to a new community. The road ahead may appear to be perilous, with many difficulties and problems. It might be a lonely road where you are often afraid and doubtful. But the Lord has led many others before you, and He will be with you, too. He will never leave you or disappoint you.

Father, I don't know what the future holds, but I do know that You hold the future in Your loving hands. *Amen.*

All peoples on earth will be blessed through you. (Gen. 12:3)

Read
Gen. 12:1-9

The early explorers who discovered Southern Africa drew up large maps of the continent. However, they did not know what lay north of the Limpopo River and simply recorded: "Here lie dragons." Many of us who have a far greater knowledge of the continent, hold a narrow worldview. We really only take an interest in what is going on around us.

Four thousand years ago, in the time of Abraham, God envisaged a way of life characterized by truth, faith, hope and an attitude of discipleship. Initially it was just one man and his family who made a start, but eventually the whole of humanity was influenced. It was a vision of universal salvation. God's worldview was universal. Because Abraham was the first person to

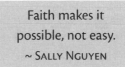

Faith makes it possible, not easy.
~ SALLY NGUYEN

embark upon this new and innovative path, he received God's blessings and gifts and passed them on to others. This was not just a vain promise – it was a promise from God!

Christians also need to broaden their horizons. The Holy Spirit drove the apostles out of the safety of Jerusalem to the furthest corners of their known world. The promise that initially came to Abraham carries through to the living Christ. It is through Him that all mankind will be blessed, because He is the living embodiment of the salvation that God envisioned.

The same Christ, who offers you faith and life, offers these gifts to people everywhere on earth. You are part of the universal fellowship. There are no dragons beyond your borders – other people live there who are also believers, and you are one with them.

Lord Jesus, help me to understand fully what it means to be a member of the body of Christ. Amen.

Read

Heb. 11:1-10

By faith Abraham, when called to go to a place he would later receive as his inheritance, obeyed and went. (Heb. 11:8)

Abraham departed. He left everything behind – everything that a human being becomes attached to: his security, associations, and safety. How did he do it? Only through faith. Abraham took all his problems, questions and dilemmas to God. God had spoken – and in the end it was the only choice Abraham had left. God allowed Abraham to hear His voice and Abraham listened and held firmly to God's Word right through the difficult days before his departure. He had an unshakable grip on God's Word. The only anchor we have in this changing world is God!

After that, Abraham didn't argue with God any longer. Instead he knelt for the last time with his family, Sarah at his side, and together they prayed their last prayer in Haran before obeying God's marching orders and venturing out into the great unknown. They rose from their knees and walked together through the land, where they had spent so many good and happy days together. Then – without any regrets or murmurings, without complaints or despair – in peace, with heads held high and pounding hearts, they left.

> The way to see by faith is to shut the eye of reason.
> ~ BENJAMIN FRANKLIN

Abraham obeyed God. God commanded him to leave his home and he did. Faith is a leap in the dark; leaving your own plans, thoughts, questions and desires behind. It is obeying the Word of God and staking your entire past and future on it. God called Abraham and he responded. That's what faith is all about.

Through Your Holy Spirit, O God, grant me the faith to obey Your calling. Amen.

Abram believed the LORD, and He credited it to him as righteousness. (Gen. 15:6)

Read
Gen. 15:1-10

How can a human find God's favor? Many people think they can do it by behaving well, staying out of trouble and keeping the Ten Commandments. Other people rely on "church work" and think that arranging flowers, handing out hymn books, taking offerings, or teaching Sunday school will earn them points with God. Some people see charity and compassion towards the underprivileged as the ultimate service to God.

Abraham, after doubting that God would keep His promises, had to fight his way back to where he had complete trust and faith in God's authority again. God favored Abraham, not because of any good deeds he had done; not because of any religious convictions he might have had, but because he came to the place where he once again put his full trust and faith in God. God was pleased with Abraham because he found his way back to Him. He repented and trusted God once more. Their relationship was restored and Abraham made his peace with God.

> Lord, grant me the ability to do what You require of me; then ask me what You will.
> ~ ST. AUGUSTINE

If you haven't already done so, follow this example without delay. Like Abraham, you cannot earn God's favor. The way to do it is to put your complete trust in the living Christ – and in Him alone. No matter how much you have struggled, how often you have failed, how many good deeds you have done, or failed to do, however far you have strayed from God – He is steadfast in His longing for you to trust Him. When you do, He will bless you.

Lord Jesus, Redeemer, I lay down all my defenses and accept Your authority over my life and over all things. *Amen.*

Read

Deut. 6:1-9

Hear, O Israel: The LORD our God, the LORD is one. Love the LORD your God with all your heart and with all your soul and with all your strength. (Deut. 6:4-5)

If the question "Who is your God?" were asked, most people would see it as a silly question. Because as Christians, they would undoubtedly know the identity of the Lord and therefore consider the question to be pointless.

However, it is necessary to ask this question from time to time – even of ourselves – because we need to be reminded of the meaning and the requirements of complete surrender and devotion to Christ. We, who are privileged to bear the name of Christ and who have been chosen by grace, ought to have our priorities straight when temptation crosses our path.

In this respect the cunning wiles of the Evil One are well known and people can tell of many obstacles he put in their way.

> Let your religion be less of a theory and more of a love affair.
> ~ G. K. CHESTERTON

Anything that threatens to come between you and your faith in Jesus, spells impending danger. It might seem innocent enough at the time, just a slight deviation, but nevertheless it still means allowing something or someone to take the place of Jesus in your life and undermining your faith.

In the strength that the Holy Spirit gives to you, acknowledge in every circumstance that "Jesus Christ is Lord, to the glory of God the Father" (Phil. 2:11).

Thank You, Holy Spirit of God, who works faith in our hearts to the glory of God the Father and Jesus Christ our Lord. *Amen.*

What does the LORD ask of you but to fear the LORD, to walk in all His ways, to love Him, to serve Him with all your heart and with all your soul. (Deut. 10:12)

Read
Deut. 10:10-22

Serving God is not a high priority in some people's lives. Everything else tends to take precedence. Spare time is devoted to some sort of religious practice, but usually without any real enthusiasm. People only pray "when they have time", and worship "when they feel like it" and then they wonder why their faith is so ineffective and weak. They give so little and expect so much; and then they become angry and critical when they find that their religion fails them in times of crises.

> Faith makes a Christian.
> Life proves a Christian.
> Trial confirms a Christian.
> Death crowns a Christian.
> ~ ANONYMOUS

True religion is a living and dynamic force, but like any other power it needs to be channeled and used to its maximum potential. It is impossible to revere God, to obey His holy commands and love Him to your utmost capacity, without this religious practice and faith impacting deeply on your life.

If you refuse to give God a place in your life, you will be forced to fill the gap with someone or something else, but there is no adequate substitute for God. You need to allow God, who created you, to take center stage if you want to lead a purposeful and fulfilling life.

By placing You at the center of my life, O God, I will lead a purposeful and abundant life. Amen.

Light on a Dark Road

It is the LORD your God you must follow, and Him you must revere. Keep His commands and obey Him; serve Him and hold fast to Him. (Deut. 13:4)

When the road ahead looks uncertain; when events take place in your life that fill you with fear and foreboding; when it looks as if the world is on the brink of chaos – then people are tempted to throw their hands up in despair and cry out, "What use is it trying to live a normal, good life? How will we ever succeed?"

Since the time of Creation people have experienced situations which appear to be hopeless. The Old Testament bears witness to the severe difficulties that frequently confronted the Israelites. The early Christian church suffered persecution, and throughout the centuries people from all walks of life have succumbed to feelings of despair as a result of the ill-fortune that has befallen them.

> I would rather walk with God in the dark than go alone in the light.
>
> ~ MARY GARDINER BRAINARD

While there is not much comfort in knowing that other people share your feelings of depression, it is extremely important to understand that, right from the beginning, God has cared for and protected those who have believed in Him and faithfully followed Him.

Turn to Him in your times of despair and trust in His all-embracing love and in the providence of the living Christ. He will lead you out of darkness and into His marvelous light.

Lord Jesus, Morning Star, shine brightly in my life and banish all my unbelief and despair. Amen.

This day I call heaven and earth as witnesses against you that I have set before you life and death. Now choose life, so that you and your children may live. (Deut. 30:19)

Read
Deut. 30:11-20

We are continuously being confronted with decisions. Sometimes the matter is insignificant and will have little or no effect on your life. But perhaps you are at a crossroad and your decision could have far-reaching consequences that will irreversibly change your future.

If at all possible, take your time before making your final decision. Impulsive decisions can sometimes prove to be disastrous. When you pray and ask for God's guidance – something that you will undoubtedly do as a Christian – you will begin to see past the inevitable short-term benefits, and discover a long-term perspective. How will your choice affect your life in five or ten years' time?

> It is morally impossible to exercise trust in God while there is failure to wait upon Him for guidance and direction.
> ~ D. E. HOSTE

Admittedly, it is very difficult to look that far ahead, so it is here that faith steps in. We cannot see into the future, but God is already there. If you honestly and truly seek to do what you believe the Father's will is, you can move into the future with confidence.

If you are genuinely seeking the will of God, you will develop a lifestyle of meditative prayer, where you are able to weigh up the choices before you and open up your life to the gentle leading of the Holy Spirit. If you need confirmation of His leading, confide in a prayer partner and you will be able to go forward into the future with the faith and assurance that God will never leave you or let you down.

Holy Master, when I seek to walk with You, assure me of Your guiding presence through Your Holy Spirit. *Amen.*

Read

Job 23:1-17

If only I knew where to find Him; if only I could go to His dwelling! I would state my case before Him and fill my mouth with arguments. (Job 23:3-4)

There is a deep-rooted longing in the human heart, and people will go to all sorts of extremes to satisfy it. It is the longing for satisfaction, contentment and fulfillment. It is the desire to leave one's mark on the community one is a part of. No one likes to think that he has led an insignificant life.

These inner drives and desires can result in great human achievements, such as the founding of business empires, the writing of great novels, and the composition of great music. Many people have creative goals because they feel that their lives have meaning when they are doing something constructive or creative.

Basically your intense drive for self-expression and fulfillment is rooted in a longing to reach out for and succeed in the things you really believe you can do. Right now your goals may seem to be out of reach, but in spite of everything you still believe in them.

> You never know how much you really believe anything until its truth or falsehood becomes a matter of life and death to you.
> ~ C. S. Lewis

When your personal goals appear to be unattainable, remember that you worship a God who is so much greater than your biggest dreams, and when you enjoy a dynamic, ongoing relationship with Him, it will bring a strong, fulfilling power into your daily life.

When you place God at the center of your life and your faith in Him is firm; when you allow His Holy Spirit to move freely in your life, you will make the exciting discovery that all things are possible through His indwelling Spirit.

With You in control of my life, Almighty God, I can attain my goals fully. Amen.

I know that You can do all things; no plan of Yours can be thwarted. (Job 42:2)

Read
Job 42:1-8

There comes a time in many people's lives when they are confronted with seemingly insurmountable problems. It is in these circumstances that people decide that matters are beyond their control and they simply accept failure and defeat.

Jesus invites everyone who feels overburdened to come to Him. He reassures us all of His help in handling our problems. He has even offered to carry our heavy loads.

However, this does not mean that you are freed from responsibility and that you can simply hand over all your problems to God and expect Him to give you exactly what you want, or answer your prayers precisely according to your desires. It rather means, that once you have handed your problems, and yourself, over to Him, and you have accepted His will for your life in faith, you will recognize God's dominion over your life. He is the Omniscient, Omnipotent, Omnipresent Being who wants the best for you.

> Happy are the meek. Happy are the yielded. Happy are those who trustingly put their lives, their fortunes and their futures in the capable hands of their Creator. Happy are those who "let go and let God."
> ~ BILLY GRAHAM

When you do this, you place your faith and trust in your loving heavenly Father's hands. You will be freed from worry and anxiety in the knowledge that God is in complete control of your life.

My Lord and my God, You hold me safely in Your hands so that I do not fall. I know that I can lay all my cares on You. *Amen.*

When I consider Your heavens, the work of Your fingers, what is man that You are mindful of him, the son of man that You care for him? (Ps. 8:3-4)

It is likely that you have admired the night sky with all its brightly shining stars and felt the awesome presence of the Creator. You may have looked into the center of a rose and wondered about the One who created it; or been confronted with some marvel far beyond human understanding and come to realize your own insignificance and ignorance.

God is a mystery to the human mind, yet man still struggles to fathom the unfathomable; remaining dissatisfied until it can attain a sufficient understanding. This is the human dilemma.

In God's perfect timing, Jesus Christ appeared on the human stage and revealed to us the character of the Eternal Creator. He demonstrated what God is really like and also what He expects from those who love and serve Him. In the living Christ we see the human manifestation of the Almighty God. In itself this is something to be grateful for, but Christ unlocked an even greater truth for us.

> The higher the mountains, the more understandable is the glory of Him who made them and who holds them in His hand.
>
> ~ FRANCIS SCHAEFFER

He lives in complete harmony with God and He invites you and me to enjoy the same relationship with His Father. Humanly speaking, this is not possible, but the impossible becomes possible when the Holy Spirit of God lives in you.

It is an amazing truth that when you acknowledge your unity with Jesus Christ, you enter into a relationship with the Eternal Father. Then your life is filled with a deep satisfaction and with a peace that passes all understanding.

Creator God, I praise and thank You that You have revealed Yourself through the living Christ so that through Him I may share my life with You. Amen.

I will praise You, O LORD, with all my heart; I will tell of all Your wonders. (Ps. 9:1)

Read

Ps. 9:1-11

There are some people who love to brag about their achievements. They very conveniently forget about their mistakes and failures, but relate with relish the story of a hole-in-one and a victory on the golf course – even if it happened ten years ago! Or they will talk about how fast they can travel from Johannesburg to Cape Town. In later years they will boast about the achievements of their children and grandchildren. We all achieve things, but some people brag about their achievements to promote themselves.

The psalmist in today's verse had a better perspective on life. He was so excited about God's achievements that he was determined to tell everyone about it. God had performed mighty deeds of salvation and the world needed to know about it. It is precisely because so many people have testified throughout the world about God's mighty deeds of salvation that there are millions of people today who know Him. The prophets related God's actions. The apostles used both the spoken and the written word to publicize what God had done through Jesus Christ. By listening to others tell of the mighty power of God, audiences also became aware of God's glorious acts of salvation and came to believe. They again told others and in this way the truth has been made known through the centuries.

> It is always right that a man should be able to render a reason for the faith that is within him.
> ~ SYDNEY SMITH

You might know about Jesus because a parent, a friend or a teacher witnessed to you about Him. If Jesus Christ has performed a mighty deed of salvation for or through you, you also need to share your experience with others. You might just speak to someone who has been waiting to hear a personal testimony about the living God.

God, help all Your disciples to share the glory of Your mighty deeds with others.   Amen.

God Most High

I will be glad and rejoice in You; I will sing praise to Your name, O Most High. (Ps. 9:2)

For many people a name is simply a means of identifying someone. Some people also have nicknames, like "Long Legs", "Shorty" or "Porky". Certain people hold high positions that carry titles like "Judge", "the Honorable", "Your Honor", or "Sir".

God has many names and titles. He was called "God Most High" by the Canaanites who lived in Israel before the Israelites arrived there after their Exodus from Egypt. The Canaanites had a number of gods, but "God Most High" was the God above all others. He far exceeded all the other gods. The Israelites liked this name and they adopted it and used it as the name of their God, otherwise referred to as "Yahveh" or "Lord".

> The whole person, with all his senses, with both mind and body, needs to be involved in genuine worship.
> ~ JERRY KERNS

It was completely fitting because God was not only elevated above the people who worshiped Him and the world they lived in, but He was also high above any other gods.

Don't be satisfied with an inferior god! Never let an idol take the place of the living God in your life: a sports hero; a film star or a politician. Things like possessions, property or the nation you belong to are also not acceptable as gods. Only the risen and living Christ is holy and deserving of your loyalty and love. Give the glory to Him – He deserves it. He will never disappoint you.

Father God, I bow in worship before You, O Most High. *Amen.*

Help, LORD, for the godly are no more; the faithful have vanished from among men. (Ps. 12:1)

Read
Ps. 12:1-8

It sometimes seems as if there are few, if any, godly people left in the world. In some parts of the planet it looks as if religion is on the decline; attending church is not as common as it used to be; and communities are becoming more secular by the day. It is encouraging to know that David, the writer of today's psalm, thought the same thing 3,000 years ago: which means that it isn't all TV's fault!

It is of course also true that bad news is always newsworthy, while good news often isn't. We hear all about terrorism, crime and drug dealing, but the media seldom, if ever, carries news of missionaries reaching out to remote new places; of churches expanding to accommodate overcrowded services; or of answers to prayer. These things occur daily but they don't make the headlines of newspapers and TV bulletins.

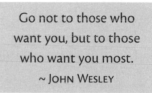

Go not to those who want you, but to those who want you most.
~ JOHN WESLEY

It is an encouraging fact that Bible study groups are popping up everywhere. Christian missionaries are very busy in many areas of the world and evangelical outreaches in different forms are frequent events. A recent report states that 20% of Russia's population converted from atheism to Christianity over the last decade. Countless churches have been established in many Eastern European countries. More than ever before, the Good News has spread out across the world. New methods of proclaiming the gospel are reaching increasing numbers of people.

If the barometer of faith is low in your area, God is probably calling you to do something about it. It takes just one believer, aflame with love for Christ, to light the candle of faith in other people's hearts.

Help me, Lord Jesus, to spread the Good News wherever I am. Amen.

Read
Ps. 16:1-11

I said to the LORD, "You are my Lord; apart from You I have no good thing." (Ps. 16:2)

Different people take pleasure in different things. Some enjoy a good book; others like to watch their favorite sports team in action, or relax with children – their own or their grandchildren. Traveling to exotic and distant places brings great enjoyment to many while others find relaxation in fishing or playing golf.

The psalmist of today's Scripture reading found joy in the company of God and fellow believers. People who share the same faith usually have similar values and joys: they enjoy worshiping together and singing praises to the glory of God. Because their faith is central to their outlook on life, they have the same attitude to the world around them. When they share their experiences, they understand what is important. When they hear other believers witnessing about how God has blessed them, it brings joy to their hearts. Bonds of love, sympathy and caring develop. Sometimes, when one believer is going through a difficult time, others will offer support.

> Shared joy is a double joy; shared sorrow is half a sorrow.
> ~ SWEDISH PROVERB

Don't ever isolate yourself from fellowship with God and other believers. Believing in Jesus and giving yourself over to Him allows you entry to the body of Christ. Appreciate the company; grow and help others to grow as you walk the road of faith together. Support them in their weaknesses and struggles. See how Christ is formed in them. When it is your turn to suffer, open your heart to receive their love because Christ will come to you through them.

God of love, strengthen and establish the ties that bind me to You and to my fellow believers. Amen.

LORD, You have assigned me my portion and my cup;
You have made my lot secure. (Ps. 16:5)

Read
Ps. 16:1-11

When you were a child, you might have thought that all good things came from your parents or from Santa Claus. When you became an adult, you made good things happen to other people. The devout person knows, however, that "every good and perfect gift is from above" (James 1:17). James also knew this without a doubt.

When you place your life in God's hands, your knowledge of what God actually does for you grows in the most amazing way. You come to understand that He gives you so much more than you can ever imagine. He gives you a rich inheritance through the culture you are born into. If you have had a good upbringing, you didn't do it yourself – it was part of God's plan for your life. It is one of the "good gifts" God has given to you.

> You can give without loving, but you cannot love without giving.
> ~ AMY CARMICHAEL

The church community where your faith has grown is another one of God's good gifts. And think about the Bible! It was written by people who were inspired by God, and later translated and conveyed by dedicated theologians. It was created by God to help you, to lead you and to enable you to grow in your faith.

The most precious "good gift" that God has given you is your salvation through Jesus Christ. He called you out of darkness and blessed you with spiritual gifts. These gifts enable you to praise Him and serve Him together with other people, so that good things can also come to them. There is no end to the "good gifts" that come from God when we truly consider and answer His call in faith.

Lord Jesus, give me the ability to appreciate the good things that God has given me, and to share them with others. *Amen.*

He Teaches Me How to Live

You have made known to me the path of life; You fill me with joy in Your presence, with eternal pleasures at Your right hand. (Ps. 16:11)

If you have ever been lost or wandered completely off the path, you will know just how despairing this can make you feel. It is easy to be overcome by panic which inevitably makes matters worse. When you are traveling far from home, it would be wise to have a map with you. Or if you are able to find someone who knows the highways and byways, you can ask him to show you the route.

King David discovered that there are different ways to get lost. He had treaties to conclude, plots and rebellions to deal with, as well as military operations to control. The king's relationship with God and the faith of the people made things even tougher. There were choices to be made. David made these choices by spending time in prayer and continually seeking God's advice.

> When we fail to wait prayerfully for God's guidance and strength, we are saying with our actions if not our lips, that we do not need Him.
>
> ~ CHARLES HUMMEL

This is exactly what you and I need to do. However confused we are and whatever the nature of our dilemma, we need much greater wisdom than our own to follow the correct plan of action. Ask the Lord for His leading and wait patiently for Him to reveal His will to you. Weigh up all your options in His presence; ask understanding friends for advice. Perhaps one line of action will appear to be a better option than all the others. Keep it in mind for a while and ask God to show you clearly if it is not His will. Ask Him to place an obstacle in your path if He doesn't want you to make that particular decision.

If God does not intervene, you can go ahead in faith and trust Him for the outcome.

Heavenly Light, lead me forward through earth's darkness. *Amen.*

Even though I walk through the valley of the shadow of death, I will fear no evil, for You are with me; Your rod and Your staff, they comfort me. (Ps. 23:4)

Every spiritual pilgrim has days when one feels down or depressed, and sometimes these feelings border on despair. For long periods you are sure of God's living presence and then, for no apparent reason, doubt creeps into your heart and a sudden lack of motivation overshadows your enthusiasm. You have no interest in your spiritual life any longer.

If this is true in your case, your spiritual vision has dimmed. You need a fresh revelation, a confirmation of the love of Jesus, to brighten up your life, and His Holy Spirit to help you guard against apathy and remind you of the wonder of His presence.

In the darkness of doubt and depression, you must hold firmly to your faith in a steadfast God. Though your emotions and your spiritual life will fluctuate, God's love for you is safe and sure. He has always loved you and even when you feel far away from Him, His love has not changed. He has not abandoned you. You can trust Him unconditionally; whatever your spiritual state.

> We are Christians and strangers on earth. Let none of us be frightened; our native land is not in this world.
> ~ St. Augustine

One of the benefits of a journey into the dark places of the soul is a greater appreciation of the light of God's love, and a more compassionate understanding of the trials and tribulations that other people go through. Even during the dark days, God can still use you in service to your fellow believers.

Good Shepherd of my life, I do not ask to be able to see the road ahead. One step at a time is enough for me if You walk with me. Amen.

Read
Ps. 27:1-14

Teach me Your way, O LORD; lead me in a straight path because of my oppressors. (Ps. 27:11)

There is a big difference between presenting your petitions to God and making aggressive demands. To be sure of God's presence in the inner sanctum of your heart, you need to obey His commands and rejoice in whichever way He chooses to answer your requests. Believe firmly that He knows what is best for you and subject yourself willingly to His judgment. Your acceptance will establish a strong bond between yourself and God, and as your faith grows, you will find yourself obeying His commands more and more readily.

When you approach the throne of God with high and mighty demands, remember that humility is one of God's gifts, as well as a fruit of the Spirit. However much faith you may have, you still do not have the right to demand anything from God. A great deal of damage has been done in cases where demands were made upon God and there was no answer. In this manner God is saying to us that our prayers remain unanswered because of our lack of reverence.

> Prayer is not learnt in a classroom, but in the closet.
> ~ E. M. BOUNDS

It is not the person who storms the gates of heaven who receives an answer, but the humble disciple who brings his requests in simple faith before the Lord and says, "Father, this is my prayer. Let Your will be done." Drawing close to God in this way is not blind faith, but rises from a belief born of the inner conviction that God knows what is best. Because He desires the best for you, it is exactly what He is going to give you.

Do Your will and only Your will in my life, Lord. *Amen.*

> "Be still, and know that I am God; I will be exalted among the nations, I will be exalted in the earth." (Ps. 46: 10)

Read
Ps. 46:1-11

The Christian faith can be a source of strength in times of weakness; comfort in sorrow; protection in temptation. It has the capacity to satisfy every need. It is basically and essentially a spiritual experience that involves us in a dynamic relationship with the living God through the love and mercy of Jesus Christ, our Savior.

Talking about spiritual experiences does not mean that we are being overemotional. It is an acknowledgment of Christian principles and the strength that God gives us to be able to obey them. In certain circumstances and situations this can be a difficult challenge. He could require you to turn aside from your hidden sins so He can free you from any feelings of guilt; He may ask you to repair broken friendships and relationships that lie shattered because of stubbornness and foolishness; or He may call you to a task you are unprepared for and where your faith in Him seems hopelessly insufficient.

> A simple, childlike faith in a Divine Friend solves all the problems that come to us by land or sea.
> ~ HELEN KELLER

A personal confrontation with the living God can be very challenging, but if you have the courage to accept the call and you obey His godly prescriptions, you will reap joyous rewards that exceed your highest expectations. A meaningful sense of purpose will define your actions; fresh revelations of the wonder of life will pervade your thoughts; you will enjoy penetrating insights that are the direct outcome of Christ's love flowing through you; and you will be blessed with sharpened perceptions. Above all you will find that life is more worthwhile now that you are spending quality time with God.

Thank You, living Master, that the time I choose to spend in Your presence renews and enriches my life. **Amen.**

Read
Ps. 56:1-14

In God I trust; I will not be afraid. What can man do to me? (Ps. 56:11)

It cannot be denied that the world is in a seriously troubled state. In some countries crime and violence have taken on frightening proportions. In spite of the fact that we are living in a so-called "enlightened century", we have proof that oppression and injustice reign supreme.

We often hear how the weak are suffering at the hands of the strong and how the rich perpetrate injustices against the poor. Generally speaking it can be said that life today is very different from the life God intended for us to have.

But there is no reason to give up hope. The answer to our problems does not lie in confrontations, retribution or conformity. It is important to know and believe that God is in control of everything and that all of humanity will one day stand before Him to account for their actions. Everything that happens on this earth is temporal in nature, but faith in the Master is eternal and doing His will is the only guarantee that your life is founded upon eternal values.

> There is no other method of living piously and justly, than that of depending upon God.
> ~ JOHN CALVIN

No matter how bad circumstances in the world may become, hold firmly to your belief in Jesus Christ, follow the road He has shown you and endure until the end. If you are willing to do this, you will experience the perfect peace and joy that comes only from the Lord.

Holy Spirit, help me not to lose courage in the struggle. Even though the road is dark, Jesus, the shining Morning Star, is a light unto my path. Amen.

Who is like the LORD our God, the One who sits enthroned on high, who stoops down to look on the heavens and the earth? (Ps. 113:5-6)

Read
Ps. 113:1-9

Throughout the centuries there have been many people whose good deeds have earned them the gratitude, praise and even idolization of others. Whatever they may have done or achieved, they earned themselves a very special place in the hearts of those who benefited from their actions.

While it is good that people are grateful for the things that have been done for them, what happens when the benefactor himself subsequently does something dishonorable? The world is full of disillusioned people struggling to cope with a situation where someone whom they greatly admired has bitterly disappointed them. The consequences of an experience like this can be very devastating for the followers of the "fallen idol".

> Christ, having sacrificed Himself once, is to eternity a certain and valid sacrifice for the sins of all the faithful.
> ~ ZWINGLI

The absolute wonder and joy of the Christian faith is that Jesus, the living Christ, will never disappoint you as long as you put your faith and trust in Him. When you accept Him as your Savior and Redeemer, you can be certain of the fact that Jesus' support and help is constant and unchanging. He will never let you down nor abandon you.

Don't ever hesitate or be afraid to seek help and support from Christ as you go through life. His love for you is holy and complete.

Savior and Master, please stand by me and help me cope with life and all its problems. I know You will never disappoint me. Amen.

I will walk about in freedom, for I have sought out Your precepts. (Ps. 119:45)

Many of us do not know much about modern science and technology and we find the various schools of theological thought perplexing. When we listen to the learned conversations of other people, we feel a bit ashamed of our own ignorance. At such times it is worthwhile to remember that no one in the world knows everything. There are limitations to what the human mind can understand and absorb.

The yearning for more knowledge is a desirable trait, but a hunger for God and for righteousness is more valuable than any desire for knowledge. Hunger for God brings a quality to your life that knowledge can never give you.

The longing to maintain an intimate relationship with God is a gift of His mercy, and His invitation is always open. It is humanly impossible to know God in His fullness and richness on a part-time basis. A good understanding of who God is, and an ever-deepening love for Him is the outcome of an ever-increasing dedication to a life with Him. If your daily life is taking up all your time and you feel that you simply don't have enough time to set aside for prayer and meditation, God is second place in your life. To arrive at the stage where it doesn't matter if you pray or not is truly a spiritual tragedy.

> Prayer, in many ways, is the supreme expression of our faith in God.
> ~ MARTYN LLOYD-JONES

Nevertheless, it is a glorious truth that you can experience the presence of God wherever you are and you can turn to Him anywhere and at any time. Those spur-of-the-moment prayers are important and inspiring and can lead you to a life of faith in the presence of God.

Because You live, Father God, the path of prayer is always open to me. Amen.

O LORD, our God, other lords besides You have ruled over us, but Your name alone do we honor. (Isa. 26:13)

Read
Isa. 26:1-15

When people speak of gods, one imagines the many idols that have formed such an integral part of the lives, culture and traditions of nations who have worshiped them over the centuries. There are rain gods and goddesses; gods of fertility; gods of war – the list is endless. Nations have lived in fear of offending them – and would even take revenge on the unlucky one who had erred.

However, idols do not necessarily have religious associations. Many people today make an idol of money in their efforts to build up a fortune; they make idols of possessions in a quest for security; or drugs and alcohol in a desperate quest for relief from the pressures and stresses of modern life. Lust, jealousy, greed and hedonism are as much idols as the statues of the heathens were. And the comparison doesn't end there –

> Christ alone can bring lasting peace – peace with God, peace among men and nations, and peace within our hearts.
> ~ BILLY GRAHAM

people today are just as frightened and anxious as they were in ancient times. They fear losing their money and possessions and they cannot face life without drugs and alcohol.

Our greatest need today is peace of mind. But the truth is that we can only find this through salvation and by putting God first. Live your life in Christ; open your heart to Him; spend quality time with Him and draw your strength from Him. Let His perfect love remove the fear from your life. "There is no fear in love. But perfect love drives out fear" (1 John 4:18).

My loving Lord Jesus, thank You for giving Your peace to me. *Amen.*

Seek the LORD while He may be found; call on Him while He is near. (Isa. 55:6)

People search for God but do not find Him. It happens quite often. Sometimes you will search for God in vain because you are not ready to receive what He has prepared for you. Sometimes you are just not looking hard enough. God is not a light that you can simply switch on and off when you want to.

The advice in today's text was given to the people of Israel while they were in captivity in Babylon around 454 BC. They believed that each nation had its own god, who only had power in that particular region. One of the outcomes of their time of captivity was that the Israelites discovered that their God, Yahveh, was still with them in Babylon. For them this was completely new and revolutionary. Their God was mightier than they had thought and He could be found wherever they were!

> Religion is the first thing and the last thing, and until a man has found God and been found by God, he begins at no beginning, he works to no end.
> ~ H. G. WELLS

The same God can still be found everywhere. No matter how inconvenient and unpleasant the circumstances, you still have full access to Him. When you are alone and far from home; when the world is collapsing around you; when you are being blamed for mistakes you didn't make; even when you have been out of touch with God for a long time, He can always be found! Search for Him; speak to Him about your circumstances and ask for His guidance. Seek Him now – while He may be found! He is always, lovingly, seeking you!

Holy God, You looked for me and You have found me. Help me to look for You and find You, and never leave You. *Amen.*

FEBRUARY

*"Simon, Simon, Satan has asked to sift you as wheat. But
I have prayed for you, Simon, that your faith may not fail."*
~ Luke 22:31

O mighty God, most worthy of praise,
I kneel in prayer before You today, ashamed.
I was convinced that I am Your child, born again.
Today I am not so sure.
My life is upside down and I am confused and in doubt.
It feels as if You are far away and out of reach;
And like You don't care about me.
I know that Satan is sifting me like wheat and I am sorely tested.
Forgive my arrogance and pride, O Lord!
I desperately want to believe
that You are the Hearer and Answerer of prayers.
Your promises are so clear in Your Word,
but in my life they're unfulfilled.
Prince of Peace, grant me the peace that You have promised me.
Please let my faith set me free.
Help me to have faith as a child and believe – and carry on believing
until the darkness disappears and the glorious light of Your love
breaks through once more.
Bless me once again with the joy of knowing that I am Your child.
Lead me by Your Holy Spirit through this barren wilderness of
agonizing doubt.
Thank You for Your assurance that You pray for me
and intercede with the Father,
because, Lord, I can't pray any more.
From the depths of my despair and unbelief I call to You:
Lord, please help my unbelief!

Amen.

Faith is the art of holding on to things your reason has once
accepted in spite of your changing moods.
~ C. S. Lewis

Read Heb. 11:1-6	Now faith is being sure of what we hope for and certain of what we do not see. (Heb. 11:1)

Faith does not mean trying to believe something you feel doubtful about or that you view as impossible. Faith is a conviction. When faith is at work, even the impossible becomes possible.

There are many things that we can be sure of. We apply the principle of faith daily in our lives. We even take certain things for granted: when you drive across a bridge, you believe that it can carry the weight of your car. When you are sure of something, you don't normally pay much attention to it; you just know and expect certain things to be true.

You can trust your emotions to the point that they control your life; your fears can paralyze you; you can have faith in a political ideology and let it rule your life; you can believe in other people and let them disappoint you time and again. Or you can have faith in God and discover that He is always completely reliable!

> It is cynicism and fear that freeze life; it is faith that thaws it out, releases it, and sets it free.
> ~ HARRY EMERSON FOSDICK

Faith is defined in various wys in the New Testament:

❖ Justification through faith – this brings us into a living relationship with God through the sacrifice of Jesus Christ. It is faith that makes us righteous and acceptable to God.
❖ Doctrinal faith – this embraces everything we believe about God. The Bible reveals to us the nature and being of God. He is the Lord and He is Love, He is Almighty, Omniscient, Allseeing, and Omnipresent. He is holy and so much more.
❖ Dynamic faith – this is the faith that enables us to live our day to day lives. Because we believe in God, we expect Him to keep His promises.

Christ my Lord, I want to believe unconditionally. Please help my unbelief and establish my faith on the Rock. *Amen.*

"The time has come. The kingdom of God is near. Repent and believe the good news!" (Mark 1:15)

Read
Mark 1:9-15

The gospel of Jesus Christ is good news. There is also the bad news that we have all sinned! "All have sinned and fall short of the glory of God" (Rom. 3:23). Each one of us is born with a sinful nature and tends towards wrongdoing. In contrast to this, God is holy, just and perfect in everything He does. Naturally, an unholy, imperfect and sinful human being cannot enter into a right relationship with God from his own strength. Something has to change before we can enjoy a living relationship with Him.

Our sins must be erased. We must be justified in the sight of God and certain that we have been fully accepted by Him.

This is possible only because of what Jesus Christ did for us on the cross. In Him, God took on human form. And Jesus came to teach us about the kingdom of God. In this way the kingdom of heaven became a reality.

> Faith alone justifies us ... because faith brings us the spirit gained by the merits of Christ.
> ~ MARTIN LUTHER

That is why Jesus Christ's public ministry began with a call to repentance. When you repent you turn from your sinful ways, back to God, and confess and repent of your sins. Then you receive His forgiveness and acceptance. It is not just about being sorry for your trespasses. Many people are sorry for their sins, but they don't change their behavior. Jesus didn't come only to teach us about the kingdom of God, but He made it possible for us to enter it and make God's kingdom a living reality in our hearts.

"If we confess our sins, He is faithful and just and will forgive us our sins and purify us from all unrighteousness" (1 John 1:9). Through our faith in the living Christ we are justified.

I praise You, Jesus my Savior, for everything that You endured on the cross for my sake. Amen.

Read
Isa. 53:1-12

But He was pierced for our transgressions, He was crushed for our iniquities. (Isa. 53:5)

In order for us to be forgiven, it was necessary for Jesus to sacrifice Himself on the cross. God has sentenced sinners to death and to eternal separation from Him. Heaven is a place for believers, not for sinners.

No one can justify himself before God and declare himself forgiven. No one can earn a place in the kingdom of God merely through works. Someone had to bear the punishment we all deserve. That someone was Jesus, who died in our place. He endured the punishment that we deserved. Blameless, He offered up His life to God for our sake. He took our place before God and carried our sins. Through this perfect sacrifice, He fulfilled the requirements of God's law.

> Three things are necessary for the salvation of man: to know what he ought to believe; to know what he ought to desire; and to know what he ought to do.
>
> ~ THOMAS AQUINAS

Believing in what Jesus did on the cross is the same as accepting that He acted for you personally – and in this way your sins are also forgiven. You are justified and acceptable before God. You have received salvation and the gift of eternal life. In this way you become a child in the kingdom of God and live in a harmonious and loving relationship with Him, knowing that He is your Father and you are His child. "Those who are led by the Spirit of God are sons of God" (Rom. 8:14).

When you give your life to God, you are born again in Christ Jesus. Your act of faith leads you to this new birth. He will never turn away anyone who comes to Him. You become a Christian through your faith. In response to that faith, the God of mercy bestows upon each believer all of life's necessities – in this world and the next.

Lord Jesus, through my own experience I know that You are truly the Savior. I praise Your name. Amen.

You also were included in Christ when you heard the word of truth, the gospel of your salvation. Having believed, you were marked in Him with a seal. (Eph. 1:13)

Read
Eph. 1:1-14

If you repent of your sins, confess them and put your faith in Christ, God is able to do amazing things in your life. Once your sins are forgiven and you are no longer condemned; your old life passes away and you become a new creation in Christ. You are no longer in the power of the Evil One and you receive eternal life. Jesus lives in you and you live in Him. You become a child of God and His heir, together with the risen Christ.

Christ Jesus is the only way to justification: and only through faith in Him can you be saved. Salvation is purely an act of God's mercy – God poured Himself out for those who actually deserve nothing. His mercy is also a gift in response to our faith. There is no other name under the sun by which humanity can be saved. No other religion or savior can restore humanity's relationship with God. "I am the way and the truth and the life. No one comes to the Father except through Me" (John 14:6).

> Since no man is excluded from calling upon God, the gate of salvation is set open to all men: neither is there any other thing which keeps us back from entering in, save only our own unbelief.
>
> ~ JOHN CALVIN

As Christians we are called to live by faith. Faith is continually trusting in God and His promises. Being born again will visibly change your life, your character and your priorities. Jesus emphasized that if you love Him, you will keep His commands. When you are born again, you begin an intimate relationship with Christ. Sanctification and justification are processes that commence with your new birth and continue throughout your life. They are the ongoing outcomes of God's mercy in your life, His response to the faith that you have placed in Jesus Christ.

Savior and Redeemer, through Your Holy Spirit please continue Your work of justification in my life and strengthen my faith daily. *Amen.*

"My thoughts are not your thoughts, neither are your ways My ways," declares the LORD. (Isa. 55:8)

The Bible reveals who God really is; His character, His nature and His personality. Many people have their own perceptions of God, but these can never be more than a figment of their own imaginations. Such a god can never save you, take care of you or answer your prayers. It is therefore important to measure your beliefs about God against the revelation in the Word of who He truly is.

God is not an idea. He is not a reason. No one can have a relationship with Him based purely on rational thought. Because He is infinitely greater than us, His thoughts are higher than ours. Therefore, it is only possible to know Him by reading His Word. We cannot live by faith if we don't know the Person we believe in.

Below are some of the revealed characteristics of God:

❖ God is holy – this is His essential nature. Our dilemma is in not being able to fully understand the meaning of "holy". But if we could explain it, God wouldn't be holy! The closest we can get to defining it is to say that He is perfect and whole.

> God's love never imposes itself. It has to be discovered and welcomed.
> ~ BROTHER ROGER

❖ God is just – He always does the right thing. Justification can only really be understood when you are in a relationship with Him. He is the standard against which all your actions are measured. It is impossible for God to make a mistake because He cannot deny His own perfect nature. When you live in harmony with Him, you are on the road to justification.

❖ God is love – although God is always right, He is also always loving. He loves all of humanity, even those who reject His love. Those who come to Him in repentance will inherit His kingdom, because "God is love" (1 John 4:8).

I thank You, Father God, that You love me and that You enable me to believe in You. Amen.

The LORD is compassionate and gracious, slow to anger, abounding in love. (Ps. 103:8)

Read
Ps. 103:1-13

❖ God is merciful – God's forgiveness is proof of His mercy. He does not deal with us as we deserve, according to the seriousness of our sins. Instead, in His mercy He made Jesus Christ a sacrifice for our sins. We can never earn anything from God. Everything He gives to us and does for us comes through the grace of His unfathomable love.

❖ God is the Judge – there will come a day when every one of us will stand before the judgment seat of Christ. Those who have put their faith in Jesus Christ do not have to fear Judgment Day, because the living Christ is their safeguard. "Therefore, there is now no condemnation for those who are in Christ Jesus" (Rom. 8:1). Those who have denied Christ, however, have every reason to fear eternal damnation. The question is whether Christ will find faith in our hearts when He returns.

> What a wonderful thing it is to be sure of one's faith! If we were to rely on our works, what would become of us!
> ~ G. F. HANDEL

Christians know that God exists, but so do demons – and they shudder! It is not so much whether or not we believe, but rather what we believe about God that makes all the difference. Let us now remind ourselves of what our faith in God has taught us as Christians: He is the Creator and He sustains Creation. He is not an abstract force but a Person we can come to know as our Father. He has revealed His nature and His character to us through His Son, Jesus Christ. He is love. He is merciful. He forgives and saves those who put their faith and trust in Him. He grants eternal life to those who believe in Him. He answers the prayers of the faithful.

I know that Jesus is Lord – He forgave my sins through His love. I was lost but now I'm found; I am at peace – I am God's child. *Amen.*

Read

James 1:1-8

When he asks, he must believe and not doubt, because he who doubts is like a wave of the sea, blown and tossed by the wind. (James 1:6)

Jesus taught His disciples in all spiritual matters. He regularly called on them to trust in God's omnipotence. Faith in the true God releases His omnipotence into our lives. This power is greater than any natural force. God is mighty to intervene in our daily circumstances and to change any situation.

There is an aspect of spiritual life that many Christians do not understand or enjoy, even though they are born again and filled with the Holy Spirit. Those who are born again have a special relationship with Him. Those who are filled with the Holy Spirit experience the inner workings of God. Yet this doesn't always mean that they are able to trust the Word of God completely.

> It is well to get rid of the idea that faith is a matter of spiritual heroism only for a few select spirits. It is a matter of spiritual manhood. It is a matter of maturity.
>
> ~ P. T. FORSYTH

People who are not already living by faith try to acquire faith when they find themselves in difficult or desperate situations. "That man should not think he will receive anything from the Lord; he is a double-minded man, unstable in all he does" (James 1:7-8). People who live in this way have an uncertain faith: sometimes strong, sometimes weak. God wants us to be steadfast in our faith in Him and not to be swayed by external circumstances.

There is a particular level of faith that God wants all believers to attain and enjoy. According to the Scriptures, this faith can be acquired in two ways: as a gift of the Holy Spirit, and by hearing the Word of God. If you want to live in this faith dimension, you must unconditionally accept the authority of God's Word. The Holy Spirit, who lives in the hearts of all believers, is the Spirit of Truth. He strengthens your faith in the Word of God in every circumstance of your life.

God of grace, grant me a dynamic faith because I hold firm to Your Word. Amen.

> "Heaven and earth will pass away, but My words will never pass away." (Matt. 24:35)

Faith is a matter of choice. It is untrue to say you cannot believe. In each situation you can choose to believe the revelation of the truth or you can give in to doubt and fear. The choice is yours. When you learn to live by faith, you also learn to make the right choices and to stand firm in your belief in God. If you concern yourself with other people's reactions rather than with God's, it will be difficult, if not impossible, to live by faith.

People who are faith-filled are very optimistic. Even in difficult circumstances they do not fall into despair because they trust that God will respond in His own time and in His own way. People who do not put their faith in Jesus have a negative attitude, torward their circumstances and others. Yet God's Word is able to deliver them. You can make the choice to focus your thoughts on God; to think in the same way He does, to agree with His Word and in so doing find peace of mind. "Set your minds on things above, not on earthly things" (Col. 3:2).

> Faith is deliberate confidence in the character of God whose ways you may not understand at the time.
> ~ OSWALD CHAMBERS

God does not want you to lead a failed life, but rather a life of faith and victory through Jesus Christ. Faith is a matter of choice. When the Holy Spirit plants the word of faith in your heart, you have the choice of accepting it or rejecting it.

The Bible asserts that God has given sinners the opportunity to reconcile with Him through Jesus Christ, and the Christian disciple must believe this unconditionally in order to be saved. A Christian who has a dynamic faith accepts the truth as God reveals it, and applies this knowledge to his own life. "Faith comes from hearing the message, and the message is heard through the word of Christ" (Rom. 10:17).

Loving Father, I thank and praise You for Your Word that is a light to my path and a lamp for my feet. Amen.

It was not through law that Abraham received the promise that he would be heir of the world, but through the righteousness that comes by faith. (Rom. 4:13)

The Bible is full of the miraculous deeds done by people who heard the voice of God and believed what He said. Moses heard the voice of God at the Red Sea; he believed and acted upon the Word, and his followers reached dry ground. The miracle happened because Moses chose not to look at the circumstances but to believe the revelation God had given him.

God is Spirit and He communicates with your spirit. The two most important ways that God talks to us are:

❖ Through the Word – ask the Holy Spirit to open up the Word to you when you read it. Scripture verses will be revealed to you in a new way, as if you had never seen them before. Then you will know that God is speaking to you.

> When the Bible speaks, God speaks.
> ~ B. B. WARFIELD

❖ Through the Holy Spirit – the Spirit can either speak directly into your heart or through an inspired word of revelation from another person.

God's Word is infallible and we are called to test words of prophecy against it. Anything that contradicts the Word of God cannot be from Him. "Everyone who prophesies speaks to men for their strengthening, encouragement and comfort" (1 Cor. 14:3). When you believe God's Word, you are truly living by faith. However, we must not only hear the Word, we must also act on it. "Do not merely listen to the word, and so deceive yourselves. Do what it says" (James 1:22).

If faith does not lead to action, it is dead. It is essential for us to affirm our faith through our actions in order to see the fruits of God's Word in our lives.

Lord, I will always believe Your Word and follow You. Make me fruitful in Your service because Your Word sets the standard for my life. *Amen.*

> If anyone acknowledges that Jesus is the Son of God, God lives in him and he in God. (1 John 4:15)

Read
1 John 4:7-21

When you put your faith in Jesus Christ, you become a child of God, alive in Christ. He also gives you the gift of the Holy Spirit. You are in Christ and Christ is in you; you live in God and God lives in you; you live in the Spirit and the Spirit lives in you. When you come to believe these truths you will no longer *try* to believe – you *will* believe!

It is possible to be a Christian for a long time without understanding what it means to live "in" Christ. The word *live* in Greek is in the continuous tense. It literally means "to carry on living in Christ". This is what God wants you to do, right where He has placed you.

The Holy Spirit empowers you to live "in Christ". This comes about through God's mercy, which enables you to live every day to His glory. Apart from Christ, you cannot receive anything from God. "In Christ" you have already received your inheritance; a portion of God's riches. Because you are in Christ, you hold a key to God's treasury.

> The main thing in this world is not being sure what God's will is, but seeking it sincerely, and following what we do understand of it. The only possible answer to the destiny of man is to seek without respite to fulfill God's purpose.
> ~ PAUL TOURNIER

God's purpose is to meet all your needs. God already had you in mind when He created the world (see Eph. 1:4-5). This is difficult to understand, but it is a God-given truth that you need to believe with all your heart. When you heard the gospel of Jesus Christ and believed, God placed His stamp of ownership on you and gave you the Holy Spirit as the guarantee of your inheritance.

What an amazing truth: that God planned your inheritance before the foundation of the world! All you have to do is claim it in faith and enjoy the wonderful life He predestined for you.

Lord Jesus, help me to always live in You. *Amen.*

Read
Gal. 2:15-21

I have been crucified with Christ and I no longer live, but Christ lives in me. (Gal. 2:20)

What was true of Paul is also true of you and me. You have been crucified with Christ. At the time of the crucifixion, Saul was an enemy of Christ. Even so, Paul realized that when Christ died, his old self, Saul of Tarsus, died with Him. It doesn't matter who or what you are before you come to faith in Christ. Your old life is crucified; Christ took you with Him to the cross and you died with Him. God's evaluation of your old self was that it couldn't be repaired, renovated, healed or made acceptable to God in any way. There was only one option: it had to die!

The cross was God's way of bringing this about. You were crucified with Christ so that your old life, which was grounded in sin and the self, would no longer exist. Your new identity is Christ living in you. Your old self could never have survived the cross. It could not have overcome death. But because your old life has passed away, you are dead to sin and all it encompasses: self-centeredness, self-interest and self-serving worldliness. The life that you now live is Jesus Christ living through you.

> Crucified inwardly and outwardly with Christ, you will live in this life with fullness and satisfaction of soul, and possess your soul in patience.
> ~ JOHN OF THE CROSS

Because your old life is a thing of the past, you are dead to the world and the world no longer appeals to you in the way it used to. You don't fit in any more. Your mind has been renewed. Through believing in His Word, you are equipped to understand the perfect will of God. God empowers you to live a new life in Christ. The Holy Spirit, who lives in all believers, makes this possible for you.

I praise and thank You, Lord Jesus, that I have been crucified with You and now I live with You. **Amen.**

We know that our old self was crucified with Him so that the body of sin might be done away with, that we should no longer be slaves to sin. (Rom. 6:6)

Read
Rom. 6:1-14

Your old life was crucified with Christ. The person you used to be was nailed to the cross with Him at Golgotha. Now you are inseparably joined to Him. Of this you can be absolutely sure. You know it is true, not because of how you feel but because God Himself said so in His Word. Never forget the truth of salvation. Your old self, full of unbelief and rebellion, has been put to death.

You have shared in the crucifixion of Christ. When He died, you died. That old life no longer has control over you. You are no longer a slave to the person you once were. Sin is no longer your master and your body is no longer an instrument of sin. You are chained to Christ. "Now if we died with Christ, we believe that we will also live with Him" (Rom. 6:8).

Because you died with Christ through faith you can now also live with Him forever. Through Him you are joined with God. The new person you are doesn't have to try to be united with Christ; you already are. And outside of your life in Christ you are nothing. "The death He died, He died to sin once for all, but the life He lives, He lives to God. In the same way, count yourselves dead to sin but alive to God in Christ Jesus" (Rom. 6:10-11).

> Our old history ends with the cross; our new history begins with the Resurrection.
> ~ WATCHMAN NEE

I bow in awe at the amazing truth that I died on the cross with You. Let me live my new life to Your glory alone. **Amen.**

Strength from on High

Since, then, you have been raised with Christ, set your hearts on things above, where Christ is seated at the right hand of God. (Col. 3:1)

Christ triumphed over all the powers of darkness. He disarmed them. They are powerless against Him – and against you because you live in Him. His victory over the demonic forces is also your victory. Therefore you can walk in Christ's victory through the centuries. Because Christ was victorious, Satan is also your defeated foe. It is not simply wishful thinking; it is the truth. When you firmly believe this, you will see the evidence:

> His incomparably great power for us who believe. That power is like the working of His mighty strength, which He exerted in Christ when He raised Him from the dead and seated Him at His right hand in the heavenly realms, far above all rule and authority, power and dominion, and every title that can be given, not only in the present age but also in the one to come (Eph. 1:19-21).

The same power that raised Jesus from the dead is at work in you. It is a force so powerful that nothing can compare to it. It is infinite and immeasurable. It is the force that was victorious over death and all the forces of darkness. That same omnipotence is at work in you daily. You are already in a victorious position. Because you share in the heavenly authority of Jesus Christ, you have the ability to rule with Him in this life.

> Faith is that strengthening power within lighting the road I trod, helping me know which way to go, pointing the way to God.
>
> ~ ANONYMOUS

You can take authority over all circumstances, over temptations, emergencies and against every evil force – through faith in Jesus Christ. Everything that is under Christ's dominion is under your dominion. You can trample under foot anything that threatens your life, because you live in Christ.

Thank You, Lord Jesus, that I may believe in You and live through faith. Amen.

May God Himself sanctify you through and through. May your whole spirit, soul and body be kept blameless at the coming of our Lord Jesus Christ. (1 Thess. 5:23-24)

Read
1 Thess. 5:12-28

Those who want to live by faith, need to learn to live in terms of relationship rather than activity. Our actions are not always in harmony with our relationship to Jesus Christ. We still do the wrong things; we often fail in our thoughts and words, as well as in our deeds. This is in direct conflict to what our relationship with Christ should be.

But God does not reject us because of this. He has a plan for each of our lives. He wants to conform you to a life of holiness, to His glory. When you walk the road with Him and with Christ, He will complete His work in you. You can afford to believe and trust this faithful God. Even when you are not doing as much as He wants you to do, He keeps on loving you and encouraging you, "My sheep listen to My voice; I know them, and they follow Me. I give them eternal life, and they shall never perish; no one can snatch them out of My hand" (John 10:27-28).

> Not only do we not know God except through Jesus Christ; we do not even know ourselves except through Jesus Christ.
> ~ BLAISE PASCAL

As long as you repent and turn to Him, He is willing to forgive you. He knows that you are not perfect and that Christ has not yet been realized in every area of your life. But the more you place your faith in the revelation of who you are in Christ, the more you will be free of judgment, fear and failure. You will be able to live as a new creation, with your faith rooted in the presence of God because your faith is pure. All His resources are available to you, in season and out of season, if you will only persevere in faith.

Dear Lord Jesus, save me from relying on my own achievements and neglecting my relationship with You. Grant that I may live in You always. Amen.

February 15

Forgiven and Accepted

Read
Rom. 8:1-8

Therefore, there is now no condemnation for those who are in Christ Jesus. (Rom. 8:1)

God's attitude towards you is one of complete acceptance, forgiveness and genuine love. You do not have to listen to the enemy accusing you of sin and failure. God rather wants you to focus on what Jesus has done for you.

Because you can never perfectly reflect God's life, the Evil One will try to make you feel condemned – like you are a hopeless failure. But there is no condemnation for those in Christ Jesus! You do not have to torture yourself about ideas about being unworthy before God. You are now living according to the truth of God's Word, and there is no need to feel defeated and depressed, "In all these things we are more than conquerors through Him who loved us" (Rom. 8:37).

> There is no more urgent and critical question in life than that of your personal relationship with God and your eternal salvation.
>
> ~ BILLY GRAHAM

You need never again be overcome by fear or difficult circumstances. Paul, of all people, knew what it was like to struggle with serious difficulties, and yet he was always able to emerge victorious. He said, "Who shall separate us from the love of Christ? Shall trouble or hardship or persecution or famine or nakedness or danger or sword? No, in all these things we are more than conquerors through Him who loved us" (Rom. 8:35, 37).

When you remain faithful, nothing and no one can separate you from God's love. God expects you to believe in what His Word says about you and to live your life led by the Holy Spirit. He also expects you to resist sin and walk in righteousness. To live in His strength and victory you must know His love, acceptance and forgiveness. God also expects you to look at yourself and others through His eyes and not through your own.

I, who have received Your forgiveness, Lord, gratefully sing my song of salvation. Amen.

"Men will have to give account on the day of judgment for every careless word they have spoken." (Matt. 12:36)

Read
Matt. 12:33-37

Here Jesus states that your words are important and have eternal meaning. Words have the power to place you under the judgment of God. If you use words of defeat and failure in every situation, you do not have faith in the power of victory through Jesus Christ. When you say, "I am expecting the worst to happen!" you show that you don't believe the Word of God which states, "We know that in all things God works for the good of those who love Him, who have been called according to His purpose" (Rom. 8:28).

Good fruit comes from a good tree and bad fruit from a bad tree (see Matt. 12:33). See yourself as a tree. God made you good. He took control of your life, placed you in His Son and gave you the Holy Spirit. Therefore, He expects you to bear good fruit.

> A little faith will bring your soul to heaven, but a lot of faith will bring heaven to your soul.
> ~ DWIGHT L. MOODY

Faith originates in the heart, "For out of the overflow of the heart the mouth speaks" (Matt. 12:34). The kind of fruit you bear, whether good or bad, depends on the state of your heart (see Matt. 12:35). Faith stems from your heart and influences your words and deeds. When your heart is full of love, you will speak in love. When your heart is full of hope, you will speak words of encouragement.

If your heart is full of faith because you believe in what God has done for you, you will speak the truth. When you believe and speak the truth, you can live in truth. You cannot live it if you don't speak it.

Savior and Master, help me through the Holy Spirit, to make my actions and words meaningful. Amen.

Victory Over the Enemy

The weapons we fight with are not the weapons of the world. On the contrary, they have divine power to demolish strongholds. (2 Cor. 10:4)

When your faith is living and active, it becomes possible to take authority over Satan and his forces. He is the thief who attempts to undermine your joy, peace and faith by trying to make you doubt your relationship with Christ. Learn to reject all his lying accusations. Stand firm against all the wrong ideas he tries to put in your mind. Use the powerful weapons of God to help you achieve this. Take each thought captive and make it obedient to Christ.

You have the spiritual authority to tear down every stronghold of negative thought and all the authorities that seek to oppose the principles of the Word of God in every area where the Enemy still has a hold on your life. Ask the Holy Spirit to show you where these areas are and then stand against them with all the spiritual authority that Christ has won for you. When you have the victory, fill your mind with His Word. "Be strong in the Lord and in His mighty power. Put on the full armor of God so that you can take your stand against the devil's schemes" (Eph. 6:10-11).

> He is victorious who triumphs over himself.
>
> ~ LATIN PROVERB

The lies of the Enemy are overcome by the truth of the gospel. When you stand firm in Christ, the Thief cannot rob you. Stand against the stronghold of the Enemy with the spiritual weapons God has placed at your disposal. Use the sword of the Spirit – the Word of God.

When you live in Christ, persevere in faith and in prayer, then the archenemy of God's children cannot oppress you. You have the godly authority to overcome the devil. Through faith you can live victoriously!

I worship You as the triumphant Christ who overcame for my sake. Support me in my struggle against evil and help me to overcome by faith. Amen.

A Prayer of Faith

"If you believe, you will receive whatever you ask for in prayer." (Matt. 21:22)

Read
Matt. 21:18-22

This statement of Christ cannot be argued away: every prayer of faith will be answered by God. It is very important to learn to apply the Word of God when you pray, because the Word is spirit and life. God's Word is the truth and will never fail. God watches over His Word to ensure that His promises come to pass. When you pray according to the Word of God, your prayers are in line with the will of God.

However, be careful not to claim the promises in the Bible without taking notice of the conditions that often accompany those promises. It is no use asking God to fulfill a promise if you are not prepared to obey the conditions that go with it.

> Our Lord is the ground from which our prayer grows; it is given us by His grace and His love.
> ~ JULIANA OF NORWICH

Faith comes by hearing the Word of God. By spending time with the Word daily, your faith will be built up and you will be encouraged. Study and learn to pray according to the Word. Take a portion of Scripture and make it your own. Assume that God is speaking directly to you as one of His children. Pray over every phrase, preferably out loud, and ask the Holy Spirit to help you to absorb the Scripture verses and let them make a difference in your life. You will be amazed at how words you have read so often before will suddenly come to life in your spirit.

The Word of God will become a personal revelation to you because you believe! Then the Word and the Holy Spirit will be able to work together and your prayer life will take on a new and exciting dimension. "Ask and you will receive, and your joy will be complete" (John 16:24).

I thank You, Lord Jesus, for all the wonderful promises in Your Word. Strengthen my prayers of faith through Your Holy Spirit. *Amen.*

Pray in Faith

"Therefore I tell you, whatever you ask for in prayer, believe that you have received it, and it will be yours." (Mark 11:24)

In our Scripture reading for today, Jesus teaches His disciples to pray in faith:

❖ He instructs His disciples to have faith in God – not in their doubts, their feelings, their reasoning or their problems. This literally means: Pray with the faith God has given you.

❖ He tells His disciples to deal with their problems: to command the mountain to cast itself into the sea. This is an act of faith and implies that you have the authority to address spiritual issues.

❖ Jesus emphasizes that when a disciple prays, he must not doubt but believe he will receive from God. Christians are not called to move mountains – but they are called to have faith when they have a problem and believe that God will solve it. Praise the Lord!

❖ Then you must believe that what you have asked for, you have already received. This is the essence of all believing prayer. Christians sometimes say that they believe God will answer them in the future. This is not faith – it is hope. Hope says, "It may happen." Faith says, "It has happened!"

> Of all the duties enjoyed by Christianity, none is more essential, and yet more neglected, than prayer.
> ~ FRANÇOIS FÉNELON

❖ Whenever you pray, pray with an attitude of forgiveness. If you cannot forgive others, God cannot forgive you. If God has not forgiven you, it is unlikely that He will give you what you ask for. He is a God of mercy, and He expects you to show mercy toward others.

❖ It is also good to pray quietly and ask for something that you know God will do in answer to your prayer. This will show you if you have true faith, or unbelief that needs to be addressed. There is also great power in prayers of agreement, "I tell you that if two of you on earth agree about anything you ask for, it will be done for you by My Father in heaven" (Matt. 18:19).

Holy Master, thank You for teaching us how to pray faithfully. *Amen.*

> The only thing that counts is faith expressing itself through love. (Gal. 5:6)

Read
Gal. 5:1-12

Paul stated very clearly in 1 Cor. 13:2 that even if we have faith that can move mountains but we do not have love, we are nothing. A life of faith and a life of love are not in opposition to each other. Just as faith without love is worthless, so is love without faith. God intended for faith to work through love and that love should come to expression through faith.

Faith is a gift from God. The first fruit of the Spirit is love (Gal. 5:22). When you live by faith and walk with Jesus, you are living in His love and this will increasingly be manifested in your life. A life of faith is sometimes viewed as cold and even heartless, yet nothing could be further from the truth. We can please the God of love only by living a life of faith. God therefore wants to bring these two principles together in your life: walk in faith and live in love.

God is love. Whatever He does in the lives of His children, He does out of love. Our faith depends on our understanding of who God is. His desire is to take care of us, provide for us, protect us, heal us and fill us with the knowledge of Him. Because He is love, He commands us to love one another with the same love that He has given us (see 1 John 4:7). James emphasized that a true relationship with God is revealed in the way we behave toward others (see 1 John 4:20-21). Your relationship with God compels you to love others.

> While faith makes all things possible, it is love that makes all things easy.
> ~ EVAN H. HOPKINS

Now you can understand why the Word says, "My command is this: Love each other as I have loved you" (John 15:12). Faith means obeying the will of God; that you not only hear and accept His will, but that you also act on it.

Help me, Father God, to hear Your will through Your Word, accept it and obey it in love. Amen.

Faith and Assumption

Read
Heb. 11:1-6

By faith we understand that the universe was formed at God's command, so that what is seen was not made out of what is visible. (Heb. 11:3)

There is a big difference between faith and assumption. God must always be the foundation of our faith: in everything He says to us through His Word and His Spirit. Faith becomes assumptions when people try to believe in God without founding their beliefs on what God Himself is saying in that particular context. Faith is the answer to God's initiative. Assumptions take this initiative away from God, so that the believer is simply acting on his own initiative. Disappointment is therefore the inevitable result of assumption.

Assumptions depend on the dictates of an individual's thoughts and feelings, while faith means listening obediently to the will of God. At best, through assumptions, you can reach only a suspicion. Through faith you will have complete certainty concerning God's will. That is why Jesus said to Peter, "I have prayed for you, Simon, that your faith may not fail" (Luke 22:32).

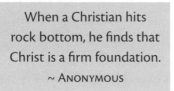

When a Christian hits rock bottom, he finds that Christ is a firm foundation.

~ ANONYMOUS

Sometimes we are disappointed with the outcome of our prayers. As far as we could see, we moved forward in faith. We believed that we were hearing God's voice through His Word and we tried to hold on to His promises. In confusion we ask, "Why didn't God answer me?"

It often becomes evident only afterwards that God's wisdom is greater than ours. Often you will be thankful, even though He did not answer your prayers in the way you thought. God always has a better plan and purpose for your life. Always remember: even when you are disappointed at the outcome, you are always safe in God's perfect love.

I declare myself completely dependent on You, O God, and I hold firmly to You in faith. Protect me from any wrong assumptions or expectations that could lead me astray. Amen.

To Give and to Receive

"Give, and it will be given to you. A good measure, pressed down, shaken together and running over, will be poured into your lap." (Luke 6:38)

Read
Luke 6:37-42

Fear and worry are the enemies of faith. Jesus told us not to worry about tomorrow, or about anything else in life. It is impossible to trust Him and still be anxious. He calls us to seek the kingdom of God and His righteousness first– then everything else will fall into place.

Whatever you give to God, He will give you much more in return. You cannot outgive God! But His kingdom principle is that you must give first. When you were born again, God gave you His rich inheritance in Jesus Christ. You did not receive it before you gave your life to Christ. First, you give your life to Him, and then He gives His life to you. The measure with which you give is the measure by which you receive. "Whoever sows generously will also reap generously" (2 Cor. 9:6).

What is God's purpose here? God wants to flood you with blessings so that you have everything you need and so that you can contribute to every good work (see 2 Cor. 9:8). Whatever you receive and own must be made available for the furthering of His kingdom. The cycle of life for a believer, therefore, is as follows: You give and God gives you more; you give even more and God exceeds your giving. You will never lack anything if you give according to God's principles.

> I have held many things in my hands, and I have lost them all; but whatever I have placed in God's hands, that I still possess.
> ~ MARTIN LUTHER

It is an act of faith to give before you receive. If you are faithful, God will remain faithful too. He is a God of mercy and wants to bless His children (John 1:16). He gives His all to those who deserves nothing. He teaches you to live according to the principles of faith. By giving to others, you learn to move in His mercy. Every time you receive from God, you can bless others.

Loving Lord Jesus, You have freely given me everything. Make me willing to bless others, to Your glory. Amen.

The Spirit of Faith

It is written: "I believed; therefore I have spoken." With that same spirit of faith we also believe and therefore speak. (2 Cor. 4:13)

You became a Christian because God spoke His Word into your life. He allowed His light to shine in your heart (2 Cor. 4:6). Before that you were in spiritual darkness, but God commanded that you receive His light, and that His light shine out of your darkness. This is His purpose for your life. Jesus said, "In the same way, let your light shine before men, that they may see your good deeds and praise your Father in heaven" (Matt. 5:16).

When Scripture says, "I believed; therefore I have spoken", it refers to God Himself. He spoke Creation into being and believed it would come into existence. During His earthly ministry, Jesus believed that He only had to speak the Word and the blind would see, the deaf would hear, the lame would walk, and the dead would rise.

> Christian worker, if you have not the Spirit of God, remember that you stand in somebody else's way; you are a fruitless tree where a fruitful tree might grow.
> ~ CHARLES H. SPURGEON

The amazing thing is that God tells us in His Word that this very same spirit of faith is at work in us. Because you have the same spirit of faith, you can also speak words of life. You can speak deliverance and healing into people's lives. "I am the vine; you are the branches. If a man remains in Me and I in him, he will bear much fruit; apart from Me you can do nothing" (John 15:5).

When we listen to the voice of the Holy Spirit speaking to us through the Scriptures, we can speak things into being because "with that same spirit of faith we also believe and therefore speak."

A life of faith comes to expression not only through our prayers but also through our willingness to exercise God's authority in the situations in which we find ourselves.

God of mercy, help me to speak words of life in faith. Amen.

"I tell you the truth, anyone who has faith in Me will do what I have been doing. He will do even greater things than these." (John 14:12)

Read
John 14:1-14

Whether we define it as a gift of faith or a spirit of faith, there is no doubt that people can have a defining faith experience which produces a dynamic outcome in their lives. This is a work of God's mercy in the hearts and lives of believers.

In the first place the believer's desire must be fervent. There must be an intense longing for a closer walk with Christ through faith. Only then can today's text become a reality in the believer's life. God always answers the call of the heart. There will be a period of testing, but during such a time, the believer will learn perseverance and the ability to hold on to God's Word with a pure heart.

The benefits of such an experience are manifold:

- a fresh revelation of God's Word to inspire our faith
- a greater submission to the authority of God's Word
- new determination to hold fast to the Word of God in spite of difficulties
- a closer walk with the Lord
- an increasingly victorious life
- freedom from condemnation
- dependence on the mercy of God
- a vibrant prayer life
- and real authority over the powers of darkness.

> I do not want merely to possess faith, I want a faith that possesses me.
> ~ CHARLES KINGSLEY

Pray to God and reach out for the gift of faith. This gift of God's love is there for you to take. You will then see many of your prayers being answered. Through this life of victory you will reign with Christ as a child of His Kingdom.

Savior and Friend, strengthen the spirit of faith in me daily so that I may use Your gift of faith to the best possible effect, to Your glory. *Amen.*

Read

Jer. 3:14-22

At that time they will call Jerusalem The Throne of the LORD, and all nations will gather in Jerusalem to honor the name of the LORD. (Jer. 3:17)

There is a fundamental difference between hope and optimism. Optimism weighs up the pros and cons and builds on future possibilities. This is often a very subjective process and is based on positive thinking. Hope sees all the negatives and believes that the positive will triumph in spite of the adverse circumstances.

In spite of the disloyalty of the people and the threat of military defeat, Jeremiah was not always a prophet of doom. His faith was firmly anchored in God. In spite of everything that was going wrong, he dared to hope that God would allow the day to come when the Israelites would be reunited once again, worshiping their God in Jerusalem. Other nations would join them and also acknowledge God as their Lord.

> O man, believe in God with all your might, for hope rests on faith, love on hope, and victory on love.
>
> ~ JULIANA OF NORWICH

Jesus showed us that hope would no longer be necessary, because God actually wanted people to worship Him "in spirit and truth" and not just in a particular place (see John 4:23). In Revelation we see the final vision – a new, heavenly Jerusalem, put in place by God, with a new heaven and a new earth. The whole of creation will be transformed and peace will reign (see Rev. 21-22).

This is a heroic hope. But when it seems as if the entire world is falling into confusion and chaos, you need to hold on to a hope that sees beyond the present day. You can believe that in spite of all the crime and violence of today, God will restore truth, peace and perfection.

Lord my God, fill my heart with the hope of Your mercy. *Amen.*

Do You Dare to Truly Believe?

He asked them, "Do you believe that I am able to do this?" (Matt. 9:28)

Read
Matt. 9:27-34

Christian doctrines almost stretch the imagination to doubt. When you think about the teachings of Christ and the high standards He demands, you are inclined to ask, like Nicodemus, "How can this be?" (John 3:9).

When you put the Master's teachings into practice, it cannot be denied that evil people become good; weak people become strong; distressed people find hope; slaves are set free; households that were in ruins become havens; greedy people become generous; people who previously shrank away from life are suddenly full of confidence; poisoned and perverted minds are restored and healed. The fact is that everything that has been rendered imperfect by sin and selfishness can be healed by the love and power of the living Christ.

> Trust Jesus, and you are saved. Trust self, and you are lost.
> ~ CHARLES H. SPURGEON

Jesus can meet your every need, but only if your faith in His ability is unshakable. Too many people come to Him with a need, but do not really believe that He can meet it. After they have told Jesus about their burdens and difficulties, they carry on in the same old way and nothing changes – because they are unwilling to be obedient to Christ.

Perhaps it is your honest desire to have an active faith, but you don't know how to achieve this. Start to exercise faith in the smaller things in life and you will soon find it easier to leave the big issues in the safe hands of the Master.

Lord Jesus, by trusting You for the little things in life, I will grow in faith until I am able to trust You completely. *Amen.*

Read
Mark 1:21-28

The people were amazed at His teaching, because He taught them as one who had authority, not as the teachers of the law. (Mark 1:22)

In our day and age, great emphasis is placed on studying and book knowledge. As the years speed by, academic standards become higher and greater achievements are required in fields of learning. The Christian realm is no different – theologians aim for higher academic achievements, and ordinary churchgoers strive for more knowledge through their studies, courses and their devoted reading of the Scriptures, and spiritual literature. In the search for knowledge of the Master and His teachings, more and more Christians are turning to books.

Knowledge that is acquired through study is invaluable and provides the student with a firm foundation – it enables a clear grasp of the subject and the opportunity to develop thinking and grow in understanding. For a Christian, however, reading and learning about Christ is not enough. To grow in faith it is essential to know the Great Author personally and allow Him to change your life. It is not enough to know *about* Him; you need to have a personal encounter *with* Him.

> A man may be theologically knowing but spiritually ignorant.
> ~ STEPHEN CHARNOCK

You must be born again.

Open your life to the leading of the Holy Spirit and ask Him to take control of your life. Give your will over to Him, so that through Him, you can enter into a personal relationship with the living Christ – not just the Christ in the pages of a book. Your experience of who Jesus really is will add a new dimension to your spiritual life that no book can give you; through the power of the Holy Spirit you will see life through the eyes of Christ.

Holy Jesus, help me in my efforts to know more about You, and to come to know You personally. Amen.

When Jesus saw their faith, He said to the paralytic, "Son, your sins are forgiven." (Mark 2:5)

Read
Mark 2:1-12

Faith is a vital component for anyone who wants to know God, ask for His help or receive His love. There are many people who sigh and say, "I wish I had more faith. Everything would be so much easier." Sometimes we try to work on our faith, like an athlete putting in some extra practice before a big race. We also accept that faith in God is a requirement before He can work in us.

Nothing in the parable of the lame man, whose friends lowered him through the roof to reach Jesus, indicates that he had that extra bit of faith that we think must have been necessary for Jesus to heal him. In fact, our text for today states the opposite: "When Jesus saw *their* faith" He for-

> Faith expects from God what is beyond all expectation.
> ~ ANDREW MURRAY

gave the man his sins. The lame man himself did not pass any great test of faith – but his friends did. How exciting it must have been for Jesus to glance up and see their anxious faces looking down at Him, hands dirty and sore as they made a gaping hole in the roof. For Jesus their faith was enough – simple, strong and unshakable.

The main point is this: Jesus is ready and waiting to do His eternal work in us, whether our faith is strong or weak – even if we approach Him in the strength of someone else's desperate hope that somehow we can be brought before Him so that a miracle of faith can take place.

I thank You today, Lord and Master, for all the people whose faith brought me to You when I was weak and needy.   *Amen.*

Read
John 8:21-30

"But He who sent Me is reliable, and what I have heard from Him I tell the world." (John 8:26)

God's kingdom is structured according to holy principles. It is a kingdom of order, while the devil's is one of chaos and disorder. To receive God's best for our lives, we need to understand these principles. God works in our lives according to the promises in His Word.

We all long for great faith. Jesus promised, "You will receive power when the Holy Spirit comes on you; and you will be My witnesses" (Acts 1:8). Paul said that God's kingdom was not a matter of words but of power. The Greek word for *power* in both these pieces of Scripture is *dunamis*. The word *dynamite* is a derivation and gives an indication of the mighty power of God that can be released into our lives. This power is seen in Creation; in Jesus' ministry; in His Resurrection, and in the power of the Holy Spirit working in the lives of the people of God.

> All the resources of the Godhead are at our disposal!
> ~ JONATHAN GOFORTH

Jesus said that we would do the same things He had done! Why are we not doing them? He had authority – even His enemies acknowledged this. Jesus exercised the authority His Father had given Him. He was able to do this because He was subjected to God (see John 5:30). Christ's authority arose out of His obedience to God. If we subject ourselves to God, we will also be exercising obedience. This will give us the ability to act in faith with the same authority as our Lord.

God expects to see growth in our spiritual lives: walking in the right relationship with Jesus, obedient to His Word. This will fill our prayer lives with faith and confidence. Justification → Faith → Authority → Power: this is God's progressive sequence. It is not just a matter of receiving power from God; we must follow the correct course to make our faith effective.

God of mercy, thank You for Your power from on high, and for the Holy Spirit who empowers me through faith to live effectively. Amen.

MARCH

For in the gospel a righteousness from God is revealed,
a righteousness that is by faith from first to last,
just as it is written: "The righteous will live by faith."
~ ROMANS 1:17

Lord Jesus, Source of all true faith,
I believe that faith is pure and true
only when You are a reality in my life.
I believe that there must be a longing to come to know You.
I believe that when I do know You,
I must desire You above all else in life
so that I can focus my energy solely on You.
Merciful Master, I believe that it is wise to begin my day with You,
to fill my heart and mind with Your presence;
to thank You for all the blessings
that come to me from Your loving hands.
I believe that prayer is an intimate conversation with You, the Father,
where we can talk and listen to You through the Holy Spirit.
I believe, O God, that the Bible is Your eternal and unfailing Word,
and therein You reveal Your will for our lives.
I believe that praise and song are indispensable parts of our worship,
feeding us and strengthening us emotionally.
I believe that You, Triune God; Father, Son and Holy Spirit, are real
and that You make an incalculable contribution to our faith lives
and also to the lives that we live in the world each day.
Thank You, Lord Jesus, that through Your gift of salvation
I can live every day by faith.

Amen.

Faith is not a refuge from reality. It is a demand that we face
reality, with all its difficulties, opportunities, and implications.
~ EVELYN UNDERHILL

Where Is Your Faith?

He got up and rebuked the wind and the raging waters; the storm subsided and all was calm. "Where is your faith?" He asked His disciples. (Luke 8:24-25)

We are so quick to become panic-stricken whenever danger threatens! How feeble our faith is when the storm threatens! Some people become anxious at the slightest sign of danger. Others lose all perspective in adverse situations.

The disciples were only human. They were Jesus' constant companions and passionately believed every word He spoke. Then a storm arose and their faith was shattered. In the midst of danger and panic, as death stared them in the face and chaos reigned, Jesus spoke.

In the same way that He spoke Creation into being, Jesus restored peace, calm and order. The Gospels tell this story to show

> Christian, remember the goodness of God in the frost of adversity.
>
> ~ CHARLES H. SPURGEON

that Jesus is Lord of the wind and the waves, and indeed of all Creation. His kingdom and His power has come and He was busy establishing His authority on earth.

It might well have been that by the time this story was written, a few decades had passed and a storm of another nature threatened the disciples – cruel persecution, torture and death under a heartless Roman emperor. They needed to be reminded that Jesus is the Almighty Lord who rules over the wind and the waves – as well as over every raging human storm.

Is your faith also weak? The storms that you have to contend with are every bit as serious as the storms of biblical times. Make sure that you have Jesus on board.

Lord Jesus, speak Your Word of authority, and calm the storms I have to face today. Amen.

That which was from the beginning, which we have heard, seen, looked at and touched – this we proclaim concerning the Word of life. (1 John 1:1)

Read
1 John 1:1-10

The voice of personal experience is very convincing. It is one thing to relate to a story that a person tells you after hearing it from someone else, yet it is another thing altogether to bear witness by saying, "I was there. I saw it happen with my own eyes." Then you will listen with more interest and respect.

The apostle John shared his heartfelt conviction about Jesus with the disciples who had never met Christ in the flesh. In our reading for today, he declares with complete conviction that Jesus is the Christ. John had more than enough time to meditate on the claims that the Master had made about Himself. John was one of the few people present on the Mount of Transfiguration when the glory of his Lord was revealed.

> Christianity is not just Christ in you, but Christ living His life through you.
> ~ ANONYMOUS

The Resurrection, the Ascension and the power of the Holy Spirit at Pentecost all supported John's belief that Jesus was the Christ, the Messiah that God promised to send to us.

Many centuries have passed since John shared his experiences with those early disciples, but what he said to them is as true today as it was back then. Time has not dimmed the glory of the Resurrection nor has it diminished the power of the gospel.

The experience that the first disciples had of the Indwelling Christ is also available to us today if we only allow Christ to come into our lives through faith.

I praise and thank You, Lord Jesus, for the knowledge that Your Holy presence dwells in me always. *Amen.*

So That All May Believe

Read

John 1:1-18

There came a man who was sent from God; his name was John. He came as a witness to testify, so that through him all men might believe. (John 1:6-7)

When you come to know Jesus as your Savior and allow Him by faith to come into your life, you join a timeless fellowship. Because this experience of coming to know Him is extremely personal, we sometimes speak of Jesus as ours alone. A preacher once referred to Him as "my Jesus".

The people of New Testament times were passionate. Their goal in life was to spread the Good News of Jesus Christ throughout their known world. The assumption that God was the God of the Jews and that other nations had their own gods, was challenged by the life, teachings and death of Jesus Christ. The coming of the Holy Spirit at Pentecost drove the disciples out of Jerusalem.

> God had an only Son, and He was a missionary and a physician.
>
> ~ DAVID LIVINGSTONE

Jesus said, "You will be My witnesses in Jerusalem, and in all Judea and Samaria, and to the ends of the earth" (Acts 1:8).

Today there are more than six billion people living on earth, of which almost two billion are Christians of various denominations. Approximately one billion others know of Jesus but are not committed to Christianity. This means that close to half of the earth's population have never even heard of Jesus. It is clear that the Great Commission, begun by John the Baptist, still has a long way to go.

However challenging the task, however powerful the opposition might seem, Christians today still have the same mission. The work will never be completed if Christians leave sharing the gospel to ordained ministers. You and I must declare our faith and become effective witnesses of the living Christ.

Lord, help Your followers all over the world to bring others to faith in You. Amen.

Through God all things were made; without Him nothing was made that has been made. In Him was life, and that life was the light of men. (John 1:4-5)

Read
John 1:1-18

Y ou have probably heard this expression often, "If you believe that, you will believe anything!" We usually say this to someone who is gullible and accepts anything, even if it just a trifling part of the whole picture.

Believing in Jesus is the complete opposite of gullibility. It is the smartest, brightest and most significant thing you will ever do. And it means so much more than simply having faith in faith. It is infinitely deeper than simply having a vague idea of the existence of a Supreme Being or just hoping that everything will work out well in the end.

It is saying, "I accept that Jesus Christ is the Son of God and that He lived and died for me. I accept and believe that He is alive today and wants to be my personal Savior and Redeemer. I accept Him as the object of my love and devotion. I will allow Him to take control of my life and reign in me according to His godly plan for my life."

> I believe in Christianity as I believe that the sun has risen, not only because I see it but because, by it, I see everything else.
>
> ~ C. S. LEWIS

Some of the greatest philosophers in the world believed in Jesus. Believing in Him is not a foolish thing to do. *Not* believing in Him means missing out on the most exciting and valuable experience that life has to offer.

When you come to believe, you embark on a journey of discovery that will keep you occupied until the end of your life on earth – and beyond!

Lord Jesus, I believe – help me when I doubt or struggle with my faith. Amen.

Read
John 1:1-18

Yet to all who received Him, to those who believed in His name, He gave the right to become children of God. (John 1:12)

People often wonder what life has in store for them. They mostly hope for good and pleasant things to happen to them, although many of us anticipate that world events will disturb our peace and disrupt our support structure. From a human perspective, we can never be certain about the future.

Perhaps you remember how, when you were little, people often asked you, "What are you going to be when you grow up?" You probably had the answer all prepared, like "A TV presenter" or "A doctor". The opportunities and choices seemed endless. But as time went on, you became more realistic as you gradually made peace with your personal limitations. Yet you didn't stop dreaming about what the future might hold for you and everything you still wanted to achieve.

> Salvation is a work of God for man; and not a work of man for God.
>
> ~ LEWIS SPERRY CHAFER

When you become a born-again child of God and put your faith and trust in Jesus, He gives you the power to become something that you currently are not. He opens up your future – He gives you eternal life! Whether you are a teenager with your future just opening up in front of you, or whether you are in the autumn of your life, you can look forward to the plans God has for you.

You may be a spiritual child or a seasoned believer, but He will always have dreams for Your future: presenting you perfect and without blemish before the Father through your faith in Him! Do you also dream of that day?

God of love and mercy, guide me into the future that You want for me and fulfill Your purpose in and through me. *Amen.*

> "I am the way and the truth and the life. No one comes to the Father excepts through Me." (John 14:6)

It is not unusual for people to ask, "What do I actually have to *do* to become and stay a Christian?" They are probably advised to read the Bible, pray and get involved in a Christian fellowship, attend services and worship God.

The reality is that *doing* all this is the result of being a disciple of Jesus, the living Christ. You first need to be passive before you can become active. You must receive. You do not come to believe through something that *you* do. It is something that *God* does. First He did something *for* you – He sent Jesus into the world as Savior and Redeemer. You didn't do anything. God acted entirely on His own initiative. Then God did something *in* you, by coming into your life and saying, "Here I am! I stand at the door and knock. If anyone hears My voice and opens the door, I will come in and eat with him, and he with Me" (Rev. 3:20).

> We are told that Christ was killed for us, that His death has washed out our sins, and that by dying He disabled death itself. That is Christianity. That is what has to be believed.
> ~ C. S. Lewis

Receiving is the way you react to God by taking this initiative and bringing Jesus into your life. If you have never consciously invited Him into your life, why not do so now?

Thank You, Lord and Savior, that You have revealed Yourself to me. I open the door of my life and welcome You in. Come into my life today and live in me. Amen.

While He was in Jerusalem at the Passover Feast, many people saw the miraculous signs He was doing and believed in His name. (John 2:23)

People sometimes long for miracles to happen. Some people pray to God for the miraculous healing of a loved one; or to make them instantly rich; or to wipe out someone they hate. Some people even try to make deals with God like, "If You will heal my mother, I will believe in You and serve You."

Yet miracles do happen! The Creation was a miracle. The Exodus of the Israelites from Egypt was also a miracle. So was the birth of Jesus – as well as many of the things that He did. The greatest miracle of all, however, was when Jesus rose from the dead.

There were certain people who followed Jesus wherever He went as witnesses of the mighty miracles He performed before their eyes. Other people came alive in the Spirit and realized that these miracles were far more than just great entertainment. They understood that Jesus really was God who became flesh.

> Miracles are not contrary to nature but only contrary to what we know about nature.
>
> ~ St. Augustine

They knew that He could perform miracles – even in and through them. Through His miracles they heard God's voice calling them to repentance and faith, and they devoted themselves to His service. Beyond the miracles, a completely new life beckoned: a life of discipleship, devotion, and service.

It is a miracle when an unbeliever comes to faith, when a sinner comes to repentance, and when a believer grows in grace and takes on the responsibilities of spiritual leadership. The miracle that Jesus wants to accomplish in you and me is no less amazing than the miracles you want Him to do for you.

God of miracles, please do a miracle today in the lives of unbelievers and believers alike. Amen.

Nicodemus came to Jesus at night. (John 3:2)

People have different feelings and perceptions when night falls. Some people are afraid of the dark, especially if they have gone through some form of crime, like a robbery. But there are other types of darkness that can descend on you too.

Sorrow can be a midnight desperation, as can doubt. Knowing that you have been disappointed by people that you trusted can also leave you in darkness. So can sickness, financial difficulties, unemployment, guilt, and confusion.

Nicodemus didn't just come to Jesus in the night, he came in the darkness of doubt and confusion. He was a religious leader but for him there were more questions than answers. He knew the Law, but he didn't know the God who had written the Law. He may have been a leading light for others, but he lived in personal darkness: a teacher who was in desperate need of instruction. He

> Darkness cannot drive out darkness; only light can do that. Hate cannot drive out hate; only love can do that.
>
> ~ MARTIN LUTHER KING, JR.

came to Jesus at night so that no one would see them talking. But Jesus turned on the light of truth and faith for Nicodemus and made a new beginning possible for him.

Whatever kind of darkness that has descended on you, do exactly what Nicodemus did. Go to Jesus, tell Him about all your problems, your fears, your confusion and your loneliness. Give your life over to His wisdom, truth and might and draw strength from His power and love, for He rules over the forces of evil.

When you came to Jesus, you came out of the darkness. Decide now to leave the darkness behind you and faithfully follow the Light of the world.

Light of the world, lead me out of my dark night into Your marvelous light. Amen.

Jesus declared, "I tell you the truth, no one can see the kingdom of God unless he is born again." (John 3:3)

Color-blind people cannot distinguish between red and green, and as a result they are totally unaware of the rich spectrum of color surrounding them. In the same way, people can be blind to aspects of life they know nothing about – music, ballet, the stock exchange and so on. For these people, such matters are a closed book.

Our relationship with God is the same. You need to become aware of Him and His kingdom. Christ calls this awakening a "rebirth". However old or young you may be, you come alive to the workings, presence and love of God only when you are "born again".

You may know a great deal about your field of work; you may be able to recite every Scripture verse, but unless you have been born again, God will not be a personal reality in your life and in your world.

> For a soul to come to Jesus, is the grandest event in its history.
> ~ JOSEPH ALLEINE

You may have achieved great things, served the church in many capacities and have an excellent reputation in your community, but you must first die to self and all your achievements and be born again before you will be able to see yourself and the world around you through the eyes of God.

Through this rebirth, God's presence becomes real to you, the Bible feeds your deepest soul, and you start living for God and grow in spiritual stature.

I am desperate to see Your kingdom, O Lord. In Your mercy allow me to be born again. Amen.

"I tell you the truth, no one can enter the kingdom of God unless he is born of water and the Spirit." (John 3:5)

Read
John 3:1-21

What is the greatest thing that God has ever done? There are endless answers to this question. One person may say, "He created the rose." Another might think, "He answered my prayers." A third could say, "He healed my loved one from a terminal illness."

Now seriously consider this: The greatest thing that God can do, is coming into the life of a person who has previously ignored and denied Him, to make that person a new creation. Some people will then say, "He has become religious," but actually it is God who has entered his life and transformed him.

It is not right to say that he transformed himself, or that he saw the light – even though these expressions

> Human salvation demands the divine disclosure of thruths surpassing reason.
> ~ St. Thomas Aquinas

are true up to a point. The Greek word that John uses for *again* also conveys the meaning of *anew*. We can therefore translate the phrase in one of two ways: "born anew" or "born again". Naturally, both are equally true. But *you* do not make it happen; God is completing the work in you.

God lets you see the emptiness and purposelessness of your previous ungodly existence. He convicts you of your sin and then He transforms you. He takes up residence in your heart and gives you a new start. He elevates your lifestyle according to His standards. This is also called salvation or redemption. Has God come into your life in this miraculous way?

Rock of Ages, cleft for me, let me hide myself in Thee. Amen.

"For God so loved the world that He gave His one and only Son, that whoever believes in Him shall not perish but have eternal life." (John 3:16)

There are people who believe that you never actually die; that you just carry on living in another form. The ancient Egyptians placed the deceased's personal belongings with him or her in the coffin to help on the journey into the afterlife.

Yet Jesus claims that the exact opposite is true. He says if we believe in Him, He will give us life as it is in heaven. If we will follow Him in this life, He will allow us to experience a foretaste of the glory to come. In Jesus the future is already here!

This future or eternal life of believers means that good has triumphed over evil. It means solving all of our earthly problems with God's solutions. It includes the healing of diseases; the piecing together of broken hearts and lives; answers to insoluble problems; overcoming the limitations of time and space; bringing all the conflicts of life back into harmony; reconciling painful differences; restoring broken relationships, and re-establishing and fulfilling relationships cut short by death. Temptation and sin will no longer exist. Human weakness will be transformed by the power and love of God.

Christ came to save all by Himself.

~ IRENAEUS

The focus of all these things is the living Christ and His pure, holy, saving love. And it all begins now!

Lord Jesus I trust You completely, not for what You give me but for who and what You are. Amen.

"God did not send His Son into the world to condemn the world, but to save the world through Him." (John 3:17)

Christ came to earth on the biggest rescue mission of all time. He came with a holy purpose. His arrival, His ministry and teachings, His healing power and friendships, as well as His death and Resurrection, were all intended for just one purpose: our salvation!

In what way do you and I need to be "saved"? Firstly you must be saved from sin. You then receive forgiveness for the sins that you have committed. Confess that you have sinned against the love and grace of God and then accept the forgiveness He offers you.

Salvation also means entering into a permanent relationship of trust and submission to Jesus, and that you seek out His help and advice to gain the victory over any evil that you may be involved in. This implies an honest effort on your part to conduct your life free of sin, according to the will of God.

> If man could have saved himself there would have been no need for the Son of God to come to earth. Indeed, His coming is proof that people cannot save themselves.
> ~ MARTIN LLOYD-JONES

Then you must be saved for a new life that honors Jesus, accepting that He is Lord of your life, and involving yourself in ministry to other people in some way. You will experience the fulfillment of fellowship with other believers and develop a sense of solidarity in this way. If Jesus was sent to save us, then you are saved to serve Him. Through ministry to others you become His ambassador, spreading the Good News of the same salvation that you received through Christ. You are saved to live a life that will continually make you more like Jesus Christ; a life where you can grow into spiritual adulthood, perfected in love. This is salvation through faith! Can you honestly say that you are saved?

I thank You, Father God, for salvation through Jesus Christ. *Amen.*

Where Can I Find This Water?

"Sir," the woman said, "You have nothing to draw with and the well is deep. Where can You get this living water?" (John 4:11)

Somewhere in London we came across a wall with the following grafitti message: "Christ is the answer." Underneath, in smaller letters, someone had written, "Yes, but what is the question?" Good interrogators know how to ask the right questions: detectives, doctors and skilled advisers.

The woman at the well did not understand what Jesus was talking about and she also asked Him the wrong question. Jesus had no need to draw living water: He already had it! She was actually the one who needed it and the right question would have been, "Where can *I* find this living water?"

She asked the wrong question because she did not realize what a mess she was making of her life through sin. She did not know how desperate she was. She did not examine herself seriously and honestly. She accepted her situation as normal and could not see how wrong she was, nor what she was missing out on. Her mistakes and her sins had distorted and dimmed her outlook on life, on God and on herself.

> "Whoever drinks the water I give him will never thirst. Indeed, the water I give him will become in him a spring of water welling up to eternal life."
>
> ~ JOHN 4:14

Each one of us must ask Christ the right question. The most important questions we can ask Him are, "What must I do to be saved?" and "How can I know that my sins are forgiven?" We can add to these, "How can I set right all the wrong I have done?", "How can I grow in love?", "How can I learn to pray?" To all these questions, Christ's answer is: Believe!

Lord Jesus, teach me through Your Holy Spirit how to ask the right questions. Amen.

"Everyone who drinks this water will be thirsty again, but whoever drinks the water I give him will never thirst." (John 4:13-14)

Read
John 4:13-26

Diabetics suffer from an extreme thirst. They have high levels of blood sugar and they often mistakenly try to quench their thirst with drinks that contain more sugar – resulting in them becoming even thirstier.

Only when their condition has been diagnosed and treated can their thirst be relieved. Some people drive themselves mad trying to overcome a feeling of emptiness, through excesses of the very activity that has led them to their problem in the first place.

Jesus was speaking to the woman at the well about *spiritual* thirst but she was talking about *physical* thirst. The "living water", or the high standards of spiritual life that Jesus offered her, would have relieved her spiritual thirst

> The spiritual character of Christ is more wonderful than the greatest miracle.
> ~ ALFRED, LORD TENNYSON

permanently. She would still have to walk to the well every day to fetch drinking water, but she would never again need to search for the living water that only Jesus could give her. The deepest needs of her soul would be met – her incessant longings would be satisfied; her thirst for love would be permanently quenched; and her own ability to love would increase and grow steadily. She would indeed have bubbled over with joy. She would have come to know a much deeper kind of happiness than she had ever known before. These are what Christians call blessings.

You and I also need the living water that only Christ can give. You will never know deep, inner peace and harmony until you drink at Jesus' well. Drink of His abundance through faith and you will never again need any other source of refreshment.

Holy Jesus, please fulfill my deepest spiritual longings today and every day. Amen.

Now Is the Time

"Yet a time is coming and has now come when the true worshipers will worship the Father in spirit and truth." (John 4:23)

One of the greatest dangers of a life of faith is to allow the notion of God's unending patience to lull us into the false belief that any time is a good time. That is why people often delay repentance until just before they die. But those who decide to wait until midnight usually die at half past eleven!

The Bible offers us a completely different idea of God. It shows how He continually intervenes. He did this with Creation, with the exodus from Egypt, with the coming of Christ into the world and He will do it again with the Second Coming.

One of the parables that Jesus told was about a farmer who returned unexpectedly and His servants found themselves in trouble because they thought that his return had been delayed. The farmer's return represents God's unexpected interventions.

> We should live every day as though it might be our last, but we should also plan as though the world might last a hundred years.
>
> ~ C. S. Lewis

Every moment is full of possibilities. Christ might return; God might appear; He might speak to one of His servants and change the history of the world. Not next week – today!

The Bible shows us how the present affects the future – the present doesn't just disappear slowly into the endless past. Jesus is Lord of the past; Lord of the future; and Lord and Master of the present. Every moment in time belongs to Him.

For the woman at the well, her daily task was to draw water and she had most probably done it hundreds of times before. But this was God's opportunity to confront her, claim her as His own and in doing so, make her a new creation. Today He comes to you. Are you ready?

I'm ready. Lord Jesus, come quickly! *Amen.*

Who Do You Worship?

A time is coming and has now come when the true worshipers will worship the Father in spirit and truth. (John 4:23)

Read
John 4:19-26

In any religion the object of worship is a matter of fundamental importance. *Who* you worship defines *how* you worship. It will determine your belief, your behavior and its consequences, and even what your outlook on the world and on life will be. It will most certainly determine who and what you are going to become.

Jesus cut short the argument of the woman at the well about where people ought to worship. Jesus told her, "It isn't *where* but *how* you worship that counts." The woman at the well missed the point. And so did the Jews in Christ's day because they elevated the letter of the Law above the Lawgiver. Furthermore, they were not in actual fact worshiping the God who was and is the Father. They were following a God they thought and expected would liberate them from Roman oppression. Consequently they were trying to tell God what He ought to be doing.

> The perfect church service would be one we were almost unaware of. Our attention would have been on God.
> ~ C. S. Lewis

It is just as easy for Christians in our day to worship a distortion of the true God. Some worship the Bible. Others worship the church that is actually designed to serve Him as His body. Others exalt the nation they belong to and presume that God exists for the express purpose of promoting their national interest.

Only the worship of God, the Father of our Lord Jesus Christ, is true worship. It is the way He must be honored and the only road to faith, salvation and sanctification.

Spirit of the Most High God, breathe life and power into the worship of Your church. Amen.

A personal recommendation of a product by someone that you know well, will often evoke your interest. When a friend sings the praises of the new car he has bought recently, it is likely that you will think about purchasing the same model. Then a salesperson will rattle off all the car's good points. Eventually you will decide to test drive it. Your final decision will depend on how the car drives with you behind the wheel, and this will determine whether you will buy the car or not.

Jesus spent a memorable two days in Sychar. The people were excited about the woman at the well's dramatic transformation and after that, they listened to Jesus Himself. They had never known anyone who taught the way He did. In spite of their uncertainty about a Jew speaking, they listened attentively while He told them parables and spoke about the kingdom of God, revealing to them the truth about His Father. He spoke with confidence, clarity and authority. They sensed that He was sincere and many of them began to say, "He is the Man for us! It's as if God Himself is talking to us. We want to hear more. This must be the Messiah God promised to send to us."

> I am convinced that the first step toward attaining a higher standard of holiness is to first realize more fully the amazing sinfulness of sin.
>
> ~ J. C. RYLEN

You might have accepted the truth of other people's accounts of what Jesus did for them. Or you could still be skeptical. Why not try it for yourself? Put your faith in Him. He is waiting to bless you with a completely new outlook on life – and the hereafter.

Lord Jesus, I have heard other people talking about You. Thank You that Your miracle of faith can become a reality in my life too. Amen.

No More Doubt

We no longer believe just because of what you said; now we have heard for ourselves, and we know that this man really is the Savior of the world. (John 4:42)

Many people are in two minds about religion. They get confused at the apparent ambiguity of certain dogmas and are often disappointed in times of difficulty by representatives of certain religions. Some people have a mixture of faith and doubt. Then there are those who do not know what they should believe and what they should reject.

It was not easy for the Samaritans to simply throw in their lot with Jesus. Yet, some did when they saw the change in the woman at the well, others took a bit longer to decide. They met Jesus, listened in amazement to Him talking, and undoubtedly discussed His words in their groups. Those who still had doubts began to see the light. There were also those who had to be convinced. And then, as so often happens with people who have struggled to grasp the truth, they embraced it with glorious certainty.

> Faith is to believe what we do not see, and the reward of this faith is to see what we believe.
> ~ St. Augustine

Everything suddenly became clear to them. They went from amazement at the woman at the well's words, to a firm understanding of what they themselves had seen and heard. Doubt had left them, skepticism had been banished, and the truth had taken hold. Jesus was not only a teacher for the Jews, but also for the Samaritans. And not only for them, but for the entire world.

Allow this truth to dawn on you today. Let it drive away all your doubts and bring you hope and salvation, in this life and in the life to come.

God of mercy, replace my doubt with the glory of true conviction. Amen.

More Than Enough

So they gathered them and filled twelve baskets with the pieces of the five barley loaves left over by those who had eaten. (John 6:13)

Some people have nothing; others have just enough; and others have more than enough. We live in a world where billions scarcely have a meal a day. A visitor to a poor country in central Africa noticed that in spite of the poverty, there was very little litter. A local resident explained, "It is because the people are too poor to afford the kind of goods that are packed in disposable wrappings – things that are responsible for all the littering in wealthy countries."

The extra food left over after Christ had fed the five thousand was an interesting phenomenon. It tells us that God doesn't just provide; He provides abundantly. In Psalm 23 we read, "My cup overflows" (Ps. 23:5). Paul wrote to the Christians in Corinth about their financial position and said, "God is able to make all grace abound to you, so that in all things at all times, having all that you need, you will abound in every good work" (2 Cor. 9:8).

> What a wonderful world this would be if we could forget our troubles as easily as we forget our blessings.
>
> ~ ANONYMOUS

In case you are busy complaining, sit quietly for a while and recall all the good things that God has blessed you with. Don't forget to include the material items. How much do you waste? Think about all humanity's blessings: family, friends, fellow Christians, professional helpers, teachers and pastors and spiritual leaders. Be thankful also for the abundance of spiritual blessing that God has given you. Charles Wesley wrote, "Bountiful mercies can be found in You, grace enough to cover all my sins."

Whatever else we may have or lack, we have received from God a super-abundance of love, grace and peace. Perhaps it is time we begin to count our many blessings from God.

Thank You, Lord, for Your abundant blessings, day after day. *Amen.*

He Is the True Prophet

After the people saw the miraculous sign that Jesus did, they began to say, "Surely this is the Prophet who is to come into the world." (John 6:14)

Read
John 6:1-15

W e all need food to survive. When people are deprived of food they think about it, long for it and even dream about it. People will even steal and murder for food.

The Bible shows us that our God is a God who provides. The Bible also says that when God returns at the end of time to reign as King, He will feed His people.

Jesus presents heaven in His parables as a banquet. The prodigal son was welcomed home with a feast. At the Last Supper, Jesus spoke of wine that would be drunk anew in the kingdom of God. The message of the feeding of the five thousand is as follows, "This is how the kingdom of God is. When God reigns there is an abundance of food for everyone." But God's kingdom will come only at the end of time.

> God's gifts put man's best dreams to shame.
> ~ ELIZABETH BARRETT BROWNING

Until then the struggle continues to feed the billions of starving people all over the world. And God plays a part in that struggle. He is present when commercial treaties are drawn up and during international negotiations. He inspires scientific research to increase and improve methods of production. We can play a part too by continuing to pray, "Give us today our daily bread."

As Christians we look forward to the day when all the starving people on earth will have enough food to eat and water to drink. It is the will of God's kingdom that this will come about. Christians pray and work in faith for that day to dawn. But just as in Galilee, we also need a miracle of faith now.

We praise You, Lord of abundance, for those who bring aid to the hungry people of the world. **Amen.**

Don't be Afraid

The disciples saw Jesus approaching the boat, walking on the water; and they were terrified. But He said to them, "It is I; don't be afraid." (John 6:19-20)

Human beings are slaves to fear. We worry about our health; our age; financial means and our children. We worry about change and whenever there is a new development we say, "The world is going to rack and ruin." Some people are already so brainwashed by fear that they are not happy unless they have something to worry about.

Time after time Jesus reassures us in the New Testament, "Do not be afraid! I am with you!" It isn't just good advice; it's a command. If big, strong fishermen could be afraid, even with Jesus near them, it is no wonder that we can also become afraid. But Jesus was there to encourage them.

> Fear knocked at the door. Faith answered and no one was there.
>
> ~ ANONYMOUS

He does the same today for you and me. You will not simply lose your fears because Jesus is nearby, but you will move past your fears when you realize that, high above the forces that appear to be controlling your daily life, there is Someone much stronger – God! Behind the rulers of humanity, whose incompetencies continually disturb your peace of mind, there is a heavenly Ruler in control. "Have I not commanded you? Be strong and courageous. Do not be terrified; do not be discouraged, for the LORD your God will be with you wherever you go" (Josh. 1:9). God is just as powerful today as He was in biblical times. Believe in Him; trust Him; listen to Him. This is the spirit of faith!

Hearer of my prayers, today I pray for everyone who is afraid in some way or another. Amen.

Take Jesus on Board

They were willing to take Him into the boat, and immediately the boat reached the shore where they were heading. (John 6:21)

Read
John 6:16-21

It is good to attribute your success in life to your faith in Jesus Christ. It is heart-warming to hear a businessman say, "I struggled to make a living. Then I gave my life to the Lord and I have never looked back. What I am today and what I have is all thanks to Christ." A successful sportsman might say, "I pray before every match and God sees me through." The message that comes through clearly is: Faith in Jesus Christ is a recipe for success. However, it is also true that many people who believe in Jesus are not successful.

When Jesus walked on the water on the Sea of Galilee toward the disciples, they took Jesus on board. Immediately the rocking boat reached the shore.

> Jesus accepts you the way you are, but loves you too much to leave you that way.
> ~ LEE VENDEN

It is always good to take Jesus on board – apart from the success or failure of a business. By accepting Him in faith, you also accept the standards you need to live by in the future. He becomes a Source of help and comfort to fall back on and you have a clear direction in which to move. With Christ on board, you will have specific values to guide you in the more important decisions of your daily life. The presence of Jesus is a constant reminder that the welfare of people is more important than personal gain.

Take Jesus the living Christ on board in your professional life. Include Him in your family relationships, your financial affairs and your leisure activities. This will not necessarily lead to success, but your faith will make a fundamental difference in improving your outlook on life.

Lord God, come into every area of my life and make my faith strong and powerful. Amen.

Read
John 6:22-34

"The work of God is this: to believe in the One He has sent." (John 6:29)

A comedian once jokingly said that he was busy recording all the donations that he had made to charity. When he died he planned to present the balance sheet to God and say, "There You have it, Lord, what do You make of that?" There are many people who think that God keeps a statement of their good deeds along with their bad ones. If you have a credit balance, then God will accept you into His kingdom; if not, then that's it for you.

This is not at all the way Jesus views the matter. What God expects is for us to have faith in Him, Jesus Christ. Faith is more important than deeds. To have faith is to believe that Jesus is the One the Father sent. It means seeing the face of God the Father in the living Christ. It also means trusting in Him as your personal Friend and Savior in the same way that a married couple support each other. It is the willingness to acknowledge the authority of Christ in your life. It means adopting a lifestyle that is in agreement with the teachings of Christ; to do good and avoid evil.

> If our confidence in God had to depend upon our confidence in any human person, we would be on shifting sand.
> ~ FRANCIS SCHAEFFER

Good deeds and actions are important, but they are merely the fruits of faith in God, and faith is what God wants you to have. Examine yourself now: Do you really have faith in Jesus Christ?

Lord Jesus, let my faith in You grow daily. *Amen.*

We believe and know that You are the Holy One of God.
(John 6:69)

Read
John 6:60-71

The way in which people deal with faith is often determined by their personalities. Highly gifted people are often prepared to reason their way through a tough intellectual challenge that an uneducated person would simply avoid.

Thomas was known among the disciples as the "Doubter" while Peter believed anything. Peter's faith was strong, genuine and straightforward. "We believe in You and we are certain of it," was his attitude. He was prepared to take risks – even to make mistakes – to affirm His trust in Christ. He had already seen the works that Jesus had done. He had listened to the teachings of Jesus. He understood and accepted deep in his heart that Jesus was the One God had sent and he was willing to stake his life on it.

> We often don't always know why things happen to us and others in a given situation or circumstance, but we know why we trust God who does know why.
>
> ~ DAVE BROWN

May God grant that your faith be as strong and childlike as Peter's. Let others struggle with the dogma and teachings of "religion". All you need to do is believe in Jesus. Let it be a simple faith: strong, real and sure. Do not beat about the bush. When it comes to faith in the living Christ, He demands your very best efforts. Half-heartedness will only lead you into confusion, indecision, uncertainty and doubt.

Even though certain things in life will continue to bother you and problems will always arise, take a leap of faith and put your complete trust in Jesus Christ.

Holy Jesus, help me to stop beating about the bush. I trust You with everything I have, now and forever. Amen.

Finding God

Jesus answered, "I am the way and the truth and the life. No one comes to the Father except through Me." (John 14:6)

All too often we hear cries of distress from people who claim that they cannot find God; or that their faith has weakened to such an extent that they are no longer sure of His existence. In many cases these are people who have shared an intimate relationship with God but have been disillusioned or hurt by an incident that affected their lives. From there the lamp started to flicker, threatening to go out all together.

One of the great joys of the Christian faith is the reassurance that we receive from the Master Himself, "Never will I leave you; never will I forsake you" (Heb. 13:5). He is always prepared to welcome you if you will only turn back to Him. His love is unconditional – His arms are always open, ready to take you back into His flock.

> If you seek Jesus in all things, you will surely find Him. If you seek yourself, you will find yourself – to your own ruin.
>
> ~ THOMAS À KEMPIS

When you return to the living Christ and allow Him to take control of your life once more, you will hear the prompting voice of the Holy Spirit guiding you to serve His holy name. It is in these circumstances – especially when you serve Him among your fellow man – that you will again become aware of the presence of God because you have found your faith again.

God of love, thank You that You are always there for me and that I may believe in You. Amen.

Don't get annoyed with someone who is always asking questions. During His earthly ministry, Jesus frequently met people seeking answers to their questions and solutions to their problems. He treated the genuine seekers with respect, but was abrupt with the sensation seekers and the hypocrites.

As a Christian you need never be afraid of the truth, even though it may squash your preconceived ideas and revolutionize your thoughts. It may even inspire you to new trains of thought.

Turning away from the truth because it requires you to reject your old ideas means closing your mind to the revelation of a deeper experience of God. You should welcome the truth – in whatever form it comes to you.

> Truth is a gem that is found at a great depth; whilst on the surface of this world, all things are weighed by the false scale of custom.
>
> ~ LORD BYRON

When Pilate asked, "What is truth?" it was a call of distress from the depths of the human heart. In Jesus he saw Truth personified and must have wished he had the opportunity to know Him better, because Jesus said that He *was* the Truth. When you accept Jesus in faith and follow His principles and teachings, you come to a greater understanding of the truth.

We must be careful that our search for the truth does not become a mere philosophy, separated from reality. It is therefore important to put your understanding into practice through the leading of God's Holy Spirit. When He is your guide, He will lead you into all truth.

O Holy Spirit, lead me on the road of truth because only then will I be able to walk in faith. *Amen.*

He said to Thomas, "Put your finger here; see My hands. Reach out your hand and put it into My side. Stop doubting and believe." (John 20:27)

It is relatively easy to say to someone else, "Just believe!" We do this often, even though the words we use differ. However, it is completely another matter when we ourselves are struggling with depression, disappointment or doubt, and are losing our own faith.

The doubt that flooded over Thomas was not dispelled by any act of will on his part. It was removed only by Jesus Christ, who appeared to Thomas in a special effort to help him.

We are seldom able to overcome our doubts by trying to rationalize them away. Usually it is the presence of God, or the visible workings of Christ in a particular manner that convinces us of the truth, love and omnipotence of the Lord. Most of the time we believe because we want to believe in something. We doubt when we don't want to believe. Jesus broke through the wall of doubt that Thomas had placed around himself and said, "Here I am!"

> Feed your faith and starve your doubts to death!
> ~ ANDREW MURRAY

We also believe because God has penetrated our consciousness and we have no option but to believe. That is why it is so important to allow God the opportunity to reveal Himself and overcome the reservations we have about one or other event in the Bible. Believe, because God is revealing Himself to you. If you are willing to do this, your faith will grow steadily.

We pray, Spirit of God, to support those who have lost their sense of Your power and love, so that once again they can honestly say, "My Lord and my God!" Amen.

Jesus told him, "Because you have seen Me, you have believed; blessed are those who have not seen and yet have believed." (John 20:29)

Read
John 20:26-31

We seem to be living in an age of skepticism. Some people ascribe this to bitter experiences, while others believe that the decline of moral standards and compromised principles have contributed to this sorry state of affairs. Whatever the reason may be, it appears as if very little can be taken at face value in today's times.

In some cases the same attitude extends to people's religious convictions and there are countless numbers of people who, like the apostle Thomas, are searching for visible proof of the existence of God. These are the people who rely on logic and intellect, instead of trust and faith. Inevitably they just get more and more frustrated.

> A man can no more diminish God's glory by refusing to worship Him than a lunatic can put out the sun by scribbling the word *darkness* on the walls of his cell.
> ~ C. S. Lewis

Jesus the living Christ calls on His followers to simply believe in God – not to try to prove that He is real. As a reward He promises to remain in the hearts of believers and take control of their lives.

This calls for an act of faith that, as Thomas discovered, leads to the peace that surpasses all understanding – the peace that you will experience when you are able to say in total surrender, "My Lord and my God!" (John 20:28).

Father God, we worship You as the Creator of the universe who has no need to prove Your existence. Amen.

Believing without Seeing (2)

Read
John 20:26-31

Then Jesus told him, "Because you have seen Me, you have believed; blessed are those who have not seen and yet have believed." (John 20:29)

We put great faith in the things we can see. When someone tells us something unusual, we always harbor a suspicion that he or she is trying to lead us astray. No one likes to be deceived. But even more than that, no one likes to give the impression that they are gullible. Because of this we usually want to see things for ourselves, as the saying goes, "Seeing is believing!"

This is exactly how Thomas felt after the resurrection of Christ. He was nobody's fool. He wasn't going to fall for the story that the other disciples had made up about Jesus still being alive. And then – before his very own eyes – Jesus appeared. The presence of the risen Savior, with nail marks in His hands and a spear wound in His side, changed Thomas's thoughts. The darkness changed to light; his skepticism was replaced by faith. Doubt disappeared and trust, amazement and worship flooded into his life like a tsunami.

> Faith is extending an empty hand to God to receive His gift of grace.
>
> ~ A. W. PINK

Thomas didn't touch Jesus. He did not press his fingertips into the nail marks on Jesus' hands or push his hand into the wound in Jesus' side. He didn't have to. He believed and fell at Jesus' feet. But many others who had witnessed the miracles Jesus performed, still did not believe – some in the crowd and some officials. Perhaps you are thinking, "If I had been there and seen it all, I would have believed."

Two thousand years later you are still called to believe. Millions believe, and millions more have done so through the ages. You can believe because the story of Thomas the Doubter sounds genuine.

Put your faith in God and surrender with renewed devotion as you say together with Thomas, "My Lord and my God!"

Merciful Lord, help me to believe even when I cannot see. Amen.

The Most High does not live in houses made by men.
(Acts 7:48)

Read
Acts 7:44-53

It is a sad fact that in many parts of the Western world, the attendance figures at church services are declining. Reports are regularly received concerning declining numbers in once flourishing communities and this is a great concern for church leaders. There can be different reasons for this – some well grounded.

One of the main reasons for the decline and deterioration of congregations, however, is the fact that so many church members approach their faith by trying to limit God to their place of worship.

The God you worship is a living God. He lives in the risen Christ and, while there is no doubt that He will be present at the worship service in your church and when you are reading His Word and singing songs of praise to His glory, you dare not limit Him to your Bible and your hymn book, shutting Him out of the rest of your life. If you do this, the light of your faith will quickly flicker, grow fainter and finally die.

> Holiness is not the way to Christ, but Christ is the way to holiness.
> ~ HENRIETTA MEARS

You are God's temple and in order for you to grow in your faith and enjoy the grace and joy of abundant life in Jesus Christ, you need to prepare yourself in your worship at church and in your prayer closet to allow Him to take complete control of your *whole life*.

In this way the living Christ will fill your entire being and as you reflect His glory, you will be able to enjoy life in all its fullness and abundance, because Christ truly lives in you by faith.

Loving God, make my life a living manifestation of Your love through Your Holy Spirit. Amen.

Read
Ps. 104:1-9

Praise the LORD, O my soul. O LORD my God, You are very great; You are clothed with splendor and majesty. (Ps. 104:1)

We always run the risk of scaling God down to the limits of our own thoughts. Often, if we cannot see how something might have happened, we convince ourselves that it could not have happened. Then we limit God even further with thoughts of what can never happen.

When your reasoning has reached its greatest peaks, and you are certain that you have examined a particular problem from every angle, always remember that beyond your thoughts lies the all-knowing presence of God. All human knowledge is fragmented, but when you join your powers of thought with prayer, you will learn to draw from the resources of the omniscient and omnipresent God.

> If God was small enough
> for us to understand,
> He wouldn't be big enough
> for us to worship.
> ~ ANONYMOUS

You can never claim that you have done everything in your power to solve your problem before you have thought deeply about it and prayed in the presence of God. When you do this, God's Holy Spirit inspires your thoughts and allows you to see the problem more clearly, revealing all the angles you might have missed. It makes sense to act in faith and put your problem under God's care because He understands it in its entirety.

Because God the Father already knows about all your problems, and because your faith in Him is firm, He will show you the road that you must take. Do not mistrust His leading but move forward in the knowledge that He understands and is working with you. In this way, through faith, you will reach a satisfactory conclusion.

Praise the Lord, because He is good!

Lord, You are bigger than my biggest problem and I believe with absolute certainty that You will lead me to a perfect solution. Amen.

APRIL

The apostles said to the Lord, "Increase our faith!"
~ Luke 17:5

Risen and glorified Savior,
You who have triumphed over death and are alive forever,
help us never to doubt Your resurrection.
Grant that it will be our source of spiritual enrichment
and the departure point of our everyday existence.
Let us be completely certain that You are always with us.
In moments of uncertainty, lead us and give us direction;
in moments of sorrow and pain,
grant us Your comfort and Your healing;
in our times of temptation, make us steadfast;
in every moment of loneliness, encourage us –
yes, be with us even unto death
and bring us to the eternal dwelling of God.
Remind us again that there is nothing in time or eternity
that can separate us from Your love.
Grant us always the blessed assurance that You have saved us;
and that through Your servanthood we have the right
to become children of God and that He carries us daily.
In so doing, we can face all the challenges of this life
with courage and without fear.
We thank You for the assurance of Your victory over the Evil One.
Strengthen our faith, hope and love daily.
We bring to You anew the sacrifice of our lives and our love;
our obedience and our trust; our prayers and our testimony.
We do all this in the victorious name of Jesus our Lord!

Amen.

There is no love without hope; no hope without
love; and neither hope nor love without faith.
~ St. Augustine

By faith in the name of Jesus, this man whom you see and know was made strong. It is Jesus' name that has given this complete healing to him, as you can all see. (Acts 3:16)

For many people, spiritual awakening or conversion comes with dramatic suddenness. These people are often fully occupied in living selfish, loveless lives, without giving a single thought to the needs of the people around them. Suddenly they are confronted by the challenge of Christ, and to their own surprise they accept Him. This leads to a transformation in their lives, and an escape from darkness, into a miraculous dawn.

Those who experience this sudden, dramatic transformation should not criticize Christians who have met Christ in other ways. There are many Christian disciples who have the Holy Spirit living in their hearts and yet are unable to give the date and time when Jesus Christ became a reality to them. For as long as they can remember they had the influence of godly parents, teachers or mentors who opened up their lives to an awakening faith. Over the years they have loved the Master and served Him – often with great sacrifices.

> Faith is from God, not from man. Man can do nothing to earn or receive it. We are right with God by faith alone.
>
> ~ MARTIN LUTHER

A slowly unfolding faith may not have the same dramatic impact as a sudden awakening, but its authenticity cannot be doubted. Like Timothy, they have inherited the faith of a mother and grandmother (see 2 Tim. 1:5). Christian faith can be awakened in us in many ways. The way in which this happens is relatively unimportant, but all people who profess to have a living faith, must manifest Christian qualities in their daily lives.

Holy Father, grant that the allegiance I may have to doctrine does not blind me to the Christian qualities in the lives of those who have come to faith in You in ways other than me. *Amen.*

All who were sitting in the Sanhedrin looked intently at Stephen, and they saw that his face was like the face of an angel. (Acts 6:15)

Read
Acts 6:8-15

Stephen was in great danger. The church was growing, but it was encountering severe opposition. However, the opponents of the early church could not find fault with Stephen's teachings or with his character, so they hired false witnesses to testify against him. In this treacherous way Stephen was condemned.

When a person has to face these kinds of circumstances, his true character is revealed. The natural reaction for someone in Stephen's position would have been to become bitter and discouraged. How is it possible to prove your innocence if lies are being portrayed as the truth?

The Scriptures declare, "Now Stephen, a man full of God's grace and power, did great wonders and miraculous signs among the people" (Acts 6:8). He had a strong inner conviction that he belonged to God and he knew that whatever happened to him would be part of God's master plan for his life. He was completely fearless because he lived according to God's will. He possessed the peace, joy, wisdom and power that is born from unity with the heavenly Father.

Stephen's experience can become part of the lives of all those who love and seek to serve Christ through faith. In whatever situation you might find yourself, always seek to determine the will of God first. This will stabilize your thoughts and give you inner peace so that, no matter how big your problems, you will know that God's presence is always with you.

> Would you like me to tell you what supported me through all the years of exile among people whose language I could not understand, and whose attitude to me was always uncertain and often hostile? It was this, "Lo, I am with you always, even unto the end of the world." On those words I staked everything, and they never failed!
>
> ~ DAVID LIVINGSTONE

Thank You, Lord my God, for the knowledge of Your holy presence and that I may always trust in You as I follow in Your ways. Amen.

Then they returned ... strengthening the disciples and encouraging them to remain true to their faith. (Acts 14: 21-22)

The world is in a critical state; this is a fact that very few people can deny. Widespread violence, poverty, disease and famine are taking a disturbing toll. In spite of scientific, technological and academic advances the situation is so critical that even the most optimistic predictions for the future are treated with hesitation.

It may sound like a small comfort, but this situation has been the same in every era of human existence. Throughout the ages people have continually expressed ever deeper concerns about the future. We tend to think that the problems we're facing now are the most serious that have ever existed. Our ancestors undoubtedly entertained similar misgivings.

> God made for us two kinds of eyes: those of flesh and those of faith.
>
> ~ JOHN CHRYSOSTOM

One factor, however, that all generations have in common, is the unshakable truth that God is always in control – in the past, the present and the future. His hand is over His children and His Creation, and we know that His eternal love will never fail for everything that is so precious to Him. Your duty and your privilege as a Christian is to support those who are weak and frightened by encouraging them to believe and trust in God; to rest in His love and find peace in Him.

To be able to do this, you must cultivate a personal relationship with the living Christ, so that His Spirit can inspire you and strengthen you to serve others in His name, through your faith.

I put my trust in You, Lord Jesus, and I continue to believe in Your plan for the world. Make me Your true witness through faith. *Amen.*

I thank my God through Jesus Christ for all of you, because your faith is being reported all over the world. (Rom. 1:8)

Read
Rom. 1:8-17

Are you perhaps one of those people who feels that your journey with God is one long, lonely, uphill struggle? It is easy to believe that you are treading a solitary and lonely road, especially if you are not part of a Christian group or fellowship.

Many of the early Christians were isolated in small groups and often had to cling to their faith in a hostile environment. But they knew that they were part of a worldwide fellowship of believers. There were Christians in Rome, in Jerusalem, in Antioch, in Ephesus, in Alexandria and in Corinth. In the towns around these larger cities there were also individual Christians who remained true to their faith.

What encouraged them to persevere? It was the knowledge that they were never alone. Their Lord had promised, "Surely I am with you always, to the very end of the age" (Matt. 28:20). They also knew that their fellow believers in every part of the world did not only endure trials for Jesus, but were also busy taking the gospel to isolated areas. They were bringing many people to faith. They were supporting the sick and the poor.

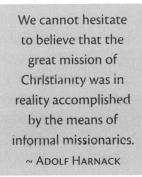

We cannot hesitate to believe that the great mission of Christianity was in reality accomplished by the means of informal missionaries.
~ ADOLF HARNACK

The faith of people in one part of the world was the inspiration and strength for people who lived in other regions.

You too, are never alone. Jesus is always with you, until the end. So are all the great multitudes of fellow believers in China, the Pacific Islands, the hills and valleys of Africa, in the hustle and bustle of India – as well as in the old villages of Europe. They are praying for you. Are you also praying for them and supporting them in faith?

Living Lord Jesus, strengthen and encourage all those believers who must fight a lonely battle today. Amen.

I long to see you so that I may impart to you some spiritual gift to make you strong – that you and I may be mutually encouraged by each other's faith. (Rom. 1:11-12)

Many church members develop a dependent relationship on their minister, pastor or priest. They think that the minister should do all the evangelizing, teaching and building up of the congregation and that their only job is to receive.

The fact is that it is a two-way street. It should be a give-and-take relationship. The pastor instructs, but the believing Christian encourages, strengthens and supports the pastor. Some Christians even instruct their pastor – and this is a fact that every pastor can confirm.

Paul writes from a remote place to the faithful Christians in Rome. He longs to see them face-to-face so that he can instruct and encourage them in their faith. There were many things (Paul calls them spiritual gifts) that he wanted to share with them. He looked forward to some inspiring interaction where he and the church members would strengthen each other's faith when he visited them. But in the end, Paul went to Rome as a prisoner. There he needed every bit of encouragement he could get from the congregation in Rome; just as much as they needed his instruction.

> It is easier to point the finger than to offer a helping hand.
>
> ~ ANONYMOUS

Perhaps you feel that you are not spiritually strong enough to help anyone. It is unnecessary to think that way. There is no monopoly on spiritual gifts. As you share with others, so you will grow – however simple the encouragement that you offer.

By giving to others, you will be more open to receive. Do you remember how Jesus longed for the disciples to stay awake and watch with Him at Gethsemane?

Loving Savior, pour out Your grace on me through Your Spirit so that I may perceive how to encourage and support my fellow man. *Amen.*

I am not ashamed of the gospel, because it is the power of God for the salvation of everyone who believes. (Rom. 1:16)

Read
Rom. 1:8-17

Sometimes people who are not familiar with the nature of the church label Christians as "religious". They may say of others, "They are very religious. They go to church every Sunday."

The gospel, which lies at the heart of New Testament faith, is not an attempt to make people "religious" as it is used in the sentence above. Many so-called "religious" people became bitter opponents of the Christian faith.

Before his dramatic conversion, Paul was such a person. But the gospel has a completely different approach. The gospel says, "Here is Jesus Christ: perfect Man and perfect God. He is God's path to salvation. All you need to do is believe in Him, and you will find the way to salvation and redemption."

> The gospel is so simple that small children can understand it, and it is so profound that studies by the wisest theologians will never exhaust its riches.
>
> ~ CHARLES HODGE

Before Jesus appeared it was written, "Salvation is from the Jews" (John 4:22). The work of Paul and the other apostles extended to proclaim the gospel of Jesus Christ and salvation through His work, also to the Gentiles. An integral part of the gospel preached salvation for all who believed the Good News and believed in the living Christ.

You do not have to be "religious" in the conventionally accepted sense of the word, to believe. It is not necessary to have grown up with any particular credos, ceremonies or religious rituals. You also don't have to be exceptionally "good". The Good News of Jesus Christ is that *everyone* who believes in Jesus has received acceptance by God through Jesus Christ. Do you believe too?

Savior and Master, thank You for the quality of life that Your gospel brings. Amen.

I am not ashamed of the gospel, because it is the power of God for the salvation of everyone who believes. (Rom. 1:16)

D o you ever feel that being a Christian labels you in some way as a weakling? Many Christians become extremely defensive and even secretive in the face of criticism.

Rome was the capital city of the Roman Empire and the center of the ancient world. Today it is referred to as the "external city". With the presence of the Vatican, it is the heart and the headquarters of the biggest Christian church. It was first a center of political and military power, as well as, to some extent, economic strength. In contrast to the might of Imperial Rome, and alongside the military legions, the trifling number of Christians must have made them look very vulnerable and unimportant.

> Christ's riches are unsearchable, and this doctrine of the gospel is the field this treasure is hidden in.
>
> ~ THOMAS GOODWIN

When Paul arrived there, he was in chains. Still he looked past the human show of authority and power, because he had already tasted the omnipotence of the almighty God. Therefore he did not take on a panic-stricken approach, nor an apologetic attitude. He was not at all ashamed of the gospel. The story of the life of Jesus, the living Christ, was the power of God and in reality infinitely more powerful than any human display of power and strength.

The gospel of Jesus Christ is still the power of God today. Jesus changes lives. He turns sadness to joy; the weak become strong; sins are forgiven; the fearful gain courage; the confused find self-confidence – all through His glorious name. That is why Paul was not ashamed of the gospel of Jesus Christ, and it is also why you and I do not have to be afraid or ashamed.

I praise You, Lord Jesus, that the power of Your gospel strengthens me with the faith to live. Amen.

A righteousness from God, apart from law, has been made known. This righteousness from God comes through faith in Jesus Christ to all who believe. (Rom. 3:21-22)

Read
Rom. 3:21-31

It would be interesting to know how many people are lost to Christianity because they find it just too demanding. They feel that they simply cannot measure up to the standards set by Jesus Christ and they give up – sometimes they don't even try to begin with! It seems to them like an unequal struggle. And so they miss out on the greatest joy this life has to offer – a personal relationship with the living Christ!

You must remember that Jesus is well aware of human weakness. He experienced this first-hand during His earthly ministry, and it is actually the reason why no one can earn the right to be a Christian and be loved by God. It becomes yours purely and only through the measureless grace of God!

> Our faith is not based on speculation, it's based on revelation!
> ~ DR. RICK THOMPSON

All that Jesus asks of you when He calls you to surrender and devotion to Him, is that you will have faith in Him and trust Him. If this seems too simple to be true, or too difficult, turn to your Bible and see how many ordinary, weak, sinful people became ambassadors for Christ simply because they believed in Him and trusted Him.

The door to this transformed life stands wide open to you and could be a dramatic turning point in your life. You dare not allow such a God-given opportunity to slip by!

At Your empty grave, Lord Jesus, I found true life. I praise You for this. Amen.

Read
Rom. 14:1-12

Accept him whose faith is weak, without passing judgment on disputable matters. (Rom. 14:1)

There are people who have turned away from the Christian faith because of the arrogant and overbearing attitude of other Christians. Although it may not be intentional, there are people whose enthusiastic witness is just a little too forceful, especially for new Christians. There is the ever-present danger that a potential new convert will feel hopelessly inadequate, and as a result, be lost to the faith.

We must remember that some people are shy, reserved and quiet. Some are too ashamed or too embarrassed to express an opinion, while others may feel useless when confronted by someone with a strong and intimidating personality. New believers may get confused and feel discouraged when they hear others freely quoting Scripture.

> Our power in drawing others after the Lord mainly rests in our joy and communion with Him ourselves.
>
> ~ J. G. BELLETT

Jesus *led* people to faith – He never forced them! His tender approach and His love for others won their hearts in the simplest ways while He taught them about the kingdom of God.

Follow the example of the Master in your witness to others and in doing so you will win followers for Christ.

Help me, true Master, to follow Your example of humility and love in my witness to other people. Amen.

Who among men knows the thoughts of a man except the man's spirit? In the same way no one knows the thoughts of God except the Spirit of God. (1 Cor. 2:11)

Read
1 Cor. 2:6-15

There is nothing dull about a spiritual life. It usually starts with great emotional enthusiasm. But like all relationships, as time goes by, a real danger exists that familiarity will dampen the zeal that started as an ardent love and eager warmth; and your faith becomes ineffective. On the other hand, you can grow into a deeper relationship with your Lord and Master through prayer, Bible study and meditation. Your spiritual state is the direct result of your efforts, or your neglect, of spiritual matters.

While natural growth requires little effort, growing in faith demands serious attention. Unless you are truly on your guard against it, your moods will dictate the quality of your spiritual life. There could come a time when life turns against you, or when you feel dissatisfied and unhappy and the

> The justified person lives and performs every act of spiritual life by faith. Everything is promised to, and is received, by faith.
> ~ WILLIAM ROMAINE

temptation to neglect your prayer life is very strong. At the precise point when you need the comfort and power of prayer the most, you stop praying and turn away from spiritual disciplines.

The highs and lows of your spiritual life are not determined by your heavenly Father, but by you yourself. And the only way to maintain a life on the spiritual peaks is to live in the continual consciousness of the presence of the living Christ. Through faith and prayer, a certain knowledge of His presence grows and through faith Christ becomes a greater reality in your everyday life.

Merciful Master, thank You that I can keep my faith alive by remaining close to You. Amen.

Read
1 Cor. 15:50-58

My dear brothers, stand firm. Let nothing move you. Give yourselves fully to the work of the Lord, because your labor in the Lord is not in vain. (1 Cor. 15:58)

Discouragement is something that many, if not all people, experience at one time or another in their lives. Well-intended actions are misunderstood; the best laid-out plans are derailed, and meaningful proposals are rejected.

The outcome of all of this is the temptation to throw in the towel. It can happen in your spiritual or secular life, but the frustrations are the same. It is generally known that discouragement is one of the most popular tools in Satan's workshop. He particularly tries to discourage enthusiastic believers to undermine the work of the Lord.

It is of the utmost importance for us to stand against this. Therefore, we need to know Jesus and allow Him to take His place as the cornerstone of our lives. Seek the will of God in any given circumstance before you tackle any project. Pray that His Spirit will lead you in all the decisions you have to make and that He will reveal His will clearly to you. In so doing, renewed by the Spirit and strong in the knowledge that God is with you, you can tackle any task with faith and trust.

> No man shall ever behold the glory of Christ by sight hereafter, who does not in some measure behold it by faith here in this world.
>
> ~ JOHN OWEN

You will still encounter stumbling blocks and there will always be those who will try to jeopardize your efforts. There will also be moments when you will experience feelings of despondency and discouragement. But call continually on the Master to support you. If you have the assurance that what you do, you do with and for Christ, it is possible to succeed against all odds and to triumph.

Living Lord Jesus, with You at my side I can face life with confidence. Amen.

You are all sons of God through faith in Christ Jesus, for all of you who were baptized into Christ have clothed yourselves with Christ. (Gal. 3:26-27)

Read
Gal. 3:21-29

When we read about the references made to Jesus as the Son of God, the majesty of Christ astounds us – unless we have no feelings. In the area of human relationships as we know them, it is difficult to grasp that the Son of God could also have lived on earth as a Man. Sometimes this concept seems totally incomprehensible to us. Perhaps it is exactly for this reason that many people, possibly including you, see it as impossible to follow the example of the Master, because He was no ordinary person – He was holy; He was the Son of the living God!

Never allow this kind of thinking to stop you from serving the Master. Remember that, by the grace of God, you have also been called to become a child of God, through faith in Jesus the living Christ, your Savior and Redeemer. The family of God is universal and every one who accepts Jesus is adopted into His family as a child of God.

> It was not *after* we were reconciled by the blood of His Son that God began to love us, but before the foundation of the world.
> ~ JOHN CALVIN

Decide once again, or for the first time, to serve God by walking with Jesus and faithfully and continuously follow His example. As you grow in grace, you will become more and more aware of God the Father as He watches over you and, through the work of the Holy Spirit, equips you to fulfill your role as His beloved child.

I rejoice, Lord my God, in the honor of being called Your child. *Amen.*

April 13

Faith Dies When Zeal Diminishes

Read
Gal. 5:1-12

You were running a good race. Who cut in on you and kept you from obeying the truth? (Gal. 5:7)

Where there is spiritual stagnation, there is also spiritual decline. There are probably more Christians than the world will ever know who feel defeated and depressed because half-heartedness has weakened their spiritual strength.

The hopes and ambitions of those who have walked the same road earlier in the company of Christ are scattered on the spiritual road. Jesus' disciples were making good progress, but their zeal and enthusiasm waned. Why?

Undoubtedly there are many causes, but there are certain basic reasons that are present in practically every "former" Christian's life. The most obvious is that he or she allowed something or someone to take their focus off Christ. They have been distracted by side roads and obstacles, and pointless arguments have taken the place of an active and real faith. While intelligent discussion stimulates the mind, it must never be allowed to interfere with, or replace spiritual growth.

> People don't ask for facts in making up their minds. They would rather have one good, soul-satisfying emotion than a dozen facts.
> ~ ROBERT KEITH LEAVITT

Another reason why a positive faith can become negative or ineffective, is when a person refuses to accept the discipline necessary for spiritual growth. Such a person puts too much emphasis on emotions and his or her spiritual life therefore fluctuates according to feelings. It is necessary to move past emotions to get to the point where God Himself becomes a living reality.

A faith that fails to make Christ the central focus; that allows controversy to detract from His glory and relies on feelings and emotions, will only weaken and in time decline and die.

Help me, Holy Spirit of God, to keep Christ at the center of my faith. Amen.

To the saints in Ephesus, the faithful in Christ Jesus.
(Eph. 1:1)

Read
Eph. 1:1-14

From time to time we hear stories of inspiring Christian disciples. Some of who were martyrs; others were mighty in their prayer lives; and others in their good deeds and righteousness. We admire their wonderful achievements, and sometimes we are overwhelmed by a feeling of inadequacy at our own spiritual struggles, defeats and failures.

The heroes of the Christian faith are called "saints". But us ordinary Christians, deeply aware of our human weaknesses, deny this status. "I am no saint," we say, meaning that we also make mistakes and even disappoint the Lord from time to time.

When the apostle wrote to the Christians in the city of Ephesus, he addressed them as "believers" or "saints". Not one of them was particularly suited to be called a saint. Some were slaves, others were businessmen, domestic servants, clerks or cleaners. Yet they were all believers. The word *saint* simply indicates their relationship with Jesus and their enthusiastic devotion to Him. They were certainly not superstars. They were not plucked out of their daily routines and replanted in a spiritual nursery. They were saints on account of their faith and trust in Jesus, right where they worked.

> God hasn't called me to be successful. He's called me to be faithful.
> ~ MOTHER TERESA

In the same sense of the word, you and I can also be called "saints" or "believers", wherever you live or work. Christ is not looking for spiritual superstars. He simply wants you to believe in Him and continue to trust in Him.

Lord Jesus, we pray today for Your disciples who live and work in difficult circumstances. Strengthen them and keep them faithful through the work of Your Holy Spirit. Amen.

Read
Eph. 5:6-21

"Wake up, O sleeper, rise from the dead, and Christ will shine on you." (Eph. 5:14)

Over-familiarity with holy truths can turn us into spiritual sleepwalkers and eventually destroy our most important experiences with the living Christ. You may have heard the gospel preached and explained in more sermons than you are able to remember. You are sure that there is nothing new to be said about the basic principles of Christianity. And because you have already heard it all so often in the past, your Spirit grow immune to the truths of the gospel.

Christ came to give you life (see John 10:10) and to pardon you through His Spirit so that your spirit can enjoy the enriching companionship of the Eternal Father. The gospel is not as much concerned with your dogmatic faith (although this is very important in its right place) but is much more interested in your relationship with God.

> As well could you expect a plant to grow without air and water as to expect your heart to grow without prayer and faith.
>
> ~ CHARLES H. SPURGEON

If your system of beliefs leads you into a living relationship with Christ Jesus, then your faith is achieving its goal. If, however, you profess that you believe in God but this confession does not succeed in making God a living reality in your life, you need to ask yourself if your faith has led you far enough down the road to God.

If you are content with a vague and undefined faith that does not bring you into God's presence, you are missing out on the abundant life that God has planned for you. Now is the time for you to awaken to the presence of the living God.

Thank You that my faith has led me to the knowledge of Your holy presence, Lord Jesus. Amen.

Finally, be strong in the Lord and in His mighty power. (Eph. 6:10)

Read
Eph. 6:10-20

World events can have a disturbing influence on you and your way of life. Particularly in times of war, people can become anxious and alarmed; recession and economic crises cause great worry; poor health or the failure of a business venture can also bring about a situation of anxiety and fear.

When you have to adjust your life as the result of a change in your circumstances, you are filled with apprehension and uncertainty. Most people will acknowledge that they have experienced these feelings at one point or another in their lives.

> God wants to be with you enough for you to make Him your refuge, your glory and your strength.
> ~ ANONYMOUS

If you don't want to be completely overwhelmed by fear and anxiety, or feelings of incompetence and inadequacy, it is essential to stay close to the living Christ and receive your strength from Him. No one else knows you so intimately and completely; no one except Jesus Christ loves you enough to care about you with the all-embracing love of the holy God.

Empowered by the knowledge that you are supported and protected by the omnipotence, strength and love of God, you will be fully equipped to cope with any situation in life knowing that you do not have to do it alone – the living Christ is by your side!

Find your strength and power in God and you will be victorious over fear, anxiety, adversity and disaster. You will be able to live in Him with faith and trust from day to day.

You, Lord my God, are my refuge and my hiding place. I will not be afraid. Amen.

The Secret of Life (1)

To me, to live is Christ and to die is gain. (Phil. 1:21)

It is unfortunate that so many people live their lives without any real fulfillment. No matter how active they are, they're still frustrated and dissatisfied. As they grow older they begin to wonder about the real meaning and significance of life.

When frustration takes hold of their spirits, they start working hard to attain those things that they think will bring them joy and satisfaction. For a while they may experience an apparent feeling of satisfaction, but then they become conscious of a gnawing conviction that they should be aiming for something better – if only they could find out what it is.

Someone once said, "We make a living by what we get; but we make a life by what we give." The secret of true life lies in giving yourself to God, to your fellow man, and to life in general. Have you ever met a miserable person who loves God; who brings joy to his fellow humans; who is always busy giving of himself to others? The secret of true life is to share with others those spiritual qualities that are born out of a genuine relationship with the living Christ. To know Christ and to have real love – this is the foundation of true life.

> I asked God for all things, that I might enjoy life. God gave me life, that I might enjoy all things.
>
> ~ ANONYMOUS

If you want to find deep satisfaction in life, put Christ at the center. Work with Him and seek to do only His will. If this seems to you like a boring exercise far-removed from the realities of life, you are seriously mistaken. In reality, it is a personal, gracious invitation from the Master to walk a path that has all the qualities that will make your life satisfying, fulfilling and worthwhile.

Thank You, Lord Jesus, for the full, rich and perfect life I have found in You. Amen.

For to me, to live is Christ and to die is gain. (Phil. 1:21)

Read
Phil. 1:12-26

Over the years a serious misunderstanding about the church has developed. Many people believe complying with Christian principles is equivalent to giving oneself over to a boring life – a life without joy, sparkle or happiness. Critics have given the impression that Christians are somber people with a comfortless existence and no fun, indeed, frowning on enjoyment.

Nothing could be further from the truth! Jesus Christ offers His followers the abundant life that can come from no other source than the Master, who Himself lived a fulfilling and complete life. There is nothing about the life of Christ that can be viewed as monotonous, boring or without purpose. In every aspect He is the Source and Origin of true life!

> The law of God and also the way to life is written in our hearts; it lies in no man's supposing, nor in any historical opinion, but in a good will and well doing.
>
> ~ JACOB BÖHME

To live the abundant life that Jesus offers you, it is necessary to lay down your life of self-righteousness and allow Him to take control. However, this does not mean there has to be any loss on your side. On the contrary, you will discover that conforming to Christ will transform your existence to one of purpose, meaning and complete fulfillment. Those who have done so have discovered life in all its fullness and abundance.

Lord Jesus, in You my soul has found a life of tranquility, joy and peace of mind. Amen.

Read
Col. 1:1-8

To the holy and faithful brothers in Christ at Colosse. (Col. 1:2)

When people emigrate, some decide to retain citizenship of the country they have left while others take on citizenship of their new country. Sometimes it is possible to hold dual citizenship and in that way have a foot in both camps.

Living a Christian life is very much like having dual citizenship. Spiritually you are "in Christ"; He is the focus of your devotion and trust; He is your Lord, Savior and Redeemer. As your Lord He rules your heart and commands your love. The closer you are to each other, the more it can be said that you are "in Christ". But you are also "in Colosse" – wherever you may live. You must earn a living there, live among the people, pay your taxes and obey the laws of the country.

> If a man cannot be a Christian in the place where he is, he cannot be a Christian anywhere.
>
> ~ HENRY WARD BEECHER

You cannot escape from the daily ups and downs "in Colosse" even if you think you could be closer to Christ in another environment. The fact is: you can remain "in Christ" only when you are "in Colosse" and that is why He does not allow you to escape the pressures of living in this world.

You therefore need to do a balancing trick. Every Christian since the time of Christ has had to do this. You can never escape from "Colosse". You are in exactly the right place, and Christ is also "in Colosse" – right there with you!

Holy Lord Jesus, help me to make You more and more of a reality in my life in the place where I live. Amen.

To the holy and faithful brothers in Christ at Colosse. (Col. 1:2)

Read
Col. 1:1-8

In the modern world trustworthiness, loyalty and determination have been moved to the background. It is acceptable to change your mind as the mood grabs you or according to circumstances. There are some people who feel that this is absolutely normal in their spiritual lives too, and they chop and change as the mood takes them.

In biblical times it was not at all easy to remain faithful to Jesus Christ. The surrounding people were hostile toward Jesus' followers. Persecution and martyrdom occurred regularly, which made it dangerous to be a Christian. So when they were confronted with the burning stake, or thrown to the lions in a "sports" arena, it is understandable that some Christians caved in and denied their faith.

> If you were arrested for being a Christian, would there be enough evidence to convict you?
> ~ ANONYMOUS

Many of those who refused to deny Christ paid with their lives. Remaining faithful to Jesus means honoring Him, worshiping Him, living – and possibly also dying – according to His teachings, and announcing your identity as a Christian; being part of a Christian community and making your contribution to His work.

Faith in Jesus can still lead to all those things. In some countries Christians are even rejected by their own families.

You have been called by Jesus to be faithful and true in your circumstances, just like the early Christians. If it is easy for you to be a Christian where you are, thank God for this and pray for all your fellow believers who must endure hardship and condemnation because of His name.

Holy Father God, I pray for all those who have to pay a high price for their faith in Jesus. Amen.

| # Learning to Know God Better

| Bearing fruit in every good work, growing in the knowledge of God. (Col. 1:10)

The devoted Christian has an inner desire to know God better. How can this be done? Some people try to achieve it by reading Christian books; delving more deeply into the Bible or by dedicating themselves to church activities or to social services in the community. All of these things are good and praiseworthy, and many people have attained advanced degrees of spirituality by doing things like these for God.

But, the letter to the Christians at Colosse spells it out clearly. A deeper knowledge of God comes into being as a fruit of the infilling of the Holy Spirit, who grants us spiritual wisdom and understanding. You do not learn to know God better by taking an advanced theological course or by rattling off Scripture verses. You learn to know Him better by "growing in the knowledge of God," when His Spirit comes to live in you.

> Mere change is not growth. Growth is the synthesis of change and continuity, and where there is no continuity, there is no growth.
> ~ C. S. Lewis

If you want to know God better, study the Word, read spiritual books, attend spiritual events and camps, and get involved in the work of the Lord; but most important of all, open yourself up to His Holy Spirit.

Only the Holy Spirit of God can help your knowledge of God grow. There must be interaction between you and the Holy Spirit; you need to respond to His influence. You ought to pray regularly for this aspect of your spiritual growth, both in yourself and in others. It is much better to ask God for spiritual knowledge than for material well-being.

Father God, let my knowledge of You and Your purpose for me grow continually through the work of the Holy Spirit. Amen.

Continue in your faith, established and firm, not moved from the hope held out in the gospel. (Col. 1:23)

Read
Col. 1:15-23

During a raging winter storm a large tree was uprooted and fell right across a busy highway. Traffic had to be rerouted. The only way the tree could be removed was to cut it up into small pieces and carry it away. It was many hours later before everything returned to normal. Just as the biggest tree can be uprooted, so the strongest faith can fail.

The storms of adversity and disaster can also uproot you and break down your faith. The simple conflicts and problems of life can weaken you. Emotional problems and doubt can eat away at the roots of your faith and leave you vulnerable to the attack of the Evil One. Suffering, unemployment, or the disruption of your family life can do the same.

> It was a Person that God gave, it is a Person that we need; and it is a Person that we accept by faith.
> ~ WALTER LEWIS WILSON

It is therefore important to feed your faith so that your roots remain strong and firm. You do this by worshiping God, reading the Bible, and studying the word of God. Christian fellowship can also strengthen your faith.

Keeping your faith deep-rooted is a lifelong task. You need to be just as serious about it when you have been following Jesus for forty years as when you have been following Him for four years. When the real storms of life break loose, your faith needs to be firmly rooted in God.

Lord Jesus, strengthen my wavering faith. *Amen.*

Read
Col. 1:24-29

I have become its servant by the commission God gave me to present to you the word of God in its fullness. (Col. 1:25)

Most people have dreams about what they want to be. A teenager may long to be a pop star or a sports champion. A businessman might dream of building an empire through his own efforts. An actresses might dream of becoming a Hollywood star. Everyone has dreams for the future. But most of us have to adapt our dreams along the way – and sometimes they must be given up altogether for the reality of real life.

God also has a dream: not so much for Himself, but for us. Sometimes God has to intervene in our dreams and schemes and replace them with His own. God's dream for Paul was that he should become a servant. This was not even close to what Paul dreamt of as a young man. No one dreams of becoming a servant; especially not someone with the intellect and motivation of Paul. Nevertheless he did become a servant, both of Christ and of the church. And in so doing he acquired fame and greatness. Following Jesus Christ Himself, he was the chief architect of the early church and of the spreading of the gospel. Paul was probably the greatest thinker of his time. God's dream for Paul bore fruit in Paul's life and work.

> To accomplish great things, we must not only act, but also dream; not only plan, but also believe.
> ~ ANATOLE FRANCE

God also has a dream or a plan for you and me. You may already know what yours is. If you do not, surrender to God in faith and ask Him what His dream for your life is. He may have great things in mind for you, or His dream may not appeal to you at all. Accept it, whatever it may be. Like Paul, you might be pleasantly surprised at the final outcome!

Holy God, make Your dream for my life a reality. Amen.

Though I am absent from you in body, I am present with you in spirit and delight to see how orderly you are and how firm your faith in Christ is. (Col. 2:5)

Read
Col. 2:1-5

Sometimes people make the mistake of thinking that as long as their faith is strong and they believe in all the right things, that it's enough. With this mindset they expect to get away with wrong behavior. Others think it doesn't matter what you believe as long as you are "doing your best". Both of these ways of thinking are incorrect.

Faith and action go hand-in-hand. You need both to be in right standing with Christ. In most of his writings, Paul went to great trouble to help people to understand how faith in Christ is directly related to solving the problems that people experience – and to correcting the wrong teachings that have been given to them. He always preached to the following effect, "Therefore, for the sake of the truth, behave in this way, avoid that, live a life worthy of discipleship in Jesus Christ."

> The world is blessed by men who do things, not by those who merely talk about them.
> ~ JAMES OLIVER

For Paul it was important to know and believe in the correct teachings so that he could live according to the example and instruction of Jesus Christ. It was as important to live correctly and obey God as it was to preach the gospel. The two aspects could not be separated – they went together.

It is still the same today: you need to behave like a follower of Christ. In order to attain this in all circumstances, you need a strong and vigorous faith in Christ. You need to know *why* you should behave in a certain way and you need the faith to know that only Christ, through His Spirit, can help you to live in the right way.

Holy Spirit of God, make my faith strong and fill my actions with love. Amen.

Read
Col. 2:6-15

See to it that no one takes you captive through hollow and deceptive philosophy. (Col. 2:8)

Since the beginning of time, people have searched the mysteries of God. From remote villages in Africa to the great universities of Western culture, people have tried to understand and explain God. But they are trying to define the indefinable. Still they never give up because people have a deep-rooted desire to find what they know exists but what they cannot prove.

No one can count the number of proposed theories of the existence of God, or the number of books written to try and confirm or deny His existence. The human mind finds it exceedingly difficult, if not impossible, to imagine an intellectual viewpoint of God that is fully satisfying.

Perhaps the reason for people's inability to get a better understanding of God is that they are looking for Him in the wrong places.

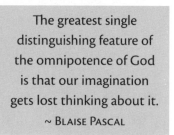

The greatest single distinguishing feature of the omnipotence of God is that our imagination gets lost thinking about it.

~ BLAISE PASCAL

We try to limit God by man-made laws, instead of simply and humbly bringing our spirits into the presence of God through prayer and the study of His Word.

God is Spirit and He can be known and experienced only when our human spirits reach out and accept His gracious invitation to take part in the challenge of delighting ourselves in God's gift of His Holy Spirit – a gift that He offers to all believers.

Through the gift of the Holy Spirit, Father God, I have the joyous assurance of Your living presence. Amen.

We continually remember before our God and Father your work produced by faith, your labor prompted by love, and your endurance inspired by hope. (1 Thess. 1:3)

One of the ongoing problems of the Christian faith is that not everyone who professes it puts it into practice. You probably know some people who make you think, "What a poor example of Christianity." Sometimes those who have much to say about the Christian faith, manage to disprove everything they have said through their unworthy behavior and actions.

It is, however, also true that the biggest majority of believers do practice what they preach. Even with their weaknesses and shortcomings, these people, who have genuinely given their lives to Christ, live lives characterized by simplicity, humility and honesty.

When Jesus came into our world, He went around preaching and teaching. He was an extremely effective communicator. Therefore it is said of Him, "He went around doing good and healing all who were under the power of the devil, because God was with Him" (Acts 10:38). This was because the things He did were consistent with what He preached. When He healed people, He gave a message of God's unending love in action. When He drove out demons, it was a clear indication of God's kingly authority over the Evil One.

> Faith without works
> is not faith at all.
> ~ ANONYMOUS

Every believer following the example of the Master is bound to put his faith into practice in the same way.

Holy Jesus, help me through the Spirit to put my faith into proper practice, for Your honor and glory. Amen.

The words *example* or *model* usually imply that something is a replica of a full-scale original. The fact is that there are many interpretations and uses of the word. In the case of our text for today, the word refers to a model of excellence or achievement.

The Christians of Thessalonica were models or examples to others in terms of their faith, zeal and works of love. The apostle Paul said that they offered the kind of example that all Christians should follow.

It is true that all believers are being closely watched by believers and unbelievers alike. Their actions, their attitude and the language they use are all noticed and often applied as a standard for others to measure and judge their own lives. Often this standard is set with positive intentions when people accept a practicing Christian as a reliable measuring-stick of good behavior. In cases where the Christian does not measure up to the right standard, it sets a bad example and can be used as an excuse for others to behave just as badly. We are models and examples to others: for better or for worse.

> Example is the school of mankind, and they will learn at no other.
>
> ~ EDMUND BURKE

Being an example for others puts a heavy responsibility on every Christian: search your heart and carefully examine your way of life. Christianity is an ongoing call to vigilance and discipline, not so that people can notice and admire you, but "that they may see your good deeds and praise your Father in Heaven" (Matt. 5:16).

Heavenly Father, strengthen all those who find that the responsibility of being a role model for You is too difficult for them. Amen.

Religion that God our Father accepts as pure and faultless is this: to look after orphans and widows and to keep oneself from being polluted by the world. (James 1:27)

Read
James 1:19-27

Faith that does not produce practical Christianity fails in its God-given calling. It is dangerously easy to become so used to credos and grand rituals that the real power of the Word leaves you untouched and unmoved.

James, in his ever-practical letter, reminds all Christian disciples how important it is for them to maintain Christ's standards in a corrupt world. They need to be fully surrendered to the Master and live their lives in the knowledge of His indwelling Holy Spirit.

Such a powerful faith has a transforming effect on everyone who confesses and accepts it. It is impossible to be aware of Christ's indwelling Holy Spirit and remain untouched by the desperate need in the world around

> There is no human power that can replace the power of the Spirit.
> ~ LEWI PETHRUS

you. James speaks of widows and orphans, the most uneducated and disadvantaged people of his day. The modern interpretation of these words would include all who are in need.

A true religion is a caring religion, extending a genuine offer of help to all who are finding the struggle of life too difficult. This offer must not be made from a sense of duty, but because your life is filled with the Holy Spirit. Unless your religion has brought you to the point of an awareness of Christ's indwelling presence and you know the power of His Holy Spirit, you will not be able to experience His transforming power.

Loving Master, through the indwelling presence of Your Holy Spirit, let my spiritual life speak of a transforming faith. *Amen.*

Read
James 2:14-26

In the same way, faith by itself, if it is not accompanied by action, is dead. (James 2:17)

Some people disregard the power of prayer because their urgent calls to God have gone unanswered. They may have been serious and devoted in their pleas, but seemingly it was all for nothing. The outcome of such an experience is often a weakening of one's faith in the power of prayer.

Genuine prayer in itself is an act of faith. It is not just a matter of telling God what you need and then sitting back and waiting for something to happen – the hoped-for miracle! Effective prayer means laying your plea before God, seeking His will for your life and then standing in faith, in obedience to the will of the Lord.

No one can possibly believe that Jesus wanted to endure the humiliation and martyrdom of Golgotha, but His prayer to His Father is an enduring and eternal example of faith and obedience, for all time and for all people, "My Father, if it is possible, may this cup be taken from Me. Yet not as I will, but as You will" (Matt. 26:39). Christ sought the will of God and accepted it in faith, to God's glory.

> Prayer is not a substitute for work, thinking, watching, suffering, or giving; prayer is a support for all other efforts.
> ~ GEORGE BUTTRICK

Follow Christ's example in your prayer life and God will answer your prayers in the manner that He knows is the absolute best for you.

Help me, O Holy Spirit, to pray prayers of faith and believe that God wants to do only what is best for me. *Amen.*

In the same way, faith by itself, if it is not accompanied by action, is dead. (James 2:17)

Read
James 2:14-26

It is not what you say or how well you argue that is really important; but it is who you are that is important. Many people are able to quote godly phrases with great ease, but the final test of faith is the quality of life and the fruit it yields for the individual and society.

Inner resources and strength, creative purpose, a natural politeness towards all people, a listening ear and an understanding heart, a mind full of constructive ideas, and a spirit that is sensitive to the leading of God: all these and other similar qualities reflect the reality of a dynamic spiritual faith that is active in a believer's everyday life.

> Let it be your business to keep your mind in the presence of the Lord.
> ~ BROTHER LAWRENCE

While the above-mentioned treasures are God's gifts of grace to you, they are ineffective unless you receive them and integrate them fully into your life. There has to be a beginning for such a life, and this beginning can be dramatic and revolutionary, but after the initial start a process of spiritual growth needs to take place. Without this growth, there can be no spiritual depth or living faith. Anything done in the name of religion will then carry the label of shallowness and insincerity.

In order to grow in the spirit so you can live out your faith in a practical way, it is imperative to spend time in the presence of God so that something of His greatness, His creativity, His love in action and His peace will become an integral part of your daily life, to the degree that you are able to receive these gifts.

Teach me, Lord my God, to make Your spiritual qualities mine and let them be expressed in my life. *Amen.*

MAY

The LORD had said to Abram, "Leave your country, your people and your father's household and go to the land I will show you." So Abram left, as the LORD had told him.
~ Genesis 12:1, 4

Eternal and Almighty God,
As You called Abram at the beginning of history,
so You call us in modern history to follow You in faith.
May it be said of us, as it was of Abram,
"By faith Abraham, when called to go to a place he would later receive as his inheritance, obeyed and went" (Heb. 11:8).
Your calling is an ongoing challenge to walk by faith and not by sight.
Your call is always to the unknown road, the unnamed destination;
It is a call to live in expectation; to dare to walk the untried road;
to watch You build something completely new in our lives.
You call us to the road less traveled,
the narrow road that leads to life.
We long so much for faith and security, but You call us to faith alone.
You do not give us any guarantees of a successful homecoming.
We want to pitch our tents in the camping grounds, with all the others,
but You want us to roll our tents up and move into the future.
Like Abraham of old, we are also pilgrims seeking the Promised Land.
Grant that we will hear Your call, clearly and distinctly,
and give us grace to be obedient – without hesitation.
You call us to spread Your love all over the world;
to carry Your joyful message to the ends of the earth.
We thank You for Jesus, the One You sent to us from heaven and who
responded in obedience and laid down His life so that the gates
of paradise can swing open for us once again
that we may inherit Canaan.
Let us then run the race as believers, sure of our purpose,
with our eyes fixed on Jesus, the Alpha and Omega.

Amen.

If you accept that Jesus is the revelation and manifestation of the
Father, then you are a follower of Christ and so a Christian.
~ BASIL HUME

Do You Believe?

Read

1 Pet. 1:1-9

Who through faith are shielded by God's power until the coming of the salvation that is ready to be revealed in the last time. (1 Pet. 1:5)

People believe in God for different reasons. Some think that their faith will bring them success and wealth; some are simply grateful for a miracle that God has performed in their lives; and others believe that faith is the only way to make sense of this disorderly world. Then there are those who believe in Him because He meets their need for a friend, a helper and a Savior.

The early Christians lived in extremely dangerous times. The people whom Peter was addressing had already suffered persecution and knew that they would most likely have to endure persecution again at some point. Their life expectancy was short. Yet they believed and trusted that God's power would always be greater than the might of their earthly rulers and that He would equip them to withstand any trials. Some Christians escaped death and others did not: They died in arenas, on burning stakes, or in the salt mines. They endured all these things because, in the face of the greatest dangers, they trusted in God and believed in Jesus Christ. To them faith was not just a matter of escaping danger and death. Faith meant facing and experiencing those kinds of trials and dealing with them with God-given courage, determination, love and faithfulness – even if the end result was death. They were able to endure because they were certain of what God had waiting for them in heaven. They also knew that whether they were with Christ on earth or with God in heaven, they would always be one with the Father in His house.

> The secret behind getting more faith, is to get to know God more.
>
> ~ LESTER SUMRALL

Let's examine our hearts. Are we able to put our full trust in Him when we are confronted with danger, disease, failure, loneliness or depression?

Merciful heavenly Father, strengthen those whose faith is being tested to the extreme. Amen.

Who through faith are shielded by God's power until the coming of the salvation that is ready to be revealed in the last time. (1 Pet. 1:5)

Read
1 Pet. 1:1-9

Your concept of time and how it works determines how you see and understand life, God and the world around you. You could see it as a circle, going round and round – history repeating itself. Or you might think of time as a straight line that begins somewhere and ends somewhere else.

While many religions think of time as a circle, the Bible shows that time as we know it, begins somewhere (with the Creation); it has events taking place in the middle, and time will end in the future. According to the Bible, God intervenes at certain points, and He will eventually let the curtain fall on human history. This final ending is called "The end of time".

It will be an act of God – the Evil One will be exposed and the truth will shine through. God will judge and separate the bad from the good, but He will judge with perfect wisdom, mercy, and compassion.

> We must never speak to simple, excitable people about "the Day" without emphasizing again and again the utter impossibility of prediction.
> ~ C. S. Lewis

Then Jesus Christ will advocate on behalf of all those who believe in Him. They will be saved, whether or not they were delivered from danger in the here and now. At the end of time the Messiah will come and take complete control; wrongs and injustices that have been committed will be set right and God will establish His kingdom over everything and everyone. Christians know and believe that God's last day will dawn. Do you believe that too?

Come, Lord, come quickly in all Your might, glory and love. *Amen.*

Read 1 Pet. 1:1-9	These have come so that your faith – of greater worth than gold, may be proved genuine. (1 Pet. 1:7)

There are few things that can change a person's values so dramatically than the death of a loved one. People who have lost a child in an accident often say, "What happened to us we do not wish on anyone, but we have learned things we did not know before. In many ways the things we regarded as important do not matter any more. And what we never considered to be important has become very meaningful. God has completely changed our lives."

Gold is considered by many to be the ultimate measure of value. If the things that money can buy are the most important to you, then this is indeed true. But there are things that money cannot buy.

> There is nothing wrong with people possessing riches. The wrong comes when riches possess people.
>
> ~ BILLY GRAHAM

Money cannot buy faith, hope or love. There are many wealthy people who have no faith, who cannot find hope anywhere and who are living without love. They are unhappy despite their worldly wealth.

Never allow the love of money to undermine your faith in God. You will lose your perspective and end up valuing the wrong things. Value God's truth and put your faith in Jesus the living Christ. Put your love for people firmly at the top of your list of priorities. View money as a utility and not as a god.

Your faith helps you to see things for what they really are in day-to-day living. Faith fulfills your hope, challenges you to love, and enriches and refines you as a person. Whatever the stock exchange says about the price of gold, remember that your faith is "of greater worth than gold".

Faithful Teacher, help me to live by faith according to Your heavenly standards and values. Amen.

These have come so that your faith – of greater worth than gold – may be proved genuine and may result in praise, glory and honor. (1 Pet. 1:7)

Read
1 Pet. 1:1-9

Setbacks, problems and disappointments can either break you or make you stronger. There are people who become broken and bitter after a tragedy or they fall in the pit of self-pity. Then there are those who emerge with the determination to overcome their disappointment and difficulties.

The trials that the early Christians had to endure were a bit different. They suffered tribulation simply because they were Christians. At any time they could be discovered and put on trial. If someone decided to follow Jesus, it was a matter of life and death. Paul and the other spiritual leaders tried to encourage the Christians to be steadfast in their faith. They knew that at any moment they too might be called to die for their faith.

> Suffering is the evidence against God, the reason not to trust Him. Jesus is the evidence for God, the reason to trust Him.
> ~ PETER KREEFT

However, they never doubted that enduring this kind of persecution would lead them into a deeper faith and a more intimate walk with Christ. It would also bring "praise, glory and honor" at Christ's Second Coming. This would form part of their reward. His glorious return would be a gift shared, because those who had been martyred stood united with Him. Having endured the cross with Him, they would therefore also partake in the glory that is His portion.

Along with any suffering you must endure, remember also, when you suffer in and with Christ, you bind yourself to the cross. And because you have joined in His suffering, He will share His glory with you. It is an enormous challenge, but what an indescribably wonderful reward He has for us!

Lord my God, help me through faith to endure all suffering with Jesus. Amen.

All Sorts of Trials

In this you greatly rejoice, though now for a little while you may have had to suffer grief in all kinds of trials. (1 Pet.1:6)

Most people have had to endure hardship at one time or another in their lives. Sometimes they bring it on themselves, but sometimes it arrives uninvited; like a thief in the night.

The grief that Peter was referring to came from the persecution and consequent suffering that Christians had to endure. The Roman emperor commanded some of these trials, while others were the work of local governors. It was truly a time of trial. Believers were only able to endure because they knew that "at the end of the age" they would be saved. That is why they were able to see past the trials and sufferings and look to the future where glory and hope shone.

You may be experiencing your own personal trials right now. These could be in the form of illness, an operation or an injury from an accident. You may be experiencing a financial setback; you may have lost your job or have fallen prey to swindlers. Some people find family problems the most difficult to cope with. Living with a gambler, a drug addict or an alcoholic can be a very big trial and must be faced on an ongoing basis. Others suffer the burden of an unmanageable workload, or the almost unbearable drudgery of a soul-destroying routine.

> Either He will shield you from suffering or He will give you unfailing strength to bear it. Be at peace, then, and put aside all anxious thoughts.
>
> ~ FRANCIS DE SALES

Deal with your hardships like the early Christians did, in the knowledge that Jesus Himself experienced many painful trials. Know today that God, like He did for Jesus, will see you through into His eternal joy and peace.

Lord, strengthen all those who have to suffer trials because of their faith. Amen.

These have come so that your faith – of greater worth than gold, which perishes even though refined by fire – may be proved genuine. (1 Pet. 1:7)

Read
1 Pet. 1:1-9

Gold-bearing ore goes through an intense process of refining before it leaves the mine as a glittering brick of yellow metal. First the ore is blasted from solid rocks and brought to the surface. Then it is finely ground in giant mills, treated with chemicals and placed in a blast furnace. The melted metal is then cast into molds and allowed to cool. After these different processes, the gold is about 90% pure. Further refining is then necessary to remove silver and any other impurities from the gold.

The killing of Christians by the authorities in the time of the early Christian church, meant that they also went through the mill. Under such tremendous pressure many of them renounced their faith. But those who were steadfast and managed to come through alive, emerged with great power and faith. And those who paid the highest price, with their lives, experienced the most intensive test of faith possible.

> God, who foresaw your tribulation, has specially armed you to go through it, not without pain but without stain.
> ~ C. S. Lewis

Hardships of any nature are a test of faith. You can either break down and lose your faith, or believe that the experience will refine and strengthen you. If you face your difficulties in the strength and grace of God, you will come through fully conscious that you have been "with Jesus". And nothing else can give you the same joy. You will be wiser and more understanding and you will see things in a completely new light. You will learn the difference between what is really important and what isn't. You will also become empathetic to the sufferings of your fellow man and, as a consequence, you will care more about others. And ... never again will you be afraid of death!

Lord Jesus, help me through Your good Spirit to endure trials with courage and with love for You. Amen.

Even though you do not see Him now, you believe in Him ... for you are receiving the goal of your faith, the salvation of your souls. (1 Pet. 1:8-9)

People try many different ways to get on the road of salvation. The most common approach is to try to be "good". Those who try so hard to be good think that God rewards people for keeping His commandments while others put their faith in good deeds. They think that God has a score card and that good deeds are rewarded and evil deeds punished. They believe they will go to heaven if they get a high score of good deeds.

Yet salvation comes through faith and not through good deeds. God saved you because He loves you. All you have to do is to trust Him completely! Accept this indescribable grace humbly and gratefully.

> There is never time in the future in which we will work out our salvation. The challenge is in the moment; the time is always now.
> ~ JAMES ARTHUR BALDWIN

But salvation is not just something for the future. "For you are receiving the goal of your faith, the salvation of your souls" (1 Pet. 1:9). It is an ongoing process as well as a one-time event. God is at work in you, both to save you from your sins and to offer you a better life in Christ Jesus, and to prepare you for a better life in heaven.

Never lose sight of your goal: to receive the complete and perfect love of Christ in heaven. But you also need to be open to receiving the grace of God on a daily basis. Not a day in your life goes by when you do not need God's grace. Even if you can accept it only in small quantities, your capacity to receive will grow and grow.

When you believe in Jesus and trust Him, you are saved, are being saved and will continue to be saved. It never ends!

Lord, renew Your love in me daily and let me receive afresh Your merciful grace. Amen.

Concerning this salvation, the prophets, who spoke of the grace that was to come to you, searched intently and with the greatest care. (1 Pet. 1:10)

Read
1 Pet. 1:10-16

D o you recall a time in your life when it seemed as if everything just fell into place for you? When you told someone about it, they probably said, "You see, it just shows you that God had something great in mind for you."

As believers we sometimes sense that God allows certain things to happen; that He has planned wonderful circumstances and has stretched out His holy hand to make sure that everything works out well for us.

The prophets of the Old Testament were convinced that God was busy doing something special. In spite of their concern for the people of Israel, they realized that God was working toward a bigger goal – something very special. They dreamt that all the nations of the world would one day embrace the gospel, accept God's truth and receive His love. He was too great a God, with too important a mission to limit His great plan to just one nation.

> Grace is the gift of Christ, who exposes the gulf which separates God and man, and by exposing it, bridges it.
> ~ KARL BARTH

The coming of Jesus to earth and the preaching of the gospel worldwide opened the floodgates of God's grace. Even in biblical times the Word went out to many people, reaching beyond the boundaries of Israel.

The grace of God is still flowing today. It pours out of the loving heart of God and changes people's lives wherever it goes. It is also destined for you. It will transform you, empower you, build you up spiritually and give you a purpose in life. It will not remove all hardships from your life, but it will give you more resources to help you cope. It is destined for you. Have you received it?

We praise and thank You, Lord Jesus, for those who have received Your grace and shared it with others. *Amen.*

When you have set your mind on doing something, whether it is big or small, it is essential to have a plan of action. The more thorough your preparation, the fewer mistakes you will make and the quicker the task will be completed.

God also planned ahead thoroughly. He carried out two enormous tasks. The first one was the creation of the universe. The second was the salvation of humanity, which He achieved through the coming of Jesus Christ. God planned the second undertaking even before He began the first. Then He gave us Jesus when the time was ripe. Jesus was part of God's master plan from the very beginning. But He came only when the world was ready to receive Him and respond to Him. In His great love, God delayed Jesus' coming until not only the Jewish people, but also the Gentiles were able to receive Him.

> Only in Jesus Christ do we have the assurance of salvation, forgiveness of sins, entrance into God's family, and the guarantee of heaven forever when we die.
>
> ~ LUIS PALAU

God also predestined your salvation. There was not a more appropriate time for Jesus to come into your life than when He did; no time was better for you to turn back to Him.

God was already planning ahead for you – even when you were completely unaware of what He was doing. Jesus made Himself known to you and now He is asking you to accept God's dream for you for a better, deeper and richer life. God has always loved you and He is asking you now to love Him in return and through faith, live the rest of your life to His honor and glory.

Father God, help me also to plan ahead and enable me to see beyond the boundaries of this life. Amen.

Through Him you believe in God, who raised Him from the dead and glorified Him, and so your faith and hope are in God. (1 Pet. 1:21)

Read
1 Pet. 1:17-25

Some people grow up in families where faith in God is taken for granted. Some people struggle through many obstacles and come to faith at last. Others notice a remarkable change in someone else's life and this convinces them that a miracle-working God does exist. A tourist visited Israel and after seeing where everything took place, was able to say, "Now I can believe!"

In the background of all these circumstances, however, the Christian faith has been built on historical events: the coming of Jesus Christ, His life, His Word and deeds, His death and His resurrection. Other religions are based on myth. Some are no more than a set of ideas. There are also those people who worship an ordinary object or create an idol, and make those the focus of their devotion.

> The essence of faith is being satisfied with all God is for us in Jesus.
> ~ JOHN PIPER

Christians have faith because God became flesh and through His life, they could see who God really is and how He works. They know that the God who became a man is still alive today and accompanies them on their pilgrimage as a close Friend, a Helper, a Healer and to show them, at last, the way to receive the gift of eternal life.

Do not base your faith on anything or anyone besides Jesus the living Christ. He specifically came to lead you to faith. That faith is not just "faith in faith". It is not merely accepting the fact that there must be a "Supreme Being". It is also not about trying to be a good person. *It is faith in Jesus Christ Himself!* It means being open to the Holy Spirit and becoming more like Christ in your nature and your character. Christian faith comes from Christ! Make sure that you are responsive to Him.

Lord Jesus, strengthen my faith daily through the work of Your Holy Spirit. Amen.

Read 1 Pet. 4:12-19	However, if you suffer as a Christian, do not be ashamed, but praise God that you bear that name. (1 Pet. 4:16)

In some parts of the world it is dangerous to be a Christian. In the last century, many more Christian believers have died for their faith than ever before.

In the early days of Christianity, Christians were punished by being thrown to the lions in arenas for amusement; or they were burnt at the stake. If, therefore, you are mocked, or ridiculed at home or at work because you are a Christian; or if you live in a community that is openly hostile to Christianity: know then that you are part of a long line of servants of the Lord who have been mocked and martyred because of their faith.

Do not be ashamed of being called a Christian, but be grateful to God that you are one. Always remember that the Christian faith is at its most glorious when it is lived out in obedience under the cross of Christ. Remember also that Christ counts you worthy to suffer for Him. There are not many people who find themselves in your position – but they are precious to God. They have a special place on the roll of honor of believers and witnesses for Christ.

> Realize that you must lead a dying life; the more a man dies to himself, the more he begins to live unto God.
>
> ~ THOMAS À KEMPIS

Never settle for cheap Christianity, a faith that is just a cultural lifestyle, easy, comfortable and popular. Do not support faith that bends its knee to the ruling political idols when they are clearly in opposition to God and His kingdom. And never envy those who look like they have it easier than you. Just believe in Christ and remain true to the name *Christian*!

Holy Jesus, help me in all circumstances to remain true to the name Christian. Amen.

For it is time for judgment to begin with the family of God. (1 Pet. 4:17)

Read
1 Pet. 4:12-19

During World War II the people of Western Europe grew used to the noise of warning sirens against expected air raids. Once the sirens went off, they knew that anything could happen and *anything* could mean bombs or rockets raining down on them.

The people of biblical times also knew that anything could happen at any time. But in their case *anything* meant a visit or a message from God. He was always intervening in their lives: to speak, to act, to love and to judge. When persecution against the early Christians broke out, it heightened the sense that God was ready to do something. As no one on earth had the power to stop the evil Roman Empire, they believed that God could come at any minute to judge their wickedness and establish His kingdom of peace, love and justice.

> I have found happiness and the fulfillment of all I have desired in Jesus Christ.
> ~ J. C. MARTIN (BASEBALL PLAYER)

But before He judged the evil in the world, He would start with the evil among His people. For them the judgment would be a process of purification.

God's arrival is always imminent. He comes in love, peace and justice. Never lose sight of that. Ask, rather, what He might find in you to judge: maybe your cold heart, your lack of compassion towards the poor; your narrow-mindedness; the brevity of your prayer life? You and I probably need to be careful about asking God to come in our lifetime!

Come, Lord Jesus, and purify, through Your Holy Spirit, every thought and deed in my life. Amen.

That which was from the beginning ... we proclaim concerning the Word of life. (1 John 1:1)

There are many, diverging points of view and philosophies on life and how best to live it. Over the centuries, scholars and people of great wisdom and experience, philosophers and many others, defended their theories on the subject. In spite of that, people today are still searching for the right answer.

There is only one way to live a fulfilling life, and that is the way of the Lord Jesus Christ. He ordained this clearly in His teachings and through His personal example. He said, "I have come that they may have life, and have it to the full" (John 10:10). Jesus' words, "I am the way and the truth and the life" (John 14:6) are as relevant and true today as when He said it to His disciples 2,000 years ago.

> The value of life lies not in the length of days, but in the use we make of them.
> ~ MICHEL DE MONTAIGNE

In order to live a meaningful life of purpose and abundance, it is essential to invite the living Christ into your heart. Let Him take control and manage your life: every corner and turn; every aspect and circumstance. Only then will you truly be living your faith.

This will definitely require self-discipline. However, when you are empowered by the Holy Spirit, you will discover a newfound joy that will bring meaning, significance and purpose to your life as you live it with and for Christ.

O love, deeply concerned for me, take me with everything that wearies me! Accept me into grace – and, my very Source of life, let Your power flow through me. Amen.

See that what you have heard from the beginning remains in you. If it does, you also will remain in the Son and in the Father. (1 John 2:24)

Read
1 John 2:18-27

There are many things that can cause you to deny your faith. Sickness or depression can cause you to think God has forgotten about you. The breaking up of family relationships can cause discouragement. The failure of a business can make you doubt the goodness of God. Conflict with your church can destroy your faith. Doubt about the existence of God can creep into your life. In situations such as these it is relatively easy to drift away from your faith.

You must, however, strictly guard against any factors that can weaken your faith. Do not allow anything to upset you; be steadfast in your faith. Endure until the end – and you will be glad that you have done so. In difficult circumstances, always remember the words of Romans 8:38-39, "For I am convinced that neither death nor life, neither angels nor demons, neither the present nor the future, nor any powers, neither height nor depth, nor anything else in all creation, will be able to separate us from the love of God that is in Christ Jesus our Lord."

> Christ is the greatest influence in the world today. There is a fifth Gospel being written – the work of Jesus Christ in the hearts and lives of men and nations.
> ~ W. H. GRIFFITH THOMAS

Most people experience highs and lows in their faith lives. We must endure trials and tribulations and have to cope with stress and pressure. You will also experience it, however strong your faith may be and regardless of your endurance. Stand faithfully in Christ, no matter what happens! He will never forsake you. He knows your circumstances and He intercedes for you, making supplication to the Father.

He is praying for you today. He will pray for you tomorrow – and every day, forever!

Savior, help me through Your Holy Spirit to remain in You. *Amen.*

Read
1 John 2:18-27

This is what He promised us – even eternal life. (1 John 2:25).

Many born-again Christians make serious promises to God. They say that they will serve Him "to the end". They solemnly promise to live a clean and honest life, to pray and read the Bible every day. Older Christians renew their vows to God from time to time. And many of us keep these vows for long periods of time before letting go of them.

The vows that we make are our response to God's love for us. On God's side of the agreement, however, is the promise of a long-term future. He promises to give us the gift of eternal life. It is a gift of quality of life in the here and now. But it also points to a future dimension beyond our human understanding. It offers us life after death.

> Once a man is united to God, how could he not live forever?
>
> ~ C. S. Lewis

This "Jesus-quality" of life means that death can never have the final say over you or any other disciple. In fact, Jesus not only opens the door to a better earthly life, but also to a perfect life beyond the grave.

Eternal life is life under God's authority and complete control. It is an intimate fellowship with God and eternal joy in His presence. It is a life filled with love and without the presence of any human sin to tarnish the joy and beauty. There will be no more suffering; old age and decay will be gloriously transformed.

Above all it is a life in Christ, in the presence of His truth, His holiness and His exceeding love. It is a future we can all genuinely look forward to.

Savior and Guide, thank You for the promise of eternal life. *Amen.*

God is greater than our hearts, and He knows everything.
(1 John 3:20)

Sometimes people behave in questionable ways and then they wonder if this will result in God denying them His favor and love forever. They may have acted out of pure desperation. They may have been misled by unscrupulous people who were trying to cover their own tracks. Or they might be so embarrassed and afraid over the possible consequences of their actions that in the end they do not know which road is the best to take.

In this way our hearts judge us and we lose all perspective in a matter. Is God also judging us? Usually we fear that He is. If you ever find yourself in a similar situation to the ones described above, try to remember our text for today, "God is greater than our hearts, and He knows everything!" Do not live the rest of your life in torment over something you have done – or something that you neglected to do. God already knows everything. He knows the pressures you are under. He knows the alternatives you have had to weigh up against each other. He knows the weak and strong points of your reasoning. Yet He still loves you – always.

> Conscience tells us in our innermost being of the presence of God and of the moral difference between good and evil.
> ~ BILLY GRAHAM

Nothing you can ever do is able to separate you from His loving care. Nothing can place you beyond the perimeters of His grace. He knows and sees the bigger picture, not only of your personal life, but of the entire universe. Leave everything to Him. Look to the future and learn from any mistakes you have made. Let a negative experience serve as a stepping stone for you towards greater spiritual growth and spiritual adulthood. And believe in God's loving forgiveness as His response to your genuine remorse.

Gracious Lord Jesus, grant redemption to those who stand accused by their own conscience. Amen.

The Command to Believe in God

This is His command: to believe in the name of His Son, Jesus Christ, and to love one another as He commanded us. (1 John 3:23)

Unfortunately there are people who claim that it doesn't matter what you believe "as long as you do your best and you are honest." Others argue, "We all worship the same God and in the end it all comes down to love." They are hopelessly wrong. It most definitely *does* matter what you believe because it determines how you will live and whom you serve.

It is of the greatest importance to identify the God in whom you believe. God the Father commands you to believe in Jesus Christ and also to believe that Jesus is the Son of the living God, the Savior of the world, and that He was resurrected from the dead and now sits at the right hand of the Father.

> God does not keep an extra supply of goodness that is higher than faith, and there is no help at all in anything that is below it. *Within* faith is where the Lord wants us to stay.
>
> ~ JULIAN OF NORWICH

If you reduce faith to a mere generalization of "faith in a Higher Being and everything that is good", you are guilty of weakening a force that began as a dynamic, powerful and world-conquering faith. It is a faith for which many believers died at the stake or in Roman arenas. You won't do this for some "Higher Being". You will endure it only for a Savior who bore your sins on a cross and triumphantly rose from the dead.

Do you really know what you believe? If you don't know, you need to find out right now. Don't listen to those who tell you not to worry about all that dogma. It is crucial to know. You ought to live according to your faith – and die in the same way. Jesus is the most glorious Truth that has ever been known to humanity. Whatever else you do in life: don't allow your opportunity to slip you by; have faith in God!

Savior and Redeemer, I believe with all my heart; please help my unbelief! Amen.

Those who obey His commands live in Him, and He in them. And this is how we know that He lives in us: We know it by the Spirit He gave us. (1 John 3:24)

How do you know that Christ lives in you and that you are "in Christ"? Can anyone know this for certain? Is it not arrogant for someone to make such a claim? As strange as it may sound, it is not at all arrogant. You *can* know, not only that you have chosen to follow Jesus, but also that He lives in you.

You cannot know this, however, by keeping a score card to supposedly reveal how spiritual you are. You do not give yourself ten points because you pray every day, and then deduct five points every time you swear. How long would you have to pray to earn ten points – five minutes? Ten minutes? How can you trust your own judgment in a subjective analysis like this?

> He became what we are that He might make us what He is.
> ~ ATHANASIUS OF ALEXANDRIA

You can know that you are "in Christ" when you are able to discern that His Spirit has taken over and He is in the process of doing a work in you that you know without a doubt is beyond your own ability and strength to perform. You feel that something unusual and outside of your own capability is happening to you. You focus more readily and easily on God. You long to reach out in love to the people whom God has placed inside your sphere of influence. You want to serve Christ.

Bit by bit you lose your reserve when you have the opportunity to talk about Him. You are no longer embarrassed to be known as His disciple. For you, it is a great joy to be able to know Him and worship Him. You *can* know for sure!

Master, help Your disciples to be certain that Your Spirit is working in their hearts. Amen.

Read
1 John 4:1-6

Do not believe every spirit, but test the spirits to see whether they are from God, because many false prophets have gone out into the world. (1 John 4:1)

It is crucial to know that what you believe about God is true, so you can be on your guard against people who try to mislead you into false teachings. This is an age-old problem for believers.

When our text for today was written, no New Testament writings existed to which believers could refer. There were no credos to set the standard. Even the insight of the local elders was limited. Because of this, people were often easy prey for fraudsters, rogues and hypocrites. There were small, isolated Christian communities that needed the guidance of spirit-filled men and women.

On occasion an apostle would pay a visit to a community and spend time helping, teaching and encouraging the people – in the same way some congregations today still invite visiting preachers to teach on mission work, charity and so on.

> By entertaining of strange persons, men sometimes entertain angels unaware: but by entertaining of strange doctrines, many have entertained devils unawares.
> ~ JOHN FLAVEL

But the local congregations of old had no way of knowing whether the preacher who arrived on their doorstep was a bearer of truth or a false prophet. And unfortunately the false prophets did irreparable damage. They often stripped people of their faith and were simply out to make money for themselves. They took advantage of the ignorance of the people and were a serious threat to Christianity.

It is the same today: false prophets still pose a huge threat to Christianity. They cause division in congregations; they establish breakaway churches. They are particularly active where people are simple and ignorant. Be on your guard! Test the spirits!

Heavenly Teacher, help me to discern truth from falsehood. *Amen.*

You, dear children, are from God and have overcome them, because the One who is in you is greater than the one who is in the world. (1 John 4:4)

Read
1 John 4:1-6

Fear can become a dominating force in a person's life. Few, if any, people are able to say that they have never experienced the paralyzing consequences of fear: the fear that robs them of their calmness and peace of mind and that, at least for a period of time, largely destroys their harmonious relationship with the Master.

When your faith in God and the fear in your mind are in conflict with one another, fear will rule because fear has its origins in our emotions, and the emotional side of human nature is very strong.

To be able to live a balanced life, your thoughts and your emotions must be in harmony with each other. This happy state of affairs can only be achieved by allowing the living Christ

> Fear is never a good counselor and victory over fear is the first spiritual duty of man.
> ~ NICOLAS BERDYAEV

to be a reality in your spirit. Feeling better is relatively easy but it requires a serious effort to bring your faith and emotions in line with each other. Until your faith can cheer you up *and* lift you spiritually, you will always be conscious of a conflict between the two.

If fear already has a hold on you and your faith seems inadequate to cope with your circumstances, wrestle against this destructive force and don't be afraid to acknowledge it for what it is. Then, read and try to memorize some of the powerful verses of the Bible until they become part of who you are.

When the promises of God have become stronger and more meaningful to you than the fear that plagues your mind, then your faith will overcome your fear.

Grant me the wisdom, Lord Jesus, to persevere in faith until I am able to overcome my fear. Amen.

The Ability to Be Victorious

You, dear children, are from God and have overcome them, because the One who is in you is greater than the one who is in the world. (1 John 4:4)

The Christian life is often described as a battle and this becomes true when a disciple is struggling against the forces of darkness of this world, the demons in the heavenly realms, and when Christians are confronted by unknown forces.

It is true that Christians find themselves in continuous conflict with demonic powers, with temptations that threaten to overwhelm them, and with subtle forces that carry out their destructive purposes even before their presence has been perceived.

Unfortunately it is also true that many disciples rely on their own strength and resources when they come face to face with forces over which they have no control. They do their best but it is just a matter of time before they break down in the face of the onslaught of the evil powers.

> Little by little, with patience and fortitude, and with the help of God, you will sooner overcome temptations than with your own strength and persistence.
>
> ~ THOMAS À KEMPIS

However, followers of the living Christ have spiritual reserves that they can call on when they are confronted by the Evil One in his many disguises. Deep within them lives a Spirit that is sensitive to the intervention of Jesus Christ and empowers them to fight confidently against any evil force that might cross their path. Never trust in your own resources, but rely on the indwelling Christ, particularly during moments when you feel weak and helpless.

In the power of Christ and through His wisdom you can overcome dark forces if you realize that your help and strength come from the Holy Spirit who lives in you. This is what faith can do for you!

Holy Master, through Your indwelling Holy Spirit I am able to live victoriously. Amen.

If anyone says, "I love God," yet hates his brother, he is a liar. (1 John 4:20)

A big stumbling block in our spiritual progress is a lack of understanding of the Christian faith; people frequently quote religious clichés they do not understand themselves. Sanctified by time and repeated use, these clichés sound correct but once examined, they are revealed to be quite meaningless.

Jesus spoke out strongly against the religious clichés so often used by the spiritual leaders of His day. These leaders often tried to cover up their religious incompetencies through these clichés, thus denying ordinary people access to a deeper spiritual walk. Christ made it clear that religious sayings that were not supported by a life of devotion were displeasing to God.

> Handle them carefully, for words have more power than atom bombs.
> ~ PEARL STRACHAN

Faith that does not reflect the ways of God in daily life cannot be used by God to serve people. What you believe about your heavenly Father will be reflected in your attitude towards your fellow man. If you merely pay lip service to God, and what you profess to believe does not come from the depths of your heart and lacks genuine conviction, your attitude will be hypocritical – and this cannot be a blessing to anyone.

Let your religious conversation convey the integrity of your thoughts and emotions. Then what you say will not only be understood by those who hear it, but they will also feel the spiritual impact of your words.

Lord Jesus, may the words of my mouth convey my spiritual integrity so that whatever I utter will have eternal significance. Amen.

Read
Prov. 16:13-21

The highway of the upright avoids evil; he who guards his way guards his life. (Prov. 16:17)

In many areas of life it seems at first glance as if the good always suffers at the hands of the wicked. Circumstances frequently occur where it seems as if those who are living righteously are the losers, while the people who live through shady practices appear to be doing well.

This results in people saying that honesty does not pay. When people embrace this kind of attitude, they run the danger of giving in to temptation, lowering their personal standards and compromising their principles.

The teachings of Jesus Christ regularly remind us that there is no point in trying just to please ourselves or other people; seeking our reward now, rather than waiting for the righteousness of the kingdom of God; compromising rather than upholding our principles.

> The righteousness of God is not acquired by acts frequently repeated, but is imparted by faith.
> ~ MARTIN LUTHER

If you long for a peaceful and fulfilling life, it is essential to remain true to the teachings of Jesus. This is infinitely more worthwhile than giving in to people around you. You will one day be called to account before God and will have to answer for the way you have chosen to live your life.

If you allow the Holy Spirit to come into your life and take control, you will discover that the strength of your willpower depends on your faith and it is this that enables you to overcome temptation. You can live like Christ – in a way that is pleasing to God.

O Holy Spirit of God, take complete control over my life and lead me on the path of righteousness. Amen.

This is the victory that has overcome the world, even our faith. Who is it that overcomes the world? Only he who believes that Jesus is the Son of God. (1 John 5:4-5)

Read
1 John 5:1-12

Never make the mistake of thinking that every dark cloud has a silver lining. Only some clouds do. If you go out and face life with a superficial, artificial optimism of this nature, you will often be disappointed. The reality is that life is tough, with evil and wickedness ruling our world.

The Bible reveals to us an ongoing life-and-death struggle between good and evil, truth and lies, light and darkness. Never underestimate the power of the Evil One. If you do so, sooner rather than later, you will be overpowered. You do not have the power to overcome evil in your own strength – however spiritually strong, experienced and mature you may be.

> The cross of Christ is God's final answer to the problem of evil because the problem of evil is in the cross itself.
>
> ~ E. J. CARNELL

You need the power of Jesus the living Christ if you want to triumph over evil. The term *world* in our text for today means the combined forces of the Evil One that are at work in communities and even in your own heart. If you try to challenge these forces in your own strength, you will be like one soldier trying to overpower a regiment of tanks with a single gun.

There is only one overcomer accessible to you in your battle against the Evil One. On the Cross and at His resurrection, Jesus dared to take on the Evil One in all his power and was victorious. He invites you to join Him on the winning team. You become a member by believing in Him, trusting Him, acknowledging His spiritual authority and bearing His name.

In this way people who were previously weak and defeated, can attain glorious victories. You can do it too.

Lord my God, help me to overcome evil in the name of the living Christ. Amen.

The Spirit of Truth

This is the One who came by water and blood – Jesus Christ. And it is the Spirit who testifies, because the Spirit is the truth. (1 John 5:6)

You probably already know the saying, "There are always three sides to a story: your side, my side – and the truth!" Arriving at the truth can be a very complicated process.

The Bible, however, cuts through to the heart of the arguments about what is true and what isn't. It accepts that whatever comes from God is the truth. It is not at all an academic issue. It is purely a spiritual matter. God is the Truth, Jesus the living Christ is the Truth, and the Holy Spirit teaches us what Truth is and is a witness to the Truth because He points us in the direction of Jesus.

The Spirit further leads us into all Truth, which is Jesus Christ. Consequently, however intellectually complex it may seem to explain that Jesus is both God and sinless Man, in reality this is a simple truth that any true believer who knows that his sins have been forgiven, can easily accept. The Holy Spirit works in our minds and convinces us that this is precisely who Jesus is.

> Where truth goes, I will go, and where truth is I will be, and nothing but death shall divide me from the truth.
>
> ~ THOMAS BROOKS

Whenever you become confused about the interpretation of a Christian doctrine, seek the leading of the Holy Spirit. Doing this is definitely not an excuse for being intellectually lazy. You also need to think about the matter – and sometimes this requires very deep and serious thinking. But if you have any doubts, choose an interpretation of the Truth that seems to you to be the closest to how you sense the Holy Spirit is directing you. Do not allow your personal desires to influence you. Remember: the Spirit points you to Jesus and to the Truth, so a simple test would be to ask, "Is this interpretation consistent with the mind of Christ according to His teachings?"

Lord and Master, enlighten my mind through the Holy Spirit so that I may know Your truth. Amen.

"I am coming soon. Hold on to what you have, so that no one will take your crown." (Rev. 3:11)

Read
Rev. 3:7-13

There may come a time in your life when you feel that everything is in the process of falling apart. Monotony has made your days meaningless, your life seems to have lost its sparkle, and you have probably adopted a couldn't-care-less attitude. Along with this unfortunate state of affairs, your spiritual life has lost its intimacy with the Father and you no longer sense the presence of the living Christ in your life.

Without a sense of unity with the living God, you will also lose your grip on life, because it is impossible to continue living in harmony with your heavenly Father once you have strayed from His path for you. In order to turn this situation around, you need to first reaffirm the basic principles of your faith. When your faith is restored to its rightful place in your life, you will find that every other aspect falls back into place.

> When led of the Spirit, the child of God must be as ready to wait as to go, as prepared to be silent as to speak.
> ~ LEWIS SPERRY CHAFER

Reaffirm your faith and give it its rightful place in your life. This means focusing on the importance of positive prayer. Prayer brings you into a more intimate relationship with the living Christ and His commands, which is far more than just an emotional experience. It is a specific act of faith that acknowledges that the Spirit of Christ lives in you and that you are allowing Him to work through you.

With the indwelling Christ living in you, you will discover that your life is being rebuilt once again and you will know without the slightest doubt that because you love Him – and He loves you – all things are working together for your good.

Holy Master, I thank and praise You once again that You equip me to face the challenges of life through the power of Your indwelling Holy Spirit. Amen.

Love That Surpasses Knowledge

Know this love that surpasses knowledge – that you may be filled to the measure of all the fullness of God. (Eph. 3:19)

Statistics show that many Christians are dissatisfied with their faith. This is not because they have turned from it, but because they have developed a couldn't-care-less attitude over issues that concern their spiritual lives. Christianity has gradually lost its appeal and they no longer acknowledge the authority of the living Christ over their lives.

How is it possible for the faith of someone who was once a dynamic Christian to diminish to the degree that it becomes a mockery? There can be many reasons for this: a lack of worship; neglecting to pray; failing to read the Bible; the challenge of peer pressure – these are just a few of the many factors that can change devotion to spiritual apathy.

> To believe in God's love is to believe that He's passionately interested in each of us personally and continually.
>
> ~ LOUIS EVELY

A well-known philosopher once said that it is possible to know everything about Christianity without actually being a Christian. There are many people who have done an in-depth study of faith, who know the credos and dogmas of the church, who can put up a strong argument on one or another theological viewpoint, but whose lives reflect nothing of Jesus Christ's life and work.

Living a fulfilling life of faith requires a personal surrender to Jesus Christ, that extends beyond theories of religion and changes a person's character and personality.

When knowledge leads to this kind of surrender, it serves a wonderful purpose, but if it merely remains book knowledge and does not result in a complete surrender to the Son of God, it is worthless.

My Lord and my God, may my knowledge of You lead me to an ever-deepening appreciation of Your holy presence. Amen.

Without faith it is impossible to please God, because anyone who comes to Him must believe that He exists and that He rewards those who seek Him. (Heb. 11:6)

Read
Heb. 11:1-10

It is impossible to please God if you do not have faith: this is the message of today's text. Ask yourself the following questions, "Am I searching for God? Do I seek Him in the Bible and in my prayers?" If the answers are yes, you are living a healthy faith life. If you claim to believe but you are not seeking out God's will, you are only deceiving yourself.

True faith demands of you one or other form of action. James puts it very clearly, "You believe that there is one God. Good! Even the demons believe that – and shudder ... You see that a person is justified by what he does and not by faith alone" (James 2:19, 24). Your faith in God must inspire your actions.

> For anything worth having one must pay a price; and the price is always work, patience, love, self-sacrifice.
>
> ~ JOHN BURROUGHS

Another truth about faith is that it is not for the weak. In Hebrews 11:13 we read, "All these people were still living by faith when they died. They did not receive the things promised." They did not receive before they died, "they only saw them and welcomed them from a distance. And they admitted that they were aliens and strangers on earth." God tests our faith and He looks at our reactions. Are we upset when we do not get what we want? The Word instructs us, "You know that the testing of your faith develops perseverance. Perseverance must finish its work so that you may be mature and complete, not lacking anything" (James 1:3-4).

To God, conforming you to the image of Christ is more important than giving you the things you want. Jesus died for His faith because He knew that His Father had something so much better in store for Him. Faith is based on truth and the Word of God is the truth. By actively living the Word, your faith will grow. How much faith do you want?

Lord, let my actions mirror the quality of my faith. *Amen.*

This is the victory that has overcome the world, even our faith. Who is it that overcomes the world? Only he who believes that Jesus is the Son of God. (1 John 5:4-5)

Everyone likes winning. We all admire winners and we enjoy being identified with them. When a sports team that we support win, we glow with pride, just as if we played a part in their victory.

The Christian faith slowly exerted an influence on the early Roman Empire. It took 300 years but at last Christianity was acknowledged as the official faith of Rome and Caesar. But the real victory took place in the people. Christianity grew in influence because Christ won the hearts and minds of all those who became His disciples.

Why is Christianity victorious? Because our faith protects us against the degrading influences of the world. The term "world" means the combined forces of evil that are involved in an ongoing struggle against God. Christ equips us with spiritual weaponry to fight against Satan (see Eph. 6:10-18).

> Attempt something so impossible that unless God is in it, it's doomed to failure.
> ~ JOHN HAGGAI

To be able to believe in Christ, we are provided with spiritual resources that give us access to the power of His victory on the cross and to His Resurrection. Our victory also comes from the power Jesus gives us to overcome those things that threaten to destroy our faith – doubt, despair, failure and sin. In this way we all have the hope of our share in the final victory of God over the Evil One.

The world has repeatedly done everything in its power to destroy Jesus and it will keep trying. But evil can never triumph because the resurrected Jesus still lives today and He is our assurance of final victory.

Help me through Your victory, Lord Jesus, also to be an overcomer in Your name. Amen.

I will instruct you and teach you in the way you should go; I will counsel you and watch over you. (Ps. 32:8)

Read
Ps. 32:1-11

It is not always easy to give up control. You might have planned a strategy down to the very last detail and then, suddenly, it becomes impossible to carry out your plans and you have to stand back and watch someone else take over. This can be very upsetting, especially when the person taking over is not as well-qualified as you.

In such circumstances you need to be on your guard against small-mindedness, because it will rob you of your effectiveness. Do not allow bitterness to take over, causing you to say unfriendly things about your successor. Grow in stature by offering him all the help, support and encouragement you can. Those who have no insight into the spiritual nature of man may find your behavior extremely foolish but you will know that by being kind, you yourself will

> The knowledge that I am not the one who is in control, gives me great encouragement. To know Him, who is always in control, is everything to me.
> ~ ALEXANDER MICHAEL

benefit by growing spiritually. Then God will guide you into new heights of true self-fulfillment.

Do not lose faith in your conviction that God will never close a door without opening another one for you. Sometimes there is a long waiting period, but being impatient is not going to change God's will, which is to carry out His purpose in His perfect time. All He asks of you is to trust and believe in Him and faithfully wait on Him.

When it seems that you have lost control, remember that God never loses control. Trusting in God will help you to have a renewed faith in yourself.

May my faith in You, Father God, help me to persevere even when it looks as if everything is out of my control. *Amen.*

Read
2 Cor. 5:11-21

Therefore, if anyone is in Christ, he is a new creation; the old has gone, the new has come! (2 Cor. 5:17)

Religion is like a magnet for those who enjoy a good argument. They tend to take a text from Scripture and waste valuable time giving it a meaning that it was never intended to have. In this way it is possible for religion to become so philosophical that it loses any sense of meaning for the average person.

A religious faith that is truly meaningful must yield practical results. It is futile to tell people about the love of Jesus Christ if you are not living in the attitude of love. Emphasizing the therapeutic value of forgiveness is not enough. You have to move beyond the theoretical and practice forgiveness.

You may be a passionate follower of Jesus, but if you are narrow-minded and insincere, your faith will count for little. It is when you are living in the presence of the Master and reflecting some of His loving and compassionate character that you show the world a faith that blesses

> The first great gift we can bestow on others is a good example.
> ~ THOMAS MORELL

everyone it comes into contact with. The world then instinctively knows that you are with Jesus and that He is blessing people through you.

There can be no effective argument against a positive and living faith. When dishonest people become honest; when people's lives are transformed by the redeeming love of Christ; when families that were once battlegrounds become heavens-on-earth; then there can be no valid argument against the influence of the living Christ in the lives of human beings.

Grant Your mercy, Lord Jesus, that the greatest evidence of my faith will be the quality of my daily life. Amen.

JUNE

Be joyful in hope, patient in affliction, faithful in prayer.
~ ROMANS 12:12

God of hope and grace,
Thank You that we can meet this month with hope in our hearts.
In spite of the fact that so many of our plans have failed,
in spite of the fact that we have disappointed You through our unbelief,
and in spite of the fact that our spiritual growth has been so slow,
there is still hope in our hearts!
We know that tomorrow lies in Your merciful hands
and that our hope is not in vain.
Lord Jesus, we know with a certainty deep in our hearts:
there is no medicine like hope, no decision as vital,
no remedy as powerful, as holding out hope for tomorrow!
O Savior, do not permit Satan to exult over us,
for when we fall Your hope allows us to get up again;
when we despair Your Holy Spirit will renew the hope in our hearts;
when we die we have hope of eternal life with You.
We take joy in the hope of this glory that will be revealed.
Our hope does not hang on the thread of "I think so!"
or "It may be possible,"
but on the strong chain of the steadfast anchor of Your holy promise
that there really is a glorious future waiting for us.
Our salvation is firmly established through the work of Jesus –
ordained by You, our unchanging God.
We thank You that the hope in our hearts lives on
as You walk with us.

Amen.

Hope in itself is a form of happiness; perhaps the greatest happiness
that this world has to offer us.
~ SAMUEL JOHNSON

"I will establish My covenant with you." (Gen. 6:18)

When people have a serious problem to solve, they usually evaluate the circumstances and then analyze their results. After that they devise a master plan; calculate the costs; set up a schedule; make sure that the required funds are available; and employ the right people to carry out the task.

When God has a problem to solve, He selects a single person, puts him (or her) in the right place and then says, "I need you to carry out a certain task for Me. I will be with you and help you. Now go ahead." Noah was God's choice to restore humanity when the flood was over. Noah was also a witness for God. God entrusted Noah with these tasks and promised to work with him and through him. Noah, therefore, was the focal point of hope in the approaching disaster. Further on in our spiritual history, the focus would be Abraham, Joseph, Moses and finally, Jesus.

> When you say a situation or a person is hopeless, you are slamming the door in the face of God.
>
> ~ CHARLES ALLEN

There is no situation so desperate that God cannot bring new hope and a new beginning out of it. After Jesus was crucified, God restored Him to life and gave the world the new gospel of the Resurrection, of spiritual power and of hope. Today He is still the living Christ. In the twilight of a world threatened by terrorism, poverty, sickness and hunger, God is always busy doing a new thing somewhere, in some way, and through someone He has specifically chosen for each task.

However bad your circumstances may seem, God is always busy looking for the opportunity to restore you and lead you into a new future and a deeper level of faith in Him. He made a covenant to do this. Let us firmly believe that He *will* do it – our hope is founded upon Him.

Lord my God, help me to hold on to hope after the flood. Amen.

"Everything on earth will perish. But I will establish My covenant with you." (Gen. 6:17-18)

Read
Gen. 6:9-22

All of us see things from a different perspective. Some people are color-blind and confuse the colors red and green. When there is a red flower among green leaves, they cannot see it. There are far too many people today who cannot see what is going on in the world around them because they have become too caught up in their own limited areas of interest.

Noah, however, could see the corruption and violence in the world around him. Everybody else thought that things were absolutely normal but Noah saw differently. His eyes were open to God and, through the insight that his faith gave him, he was able to perceive both danger and hope in what was going on around him. In and through all of the dark calamity around him, Noah knew that the situation was dangerous, but he dared to trust in the promises of God and hope that there could and would be a better world in the future.

> If you do not hope you will never discover what is beyond your hopes.
> ~ CLEMENT OF ALEXANDRIA

Faith in God places you in a position to see things that other people cannot see. In the dark times of World War II, Bishop Berggrav of Norway smuggled a message out of his Nazi jail cell to the Christian church that read: "God has planned a victory in the night." Others saw only the darkness, but he saw a glimmer of the dawn breaking through. And the light did break through shortly afterwards.

Whatever darkness and destruction is going on around you, either on a worldwide or on a personal level, look past the outward appearances for the possibility of God's sovereign grace and intervention. He stepped in and sent us Jesus. And He will come again – so be of good courage and persevere in hope, no matter what happens around you.

Creator God, through Your Spirit open my eyes so I can truly see. Amen.

Read
Gen. 13:1-18

"Lift up your eyes from where you are and look north and south, east and west." (Gen. 13:14)

There are many advantages to doing a "stocktake" of your life. This means that you must come to a standstill and think about who and where you are and what your future options look like. Most people tend to get sucked up into a torrent of activity, or caught up in a stream of problems, and then all they can think is that things have become very difficult for them. Assessing where you are in life can be of great value in circumstances like these.

God commanded Abraham to look around him. The surrounding highlands were lush and fruitful and able to provide Abraham with everything he needed to live a good life. But instead of searching for the best land and seizing hold of it, as Lot did, Abraham stood still for a moment and took stock. At God's command he looked up for a while and scanned the horizon in all directions. He needed time to take it all in. He needed time to evaluate his situation, to see where he was – and to see what the land looked like.

> Where there is no hope, there can be no endeavor.
>
> ~ SAMUEL JOHNSON

Perhaps you, too, need to lift your eyes from the position you are in now and take stock of yourself. Ask yourself where you are coming from and why? Perhaps you should also ask why you have never taken the trouble to achieve anything worthwhile – and why not? At a certain stage Jesus inquired of His disciples, "Who do the people say I am?" He was in the process of assessing the value of His ministry and was trying to determine how effective He had been and how well the disciples understood His mission. Where do you stand spiritually? How much have you personally grown in grace? How true are you to Christ's expectations of you? How big is your hope of a future with God?

Holy Father God, let me take stock for a while, look up and listen to what the voice of Your Spirit is saying to me. Amen.

"All the land that you see I will give to you and your offspring forever." (Gen. 13:15)

Read
Gen. 13:1-18

It is strange to think that out of all the regions of the earth, God chose to do something so important on a small corner of land on the eastern side of the Mediterranean Sea. He chose to work from that small corner of the world with a small nation at a specific time in human history.

God gave that small piece of land to Abraham. Abraham knew that this was not something that had happened to him by chance, he knew he had not arrived at that place by accident. As he looked at the land, he knew that it was God's gift to him. So he took possession, admiring it as one admires a new house or car. He saw it as his inheritance: the place where his descendants would make their home; raise their families; live – and die. He undoubtedly had a feeling of great joy, and humbly acknowledged that God had given the land to him. He probably also wondered what great events would take place in the future in that land.

> Each one of us, as members of the Body of Christ, has been given at least one spiritual gift.
> ~ BRUCE KEMPER

God also gives you opportunities. The gift of life alone is enough to glorify and serve Him forever. Salvation through Jesus Christ is the most precious gift of all. God also gives you material benefits; and relationships with the people you live and work with. Carrying on the long Christian heritage and passing it forward to others is also a gift of God. You receive it, make your contribution and pass it on. The Bible is a gift – deep, rich and precious. So also are all the spiritual fruits that you receive: among which one of the most important is hope. What is your gift to God?

Holy God, I thank You ceaselessly for all Your gifts to me. *Amen.*

Go back to your mistress and submit to her. (Gen. 16:9)

When you are driving in your car and you land up in a one-way street, facing the wrong way, you are in trouble. You either have to proceed slowly forward until you can turn off into another road, or reverse all the way back to where you first made the wrong turn.

Hagar, the maidservant of Abraham's wife, Sarah, was commanded by the angel of the Lord to return to Sarah after she fled into the wilderness. After God said to Abraham, "Go forward!" He told Hagar, "Go back!"

God may also say to you, "Go back!" He does this when you take the wrong road or when your life has been completely derailed. When the Prodigal Son came to his senses, he decided to go back home, where he received mercy, forgiveness and a warm welcome. If you decide to try to run away from your responsibilities and take the easy way out, God may well tell you to turn around and once again battle up the steep road of service in difficult circumstances, back to the situation that God has placed you in.

> Nothing worth doing
> is completed in our
> lifetime; therefore we
> must be saved by hope.
> ~ REINHOLD NIEBUHR

It is never easy going back. It means acknowledging that you made a mistake in the first place, and that is never an easy thing to do. Going back might mean a change in your outlook, showing remorse and beginning all over again. But it also means that God is giving you a second chance; that you can start off once again on the right foot and you can leave the past behind you. It means that your hope will never die. Is it perhaps the right time for you to turn around and place your hope in the mercy of Christ?

Lord Jesus, support all those who must turn around and start over. Amen.

The LORD has heard of your misery. (Gen. 16:11)

Read
Gen. 16:1-16

Many people who take refuge in God in times of crisis find great relief in the fact that they can leave their problems in His hands. Their hope is placed in their God. Others, whose requests have not been answered, feel disappointed and let down by God.

When the angel of God spoke to Hagar at the well in the wilderness, He commanded her to return to her mistress, Sarah. But at the same time he assured her: "The LORD has heard of your misery."

If you are in the wilderness of despair and have lost all hope; if you fear the future and are trying to run away from the past, you need to pray to God for help. God will not necessarily give you what you ask of Him, but He *will* hear you. Countless people can say together with the psalmist, "God is our refuge and strength, an ever-present help in trouble" (Ps. 46:1).

> A religious hope does not only bear up the mind under her sufferings, but makes her rejoice in them.
> ~ JOSEPH ADDISON

God always hears your cries of distress and, even if He does not immediately relieve the pressure you are under, He will give you the strength to cope with your difficulties. As a result you will be strengthened and enriched through your trials and pressure. Some people have found that their trials served as a turning point in their lives on the road to hope, faith and salvation.

Jesus also prayed to God in Gethsemane when He was struggling with His impending crucifixion. The cup of suffering was not removed from Him. But He endured the cross and sacrificed His life, thereby bringing a living hope to humanity, everywhere that God brings salvation through suffering.

God of grace, please hear the cries for help of all who run to You today. Amen.

Read

Deut. 20:1-8

When you go to war against your enemies and see an army greater than yours, do not be afraid of them, because the LORD your God will be with you. (Deut. 20:1)

Fear thrives on half-truths and ignorance, and when alarming occurrences seem to confirm what is already beginning to be believed, fear starts to dominate the mind. Then your ability to reason calmly disappears and you can fall prey to wild rumors that eventually destroy both your hope and your faith.

It is during these days of rising tension and pressure that your hope and faith in the living God must be bigger and stronger than any fear that can attack your mind and spirit. This is possible only when your concept of the heavenly Father is so strong that no element of fear can take root in your life. However, it is not easy to maintain the right focus when fear is trying to achieve exactly the opposite.

> The fear of God kills all other fears.
>
> ~ HUGH BLACK

The forces of evil that are trying to unnerve you rely for the most part on fabrications. When you see might and power assembled against everything that is precious to you, your courage will fail you unless you use your spiritual eyes and look past reality to perceive the great truths of the Spirit.

You must remember that evil can never overpower the holiness of God: this is our hope. Even though there will be moments when the Evil One is aggressive and triumphant, the final victory always belongs to God. It must also be remembered that in the darkest moments, when it seems as if the battle is going against you, the holy Father is closest to you, His child.

Heavenly Father, I reaffirm my full faith in You. My hope in You is steadfast. Amen.

"I am the resurrection and the life. He who believes in Me will live, even though he dies; and whoever lives and believes in Me will never die." (John 11:25-26)

Read
John 11:17-32

For many people these words might sound somewhat contradictory. In fact, many of the teachings of Christ appear to be inexplicable when we try to interpret them purely from an intellectual viewpoint. The Scriptures and wisdom of thousands of devoted and experienced Christians prove that hope, trust and faith in God Almighty always form the basis for wonderful events that challenge human logic.

Through the years people have endured challenges and trials in numerous forms, and it was always those with a strong hope and faith in the living Christ who have been able to endure the onslaughts in whatever form they took.

> The word "hope" I take for faith; and indeed hope is nothing else but the constancy of faith.
>
> ~ JOHN CALVIN

In the times we live in today, the attacks on our faith and hope grow ever more serious and fiery. They manifest in so many different forms. Some suffer persecution, others suffer financial difficulties, illness and a whole variety of personal setbacks.

Whatever your situation might be, always remember that God is with you and He will support you and help you through everything. Do not let go of your hope and faith in His continued presence in your life. Fix your faith on Christ and He will inspire you to lead a life of hope and assurance in all circumstances.

Through Your love, Lord Jesus, I find lasting hope and joy. *Amen.*

Read
Job 32:1-12

But it is the spirit in a man, the breath of the Almighty, that gives him understanding. (Job 32:8)

If you really want to enjoy life, you need to understand that there are many hidden sources of inspiration to be found along the path of life – and they are just waiting to refresh and inspire you and encourage you to greater heights. Denying their existence would be to rob yourself of something of great value, for which there is no substitute.

The problem is that most people rush through their daily tasks with no time or desire to be stimulated by the elements of their own actions or by their own discoveries. Whenever something big and noble comes to them, they are momentarily excited, but soon fall back into their old rut. In their failure to appreciate these small inspirations that pop up into their lives, people alienate themselves from the stream of creativity that hope, beauty and power can bring them.

> He that lives in hope
> danceth without music.
> ~ GEORGE HERBERT

The pure joy of these small inspirations lies in discovering them for yourself. They will not force themselves upon you, they must be picked like beautiful flowers out of the everyday experiences of life. Think of how the average person reacts to a friendly word or approach. Have you forgotten the quiet joy and satisfaction you experience when you comfort someone who is suffering? Have you become too used to the beauty and splendor of the rising and setting of the sun?

When someone shows faith in you, you feel that you have value. There are also numerous other inspirational blessings just waiting to be enjoyed. To get the best out of life, you must make sure that you do not miss out on them.

Grant, gracious Savior, that the hope of inspiration in my life will never die. Amen.

To the LORD I cry aloud, and He answers me from His holy hill. (Ps. 3:4)

Read
Ps. 3:1-9

Most big companies that deal with the public have a helpline system. If something is wrong with a product that you have bought, you can call the helpline.

When you place your hope in God and believe in Jesus Christ, you have a completely different sort of helpline available. The person who wrote our text for today knew all about it. In difficult times of stress, tension or misfortune he called on the Lord for help. The people of ancient Israel thought that God lived on Mount Zion in Jerusalem, where the temple was built. Therefore, the temple was their spiritual "call center."

No one goes through life without experiencing problems. Difficulties are an integral part of life. But you can always ask the Lord for help. His helpline is open, twenty-four-seven.

When you are suffering from an illness, you can call on Him for help. When you are in trouble; when you experience financial problems; when you feel hopeless; when you are exhausted by worry; when you are concerned about the future; when your friends turn their backs on you; when you have been cheated and robbed – you can call on God and nurture the hope and faith in your heart that He will be there to assist you. He will come to your aid and stand at your side. Test Him in this if you cherish a living hope in your heart.

> The natural flights of the human mind are not from pleasure to pleasure, but from hope to hope.
> ~ SAMUEL JOHNSON

Help those who turn to You today with hope in their hearts, beloved Lord. Amen.

What Keeps You Going?

Read
Ps. 3:1-9

I lie down and sleep; I wake again, because the LORD sustains me. (Ps. 3:5)

Different things keep different people going. The mother who is dedicated to her children is motivated by their need for her love. The athlete dreams of an Olympic medal and this is what drives him through the long and difficult months of training. A scientific researcher experiments patiently to find a remedy for a disease. The hope of success keeps them all going. Many Christian disciples have endured illnesses, in the hope that they will meet Jesus and their loved ones in heaven.

The writer of our text for today took note of the natural process of sleep: sleeping and waking up again. But he also knew that the renewed strength that he received through sleep came from God. God restored him with each sleep and kept him going. God will also preserve you in the same way.

> If it were not for hopes,
> the heart would break.
> ~ THOMAS FULLER

When you are overworked and tired, Jesus will refresh you. If you feel lonely and abandoned, God will stay with you. Throughout the years He has been with you – even when you were not aware of His presence.

If you don't know where to turn to and you feel that life no longer has any sense or meaning – He will still keep you going. When you are flat broke and don't know where your next meal is coming from, He will somehow see you through. If your life is busy falling apart as a result of mistakes and misunderstandings, He will restore your balance. When you fear the future, keep hoping that Christ will meet you, because He is already there.

Lord Jesus, restore hope to those people whose lives are busy falling apart. Amen.

I lie down and sleep; I wake again, because the LORD sustains me. (Ps. 3:5)

Read
Ps. 3:1-9

How deep do you sleep? Some people sleep so deeply that they make strange noises. If you have ever been kept awake all night by a roommate's snoring, you will know just how deeply some people can sleep. Restful sleep is one of the most valuable blessings God gives to His children. To lie down, tired and worn out, and to then awaken refreshed and strengthened is a wonderful experience. You will sleep even better if you trust God and hope for His continued presence throughout the night. Then you can hand over your daily stresses and tensions to Him, as well as your worries and anxieties. You will know that the problems and difficulties that life throws at you can do you no harm in the end.

> If you can't sleep, then get up and do something instead of lying there and worrying. It's the worry that gets you, not the loss of sleep.
> ~ DALE CARNEGIE

You can feel quite sure that when you lie down to rest, you are in the arms of Christ. Remember also that when you go "off duty" and fall asleep, that God neither slumbers nor sleeps (see Ps. 121:4). He keeps watch over you all day and all night. This 24-hour watch is very unpopular with military personnel, because it means that they do nothing for a whole day and yet they are exhausted at the end of it. For God it is a service of love. He is happy when He is protecting and preserving you. Possibly His watchfulness is even more focused when you are sleeping than when you are awake, because while you are sleeping you can't defend yourself.

Jesus slept well. He slept through the storm on the Sea of Galilee. He will keep you safe when you are asleep – if your hope is fixed on Him. And when you cannot sleep, don't count sheep – talk to the Shepherd!

Holy Father, bless those who suffer from lack of sleep. Amen.

You made him ruler over the works of Your hands; You put everything under his feet. (Ps. 8:6)

With the advancement of science and technology in our time, there are people who think that there is little or nothing the human race cannot do. And yet famine, poverty, disease, terrorism and war remain huge problems. There is still a long way to go towards resolving these issues. Were it not for these problems we might think that the human race had the universe under control. Even so, God has appointed humans as the rulers of His Creation.

While the universe belongs to God, He has given it over to people. We need to farm to provide food; we must mine the minerals that are there for us. We must accumulate the good things of life and enrich our human existence. We must create beautiful things so that we can enjoy life. We must handle international affairs in a way that will bring peace and well-being to all nations. Through it all we must give honor and glory to God who delights Himself in happy communities and in the growth and development of humanity.

> Totally without hope one cannot live. To live without hope is to cease to live.
> ~ FYODOR DOSTOEVSKY

Your daily task, and that of your family, plays a small role in this dominion over the Creation. It is where your skills develop, where you earn a living, and where you grow and mature as a person.

In your field you also do things that are of benefit to the community. When Jesus worked in the carpentry shop in Nazareth, He sanctified it, as well as the day-to-day work of His followers throughout the centuries. Our hope in the continued existence of our universe is fixed on God the Creator and Jesus the Transformer.

Lord Jesus of Nazareth, grant me Your grace to see how my work fits in to Your greater plan for the world. **Amen.**

The LORD is a refuge for the oppressed, a stronghold in times of trouble. (Ps. 9:9)

Read
Ps. 9:1-11

Everyone needs a refuge at some point in their lives. A hospital is a safe harbor for those who are ill; a holiday resort is the perfect getaway for people who are under stress or are overworked. Churches have often served as refuges for people who have lost everything in floods or who have fled in fear during wartime. A refuge is a place where you can retreat and feel safe; where you can recover from whatever difficulty you had to bear.

In biblical times the greatest oppression originated from military action. Civil strife was also common, personal conflict between families and friends was an everyday occurrence, and rocky hills and caves served as places of refuge from military danger. The psalmist, however, knew that God Himself is always a safe harbor of refuge in times of danger and need.

> There is no better or more blessed bondage than to be a prisoner of hope.
> ~ ROY Z. KEMP

God remains a refuge and a hiding place for those whose hope is in Him. We all need a safe harbor during a personal crisis. When you are plagued by doubt, there is no safer place than in the arms of Christ.

If you are upset or confused, you don't have to flee to the mountains and look for a place to hide. Fix your hope on Jesus; seek His peace, joy and love. You will find rest and safety in Him. Draw strength from prayer and seclusion with Jesus.

God is a refuge for those in need, He is like a rock that always stands firm. Amen.

Read
Ps. 9:11-21

Sing praises to the LORD, enthroned in Zion; proclaim among the nations what He has done. (Ps. 9:11)

Usually when you are powerful, rich, and successful, you either have many friends, or no friends at all. Fair-weather friends are always plentiful. But when the tide turns you need true and honest friends to stand by you.

The writer of today's text knew adversity. Enemies attacked him but God helped him to conquer them. This strengthened his hope in God and deepened his faith. There is nothing like overcoming difficulties to run a thread of steel through your hope. The psalmist felt that he had come to know God better. He discovered that, while certain human friends could not cope with problems, God not only could, but *would*.

It does not matter if you have never searched for God before. If you turn to Him in the midst of your crisis, He will turn to you. He is waiting to find you in your trouble. Those who know Him can confirm that God has never left them in the lurch; however difficult the circumstances were.

> Hope is the pillar that holds up the world. Hope is the dream of a waking man.
>
> ~ PLINY THE ELDER

Jesus has also promised to always be with us. When you are fighting an uphill battle; when your health is falling apart; when enemies are plotting against you, Jesus will stay with you. When your loved ones reject or abandon you, He will hold on to you. When you are about to lose all hope, He will lead you into new heights of faith. Never let the hope in your heart die.

God of hope, remain with me, no matter what happens in my life. Amen.

Arise, O LORD, let not man triumph; let the nations be judged in Your presence. (Ps. 9:19)

Read
Ps. 9:12-21

When James Wolfensohn retired as president of the World Bank, he was described as "the banker who cared about the poor!" In his ten years as president he tried to guide world leaders into recognizing the complexity of poverty and he advocated its reduction. He liked to say that poverty anywhere meant poverty everywhere. There is no simple and easy solution to poverty and the poor and rich nations have to work hard together to have any hope of raising the standard of living of the poor.

In the Bible the poor did not put their faith in, politicians, economists or bankers. Their hope was fixed on God. One of the marks of His righteousness was His pity and compassion for the poor of the world. He was always on the side of the poor. One of the future visions in the Bible is that God will allow a time of abundance. The poor will be fed, the thirsty will have more than enough to drink, and there will be enough space for everyone. In biblical times they had the insight to understand that poverty was far more than just an economic issue – it also had an important religious dimension.

> No society can surely be flourishing and happy, of which the far greater part of the members are miserable.
> ~ ADAM SMITH

Left to its own devices, humanity is sinful and uncaring towards each other. God had to tell His servants to give priority to those things that were of most interest to Him. God needs the James Wolfensohns of this world to use their skills to resolve the problem of poverty. He needs the hope of the poor (and not their despair). He also needs your pity and compassion and concern – and possibly also your skills – to maintain this hope.

Lord, God of mercy, I pray today for all the poor in the world and ask that You will show me through Your Spirit what You expect from me. Amen.

When God Feels Far Away

Why, O Lord, do You stand far off? Why do You hide Yourself in times of trouble? (Ps. 10:1)

One of the most serious aspects of hardship is the feeling of complete hopelessness. You feel as if there are people out there plotting your downfall behind your back. You also feel lonely because you think that the whole world has turned against you. The most serious aspect of all, however, is the feeling that God has abandoned you.

If you have ever experienced this feeling, remember, it is completely normal. The writer of Psalm 10 felt the same way, as well as millions of other people all over the world. The psalmist was surrounded by evil people who were trying to harm him. They were cunning henchmen who were making life difficult for him. The psalmist felt that God, whom he expected to protect him and destroy his enemies, had hidden Himself just when he needed Him the most.

> Religion is the first thing and the last thing, and until a man has found God, and been found by God, he begins no beginning and works to no end.
>
> ~ H. G. Wells

He was busy learning one of the most difficult lessons – that problems and difficulties are a part of life for everyone. Evil is so strong and so widespread, and its trickery so subtle, that anyone who underestimates it is living in a fool's paradise. Even so, the psalmist did not abandon his hope in God. He prayed for God to reveal Himself and to help him with the evil circumstances he had to deal with.

You also need to know and believe that, however difficult life might be for you, God *will* reveal Himself. He wants you to seek Him in the dark times too, so that you will know without a doubt that He loves you. And if you persevere in hope, He will bless you richly.

Lord Jesus, let the ones who have gone astray seek You until they find You. Amen.

You hear, O LORD, the desire of the afflicted; You encourage them, and You listen to their cry. (Ps. 10:17)

Read
Ps. 10:12-18

When the international advisory service, Lifeline, began working, they let the world know, "Help is just a phone call away!" Anyone with a problem or the need to talk could dial the easy-to-remember number and be sure that there would be a friendly, listening ear on the other side. There would be no shocked reaction, disapproval or judgment – no matter what the caller said. And the call would be treated completely confidentially.

The writer of our text for today knew that whatever trouble he might be in, he could turn to God and God would listen to his problem. God would know about and understand his pain and He would listen to his call.

> The first duty of love is to listen.
> ~ PAUL TILLICH

You can also make the call, because God will do the same for you. However foolish you may have been, however upset you are at the moment, however guilty you may feel and however low you may have sunk, however frightened you may be: Jesus will always listen to your story. He listened to the thief next to Him on the cross; He heard the cries of distress of the blind Bartimaeus on the road to Jericho; He listened to the cries for help from the lepers. You can come to Him with any grievance, problem, injustice, illness, fear or hope; with your mistakes, your failures, your pain and your dilemmas.

Leaving your troubles with Him will do you the world of good. And you may find a way forward just by talking things out with Someone who has a sympathetic ear to lend. It is no vain hope.

Let everyone who has heavy burdens to carry, Lord Jesus, approach Your throne of grace. *Amen.*

In the LORD I take refuge. How then can you say to me: "Flee like a bird to your mountain." (Ps. 11:1)

You have most probably felt that the situation on earth is so oppressive and depressing that you just want to cry out, "Stop the world! I want to get off!" The world is facing enormous problems: global warming; poverty; terrorism; globalization; the lowering of standards; and the depletion of the earth's natural resources, to name just a few. Then there is your personal situation, the circumstances that choke your hope and optimism to death. Sometimes things are so bad that you feel like you just want to run away from it all.

The psalmist also experienced danger and threats to safety. These were caused by the evil plots and plans of his enemies. But he did not crack. Even less did he give in to the temptation to run away and hide out in the mountains. He fixed his hope on God as his refuge and his hiding place. He might well have said, "Don't tell me to flee. My God is not to be found in running away from my problems, from danger and from pressure. I am staying right here, because I know it is where God wants me and where He will strengthen and empower me with hope."

> God proved His love on the cross. When Christ hung, and bled, and died, it was God saying to the world – I love you.
>
> ~ BILLY GRAHAM

However overwhelming the circumstances may seem to you, do not become a runaway. Place your hope and trust in the God who is right there with you in the center of the problems and the pressures of the real world. Jesus struggled against Satan in Gethsemane before He went to Golgotha – but He did not attempt to escape the cross.

Jesus of Golgotha, thank You for the cross; help me, please, to carry mine. Amen.

Hope Only in God for Safety

O Lord, You will keep us safe and protect us from such people forever. (Ps. 12:7)

Read
Ps. 12:1-8

The human race longs for security. We want to know that when a foreign power threatens our country, our army will protect us. Of course we hope that our politicians will be able to solve the problem before it comes to a military confrontation. We also long for financial security, safety in our homes, healthy food and emotional security.

There is, however, no absolute security for any of these areas. War, crime, economic uncertainty and the unpredictable nature of the human personality all undermine the stability that we need. In the end our hope of security can be established only in God.

> Those who desire to give up freedom in order to gain security, will not have, nor do they deserve either one.
> ~ THOMAS JEFFERSON

The poor are much more vulnerable to the changes that come about. They most likely have more need of God because they have no authority. They have little to negotiate with. The Bible explains that God hears their cries, that He knows their needs and He feels their pain. Unlike the empty promises of some politicians, God does indeed do something for the poor. They know that His promises are reliable. His words are the truth, not just superficial clichés that hold no substance.

You should also place your hope in God for your security. No matter how well you may provide for every aspect of your material needs, eventually you will need the security that only God can give you. This security flows from His promises, from the fact that He knows you, loves you, is holding on to you and will never let you go. It is definitely worth your while to put your hope firmly in God.

Lord my Security, I place my renewed hope and expectations in You alone. Amen.

Thankful and Safe

Read
Ps. 16:1-11

Therefore my heart is glad and my tongue rejoices; my body also will rest secure. (Ps. 16:9)

You have probably already noticed how different people react to what life dishes up for them. No matter what circumstances some people find themselves in, they react negatively and unhappily. Other people have joy in practically every situation; even in serious and sad circumstances. If you have set your hope firmly on God, you probably belong to the second group.

King David wrote our text for today about 3,000 years ago, when he was surrounded by enemies and was experiencing problems and making many mistakes. Even so, because of his steadfast hope in God and his faith, he was still thankful and safe. He knew without a doubt that God is the King of kings and that eventually He would triumph over all his enemies and wipe out evil. The few arrows of adversity that came David's way could not overpower him. As a result he felt completely safe.

> Let us be grateful to people who make us happy – they are the charming gardeners who make our souls blossom.
> ~ MARCEL PROUST

This can also be your happy lot. You have the choice of letting your problems, big or small, get out of control until they look like high mountains and you feel miserable, worried and afraid. Or you can put your hope in Jesus and remember His words, "In this world you will have trouble. But take heart! I have overcome the world" (John 16:33). Just keep your spirits up and hope in God: even in the most difficult and darkest circumstances there is always good reason to thank God. Thank Him for the opportunity to accept the challenge and praise Him for the thankfulness that will be born out of your misery. The difference lies not in the circumstances, but in your attitude! Put your hope in God and feel thankful and safe.

Loving Master, help me through Your Spirit to always feel thankful and safe with You. Amen.

You will not abandon me to the grave. (Ps. 16:10)

As the years of your life slip by, many things change. People we have known die and those special relationships are broken. Some residential areas deteriorate and become unrecognizable, while others develop with unusual speed. Science and technology bring many changes, some of them very exciting. Social customs and conventions also change radically.

But there are some things that never seem to change: the seasons come and go, true to their appointed time; trees grow and flowers blossom. People still fall in love, marry, and innocent and loving little children are born.

> Death is as the fore-shadowing of life. We die that we may die no more!
> ~ HERMAN HOOKER

The author of our text for today knew that the God he served was unchangeable. His hope and faith in God were eternal and the grace of God always remains unchanged. Because God is not bound by time, His love is timeless. The psalmist sensed that not even death could bring the mercy of God to an end.

Christian believers know only too well that because Jesus Christ rose from the dead, not even death can break the bond between God and His children. You can view death as a way of getting to know God better, for then His love will dry the tears in our eyes; pain and suffering will be a thing of the past, and the heartache and disappointment will be transformed into victory. Sorrow will change to joy; work will be replaced by praise; and defeats and failures will become fulfillment – and hope that goes beyond death!

Living Lord Jesus, thank You for the hope that makes me strong in the face of death. Amen.

My Hope and My Shelter

The LORD is my rock, my fortress and my deliverer; my God is my rock, in whom I take refuge. He is my shield. (Ps. 18:2)

You may think that you have no enemies, but you do. The criminal who watches your house for an opportunity to break in is your enemy; the drunken driver is a danger on the road and therefore your enemy; the scoundrel who wants to trick you out of your hard-earned savings; the drug dealer trying to lead your children astray – these people are all your enemies. You can probably think of others yourself.

You may pray daily for protection against the Evil One and even quote Jesus' very words from the Lord's Prayer, "Deliver us from the Evil One" (Matt. 6:13). You should do this. You can, however, think of all these things in a more positive light if you think of God as your Protector and your Shield. A soldier uses his shield to deflect the arrows of the enemy. God is your source of supernatural strength. Jesus strengthens you for battle. The fortress was a safe place where the soldiers could withdraw to regroup after battle. Often the entire area was defended by such a fortress.

> The most important of life's battles is the one we fight daily in the silent chambers of the soul.
> ~ DAVID O. MCKAY

Jesus is your Shield, your safe Fortress, your Rock where you can hide away. You are not alone in your battle against the Evil One. You do not have to try and overcome in your own strength, Jesus has already overcome all the forces of the Evil One. And He is on your side if your hope is fixed on Him!

Almighty God, You are my safe fortress against the onslaughts of the Evil One. Amen.

He reached down from on high and took hold of me; He drew me out of deep waters. (Ps. 18:16)

Read
Ps. 18:17-28

You might remember the devastating flood that hit Mozambique a few years ago. In the midst of such a huge crisis the South African army sent helicopters to bring the people to safety. Because of this a baby was rescued from a tree and many others were also saved by miraculous rescue efforts.

David, who wrote this psalm, was persecuted by King Saul. He was forced to flee for his life and found himself in danger of death every day, yet he survived to become one of Israel's greatest kings because the hand of God saved him.

If you have recovered from a life-threatening illness, God has stretched out His hand to you. If you have survived an armed robbery; lived through a terrible accident; or escaped a political uprising, then you can also confess, "He reached down from on high

> The Lord is loving unto man, and swift to pardon, but slow to punish. Let no man therefore despair of his own salvation.
> ~ CYRIL OF ALEXANDRIA

and took hold of me; He drew me out of deep waters." Even when you have survived an economic crisis, an emotional trauma, or a family break-up, be thankful that God saved you. He has worked through other people and used them to save you from disaster.

Jesus came from the Father to save and redeem us and lead us on a godly path. How thankful you should be to God who pulled you out of deep water. Keep your hope focused on God and you will experience His saving grace every time.

Holy Father, we pray for those who find themselves in deep water, especially those who do not know of God's saving grace. Amen.

Even though I walk through the valley of the shadow of death, I will fear no evil, for You are with me; Your rod and Your staff, they comfort me. (Ps. 23:4)

Many people's lives are governed by fear. Death, poverty, hurtful relationships, jealousy and malicious gossip are just a few of the fears that plague humanity.

If you are afraid of the future, think about and remember the past. When you look back on the road you have traveled, think of those times when your faith and hope were strong and your attitude positive. Most of all, think about how real God has been to you. Your whole life may not be blessed with such lovely memories but at the time they existed they confirmed the truth of His presence in your life.

God was with you in the past and you allowed Him to lead and inspire you. You were deeply conscious of His holy presence. When you turned away from Him to please yourself, the fear and depression began. You were afraid that you were too inadequate to live a successful life.

> I don't know what tomorrow holds, but I know Who holds tomorrow.
> ~ ANONYMOUS

The future is yours to do with it what you will. You can either go forward, afraid of everything that could happen to you and just succeed in making your life miserable. Or you can go out to meet life with hope, confidence and faith, and believe with certainty that you can never be separated from your Father God's grace and care. God cares about you, therefore, you have absolutely no reason to fear the future.

Father God, I am not afraid of the future, because You are already there. Amen.

O LORD, You have searched me and You know me. You know when I sit and when I rise; You perceive my thoughts from afar. (Ps. 139:1-2)

Read
Ps. 139:1-12

Most people refuse to accept an honest evaluation of themselves and, because meditative self-examination can be so uncomfortable, the majority of us refuse to practice it. Hidden weaknesses, perverted attitudes and many other bad habits are revealed when you set aside time for quiet self-examination.

The depth and quality of this self-examination depends on your personal standards. If you have low standards, you will find that they manifest in a low lifestyle. It is when you instinctively realize that God has His own standards according to which you should live, that you will start to make a serious effort to conform to His plan for your life. It should be the hope of every follower of the Master to conform to His standards.

> The ultimate measure of a man is not where he stands in moments of comfort and convenience, but where he stands at times of challenge and controversy.
>
> ~ MARTIN LUTHER KING, JR.

This could become a problem for you. Can anyone measure up to God's standards? In your own strength such an achievement is impossible, but if your hope lies in God He can transform your inability through His omnipotence. Whenever you delight in His forgiveness in simple hope and faith, receive His Holy Spirit into your life and live in the knowledge of His indwelling presence, the true value of self-examination will become very clear to you.

The Holy Spirit leads honest and serious disciples into the discipline of self-examination. He enables them to see themselves in the light of the holiness of God and, as the residue of the weaknesses of bygone years moves before your spiritual eyes, it is replaced by the purifying strength that is the living Christ's alone. It is a glorious hope which we need to cling firmly to.

I praise and thank You, O Holy Spirit, for giving me the courage to face the challenge of self-examination. *Amen.*

Blessed is he whose help is the God of Jacob, whose hope is in the LORD his God. (Ps. 146:5)

According to the dictionary the meaning of the word *joy* is "reason for happiness." On *happiness* the dictionary says: "situation of satisfaction." This is something that most of us, if not all of us, greatly desire. Particularly in these fast-moving and uncertain times we live in, people are tired of the rush and confusion of the world, and their hearts are crying out for rest and the joy of peace. Many of us try to find these things through man-made methods but, as we so often find out at the cost of our own happiness, these methods are not at all adequate to meet the need of our hearts.

There is one certain way to live a life of joy and happiness and that is to live according to God's plan for your life. You need to subject yourself to His authority in every aspect of your life. Whatever it is, open your life to His leading and influence so that He can guide you.

> Joy is the experience of knowing that you are unconditionally loved.
> ~ HENRI NOUWEN

The Scriptures and history itself will prove to you that the person "whose hope is in the LORD his God" is also the one who comes to know joy and satisfaction in every aspect of life. Fix your hope in the living Christ and you will be able to live with the same joy and satisfaction.

Whatever You decide for me, Father God, it is for my good because You will never deceive me; You lead me on the paths of righteousness and will never leave or forsake me. I accept with joy and satisfaction what You give me from Your hand and I hope patiently for Your grace. Amen.

Blessed is he whose help is in the God of Jacob, whose hope is in the LORD his God. (Ps. 146:5)

Read

Ps. 146:1-10

When you start a new business, without exception moments of doubt and uncertainty will come. Because human nature is what it is, most people experience these times of worry and anxiety every time they move into an unknown future. Some people are overwhelmed by fear and doubt in these circumstances and they fail in their endeavors – sometimes even before they have started.

The biggest and most important business of all is naturally life itself. The prospect of an exciting future, with all its potential promise, stretches out before us. How will we cope with it? Will you move forward in trust and hope to achieve your goals; or will you be overwhelmed by your fear of the unknown and settle for second best instead: a mediocre and unfulfilled life?

> Come, my Way, my Truth,
> my Life! Such a Way as
> gives us breath, such
> a Truth as ends all strife,
> such a Life as killeth death.
> ~ GEORGE HERBERT

The living Christ invites you into partnership with Him in the business of life. He has assured you of His presence at all times and He has promised to give you a full life. He will never let you down or turn away from you when you need Him.

With this hope and certainty, you can move forward into a richly abundant life in the power of the Holy Spirit. Give Him full control over you and over your life and you have the guarantee that your life will be successful and completely satisfying.

Lord Jesus, when I depend upon myself I am engulfed by doubt and uncertainty; but with Your arms around me, I have the most wonderful partner anyone could desire. *Amen.*

Jesus' Friendship

"You are My friends if you do what I command." (John 15:14)

Jesus had an enormous capacity for friendship. Children loved Him without reserve; the outcasts of society were relaxed in His company; a corrupt tax collector became His disciple; an impulsive fisherman became His special friend. It is impossible to knowingly spend time in the presence of the living Christ and remain untouched by His love.

This holy friendship is the outpouring of God's love in your life. If He did not love you, you could not react to Him. But He does, and you do, and an exquisite intimacy develops that is reflected in your new attitude towards life. You see people in a different light; you are less critical and develop a deeper understanding of people's problems. The spirit of forgiveness dominates the spirit of bitterness of your previously unforgiving spirit. And because the Spirit of holy friendship, which is the Spirit of love, takes over your whole life, you will find to your surprise that you spontaneously act in love in situations and circumstances where you never thought it could be possible.

> The dearest friend on earth is a mere shadow compared to Jesus Christ.
>
> ~ OSWALD CHAMBERS

The friendship that Jesus offers you and the friendship that you share with Him must find practical expression in your daily life. It may never be selfish but must be willing to grasp the hand that reaches out to you, to share the friendship of Jesus with anyone who wants to receive Him. This is a joy and a privilege of fulfilled hope. Introduce your heavenly Friend to other people and see the phenomenal results. Then they can also experience the life-changing love and know the joy of friendship with the living Jesus.

I thank You, my Savior, for the life-changing power of Your glorious friendship. Amen.

"Woe to me!" I cried. "I am ruined! I am a man of unclean lips, and I live among a people of unclean lips, and my eyes have seen the King, the LORD Almighty." (Isa. 6:5)

Read
Isa. 6:1-9

There is an old African proverb that contains an amazing truth, "It takes a whole village to bring up a child." You and I are products of the community we grew up in. Your parents gave you your biological form and your family raised you; but the broader town or community also had an impact on your life. You had the benefit of their strength; you suffered their shortcomings and you were shaped by some of their influences.

After he had seen the holy God, Isaiah saw himself in a whole new light. He saw himself as an unworthy and heinous sinner. However, he took the townsfolk into the temple with him. He perceived his own sinfulness but he also acknowledged the involvement of the broader community in his guilt. What chance did he stand? What hope was there for him?

> Our ground of hope is that God does not weary of mankind.
> ~ RALPH W. SOCKMAN

There *was* hope! He had seen the King: the Lord, the Almighty. It was that vision of God in His holiness that convinced the prophet of his sinfulness. Indeed it was that very same vision of God wherein his hope lay. For God is always Judge and Savior; Surgeon and Healer; Prosecutor and Friend. He is also all of this for you if your hope is established in Him – through the merit of Jesus Christ, our Savior and Redeemer.

Thank You, Lord my God, for the community I come from. Help me to be part of the solution to their problems and a contributor to their hope for the future. Amen.

JULY

If only for this life we have hope in Christ, we are to be pitied more than all men. But Christ has indeed been raised from the dead, the firstfruits of those who have fallen asleep.
~ 1 CORINTHIANS 15:19-20

Loving Father God, I worship You as the Source
of infinite hope and grace.
The glorious promises in Your eternal Word
light the flame of hope in my heart every time.
Because I have found my refuge in You, I can continue to hope.
However furious the storms of life, raging and devastating,
You remain my anchor of hope!
Lord Jesus, Your life, suffering and death,
Your resurrection from the dead, assure me of the hope of eternal life
together with You in our Father's house.
Holy Spirit of God, Your comfort gives me hope in my darkest hours
and guards me from despair.
Triune God, by Your grace I have the lasting hope of my eternal
inheritance, which is being kept safe for me. Miraculous grace!
Even in this life You keep me safe in Your Almighty hands.
You have taken me into Your care – what inconceivably great mercy!
You are my hope; in life and in death.
Your Son also died for me, an undeserving sinner saved.
Therefore I am absolutely sure of my inheritance.
Thank You, wonderful and loving Jesus, that Your love has transformed
my hope into conviction.
You are my guarantee against despair!
Father, Son and Holy Spirit, keep the flame of hope burning
in my heart.
I pray this in the name of my Savior, my Hope, the living Christ!

Amen.

Practice hope. As hopefulness becomes a habit,
you can achieve a permanently happy spirit.
~ NORMAN VINCENT PEALE

Read
Isa. 28:23-29

All this also comes from the LORD Almighty, wonderful in counsel and magnificent in wisdom. (Isa. 28:29)

The twentieth century has experienced rapid progress and development in almost every area. In the fields of science and technology, engineering and architecture, business and leisure, great steps have been made forward in unimaginable ways. In many instances this has been of great benefit to humanity, but there have also been occasions when things have gone wrong and caused pain and suffering. This was mainly because of people who were motivated by greed and worked to achieve their own glory.

One of the dangers experienced in the application of the new methods and inventions was giving in to the temptation to discard older, proven methods because they were viewed as old-fashioned and obsolete. While change in certain circumstances may be necessary and advantageous, there is no point in making changes if they are not needed.

> Hope is a waking dream.
> ~ ARISTOTLE

When the need to make changes in your own life is staring you in the face, first lay your plans and ambitions before God. Trust in Him as your friend and follow His wise advice for your prosperity, progress, happiness and peace in life. He knows what is best for you.

Be sensitive and open to the influence of the Holy Spirit and respond to His inner whisperings. With God's watchful hand over you, you can always be hopeful of success.

Trusted God and Father, through all the changes in my life, through joy and sorrow, Your grace has always guided me along the right path. I praise and thank You. Amen.

The fruit of righteousness will be peace; the effect of righteousness will be quietness and confidence forever. (Isa. 32:17)

Read
Isa. 32:9-20

We all desire good government, perfect health, prosperity and peace. Humanity's long journey through time is interspersed with battles, wars and bloodshed. However, very few wars attained the purpose fought for. Most wars result in unforeseen and unexpected consequences for the people involved. All wars lead to indescribable suffering and are stains on the conscience of humanity; marks of our collective sinfulness. War symbolizes and emphasizes our failure to live together in peace; it is an insult to God.

The Bible contains a rich variety of ideas on hoping for peace. Peace means much more than the absence of strife. It is the freedom of people to live a full life and to grow. It means mutual respect and love for one another and it is the "fruit of righteousness." Peace will come about if people live their lives honestly and devoted to God: not only as individuals but also as communities and nations. It is impossible for injustice and peace to co-exist as injustice is one of the causes of war.

> Hope means hearing the melody of the future. Faith means to begin dancing to the beat now.
> ~ RUBEM ALVES

Because people are unable to live righteously in their own limited abilities, we can only hope for the peace that comes as a gift of grace from God. Like righteousness and prosperity, it is one of the blessings God leads us into, as part of our hope for the future. Perfect justice, abundance and peace will most probably only be attained at the end of the age when God reigns in His final kingdom. We must therefore set up a steady stream of little road signs of hope and peace along the way.

Lord and Master, may the hope of peace never diminish in my heart. Amen.

Hope in the Jubilee of Nature

The desert and the parched land will be glad; the wilderness will rejoice and blossom. (Isa. 35:1)

Enormous growth in the world's population over the last few decades has placed immense pressure on the earth's natural resources. There are more mouths to feed than ever before. As a result, the United Nations has to keep developing new ways of utilizing the world's oceans, rivers and forests more effectively.

It is very easy to become discouraged when considering these facts. Problems and difficulties seem to be increasing at a greater rate than solutions can be found. Yet the faith and hope found in the Bible concerning this is very positive. God is the Source of new life – and not only on personal and spiritual levels; He also renews the earth. The desert is glad because "Israel will see the glory of the LORD, the splendor of our God" (Isa. 35:2).

> Hope is a feeling that life and work have meaning. You either have it or you don't, regardless of the state of the world that surrounds you.
> ~ VACLAV HAVEL

While humanity may be at its wits' end trying to deal with these problems, this is not at all the case with God. He is still the Creator and the Renewer of life! He has more miracles to unfold than humanity could ever dream of. Some of these miracles demand skilled human cooperation to come to pass. When this happens, people can join together with nature in a joyous song of hope to the glory of God.

In hope the prophets looked forward to what they expected and believed God was still going to do in the future. Let this also be our vision, hope and expectation!

Creator God, we pray today for scientists and technologists who are creating initiatives to sustain life on earth. Let us never give up hope. Amen.

Say to those with fearful hearts, "Be strong, do not fear; your God will come. He will come to save you." (Isa. 35:4)

Read
Isa. 35:1-10

There are many people who fail to reach their full potential in life because they are either too afraid or too reserved. They might well possess the required ability, but when the time of testing comes, they are shy or embarrassed and then they withdraw.

Many people who can give a good account of themselves when it comes to their chosen area in life, fail in broader contexts because of a weakness in their characters. The outcome is often a feeling of failure and inadequacy that only serves to strengthen the sense of worthlessness already felt.

A Christian need never feel inferior. As a child of God you have the promise that His Son, the living Christ, will be your constant companion and friend throughout your life. He has

> Man's way leads to a hopeless end God's way leads to an endless hope.
> ~ ANONYMOUS

undertaken to help you carry the burdens of your sin, responsibilities, suffering and worry. You have His word that He will never leave you nor forsake you (see Heb. 13.5).

With this promise of God's support, and the assurance that the Son of God is with you at every moment and in any situation, you can move forward in life with hope – full of faith, self-confidence and without fear.

With You at my side, Lord Jesus, I can go out to meet the future with hope and trust. Amen.

And a highway will be there; it will be called the Way of Holiness. (Isa. 35:8)

It's always exciting to travel on a new road. It is smoother, shorter and more pleasant than an old one. Usually it also has a much better surface. Expensive as they are to build, and as slow as they are to materialize, highways are one of the great achievements of the modern world.

You may have never thought of God as an Engineer, but the prophet of the past thought so! He foresaw that God would allow all sorts of miracles to take place that would enrich people's lives. One of these was a road – and it would also be a safe road. It would be the road to Zion in Jerusalem. The redeemed would return, "They will enter Zion with singing" (Isa. 35:10).

> There are no hopeless situations; there are only people who have grown hopeless about them.
> ~ CLARE BOOTHE LUCE

If you have given your life to Jesus Christ and have dedicated yourself to Him, then you are one of the redeemed souls for whom God built this road. This road indicates that it is for those who are devout and, therefore, you must qualify accordingly in order to be able to walk on it.

The Holy Spirit gives God's characteristic of holiness to you. This is not something that you earn or can attain through achievement, or something that you need to score points for. As the Holy Spirit brings Christ forward in you, you begin the journey on this path. And at the end of it those who have journeyed with you along the road of hope will be waiting.

Heavenly Father, we come before You today as we think of everyone who is traveling on the roads in our land. Protect them and bring them home safely. Amen.

A voice of one calling: "In the desert prepare the way for the LORD; make straight in the wilderness a highway for our God." (Isa. 40:3)

Read
Isa. 40:1-11

Before Jesus Christ came to earth, the world was in disarray. Violence was rampant; people were suffering at the hands of cruel rulers; the rich were very wealthy and the poor were extremely poor. For the average person the future looked bleak. They had little hope.

Through the darkness of despair, however, came the voice of God calling His people not to give up hope and to prepare themselves for the coming of the expected Messiah – He who was destined to save Israel.

History has proved how, to fulfill His promises and out of His great love for the world, Almighty God sent His Son, Jesus Christ, to save His people.

Circumstances in today's modern world leave much to be desired, and like the people of old, there are many people today who waver on the brink

> Hope is necessary in every condition. The miseries of poverty, sickness and captivity would, without this comfort, be insupportable.
> ~ SAMUEL JOHNSON

of despair. But the promises of God are just as relevant today and will be fulfilled if you keep your faith and hope in the living Christ.

Persevere in your hope in Jesus Christ; His perfect love will drive all despair and fear from your life.

Holy Spirit of God, help me to walk the road of hope together with You until I reach that perfect day. Amen.

Read Isa. 55:1-13	The mountains and hills will burst into song before you, and all the trees of the field will clap their hands. (Isa. 55:12)

We have probably all experienced the sheer joy of a perfect day: You wake up refreshed after a good night's sleep, the sky is blue, the sun is shining, birds are singing and a light breeze cools the day down. You think to yourself, *How perfect! I wish that every day could be just as lovely as this one.* On such a day it seems as if nature is bursting out into a song of praise.

In the musical, *The Sound of Music*, Maria sings, "The hills are alive with the sound of music, with songs they have sung for a thousand years." Maria expresses the same joy and gladness as the prophet in the Old Testament.

The prophet sang out his own joy at the redemption of the people of Israel from exile. They would return to their homeland around Jerusalem. The prophet thought that the hills were rejoicing with him in this wonderful moment of God's greatness and goodness. Even the trees wanted to take part in the festivities for the salvation of God's people!

> Hope is patience keeping its lamp aflame.
> ~ TERTULLIAN

You can also burst out into joy. When you worship and truly praise God and hope for His promises, the whole of Creation celebrates with you. Therefore, rejoice in the midst of the struggle. When the whole world is steeped in joy – hope and rejoice! When trouble strikes – still hope and rejoice! Celebrate God's kingly authority and celebrate Christ's work of salvation for all of humanity!

Let all of Creation resound with songs of joyous hope, to Your honor, O Father. Amen.

Instead of the thornbush will grow the pine tree. This will be for the LORD's renown, for an everlasting sign, which will not be destroyed. (Isa. 55:13)

Read
Isa. 55:1-13

There are many monuments in this world that bear witness to great people and events. St. Paul's Cathedral in London bears witness to the architectural talent of Christopher Wren. The Pyramids attest to the engineering ability of the early Egyptians. Many roads built by the ancient Romans still exist today – evidence of their engineering skill. Certain orders of monks and nuns are a lasting testimony of the devotion to Jesus Christ by the founders of the church.

In our text for today we read the thoughts of the prophet on the people of Israel's return from exile to their homeland. This event took place in the year 538 BC. During their absence their land was plundered and became overrun by thorn bushes: symbols of neglect and decay. When God redeemed His people, He also restored their land. God's touch is always complete and renewing, and ensures a new life of hope.

> In our sad condition our only consolation is the expectancy of another life. Here below all is incomprehensible.
> ~ MARTIN LUTHER

In today's world we are extremely conscious of environmental pollution, so it is a comfort to Christians to know that God renews His Creation even today. Therefore, there is still hope for the earth.

God does not only restore His creation, however, He also restores people! "Therefore, if anyone is in Christ, he is a new creation; the old has gone, the new has come!" (2 Cor. 5:17). You are made new by Jesus Christ – especially as you grow towards adulthood. Then you, too, become a lasting witness of hope and of God's undying love.

Holy Father, let Your Spirit work deep inside me so that my life can be a testimony of Your salvation. Amen.

Hope Lights up Your Life

The sun will no more be your light by day, nor will the brightness of the moon shine on you, for the LORD will be your everlasting light. (Isa. 60:19)

There are times in each person's life when he or she urgently needs encouragement and strength. Problems get us down and life looks particularly empty and meaningless; our hopes are shattered and plans fail before they even have the chance to be completed. At times like these, people search for something to lift them out of their despair and depression and give new meaning to their lives.

Without the slightest doubt, the answer lies in accepting Jesus Christ as your Savior and Redeemer. Christ came into this world as a light and He brightens the lives of everyone He touches. The healing power that flows from Him does not only bring health to the body but also to the mind and the soul. Those who come into contact with Him find that their lives are transformed by His godly influence and they experience a feeling of hope and peace that they have never known before.

> Hope is the only bee that makes honey without flowers.
> ~ ALEXANDRE DUMAS

If you feel that the light has faded from life, turn towards the living Christ. Seek Him in prayer and meditation, in the stillness of His presence. Gradually He will impart His strength and hope to you. His light will brighten up those dark areas of your life and His peace will bring new hope and rest to your soul. Jesus offers you life in all its abundance – receive it and live!

Light of the world, drive all the darkness and despair out of my life and make it bright as day. **Amen.**

> "Behold, I will create new heavens and a new earth. The former things will not be remembered, nor will they come to mind." (Isa. 65:17)

Read
Isa. 65:17-25

We often hear people complaining about the deteriorating situation of the world and life in general. They long for "the good old days" where things were much simpler than they are at present. Having a pessimistic attitude will not improve the situation, yet you must acknowledge, if you make an honest assessment of the events of past years, that there is a great deal of room for improvement.

There is no reason to lose all hope, however; to do so would be foolish. The Lord is completely in control of everything. His love for His Creation is so great and all-embracing that, notwithstanding the actions of the people who sully and undermine the work of God, He will restore His Creation to perfection – for His faithful followers who trust in His name.

All who follow Jesus have the responsibility to hope and trust in His promises and the Almighty power of God. It is your duty and your privilege to live in obedience to His commandments and allow Him to use you to help in the restoration of His Creation to perfection once more.

> One day we will meet beside the river and our Lord will dry every tear. For now, we must live in the joy of that promise and recall that for every generation life is hard, but God is faithful.
>
> ~ BODIE THOENE

Savior and Master, use me in the restoration of Your Creation and grant that I will never be without hope. *Amen.*

"Behold, I will create new heavens and a new earth. The former things will not be remembered, nor will they come to mind." (Isa. 65:17)

Yesterday has gone forever and tomorrow is approaching fast. If you look back into the past, you will be reminded of events that happened long ago. That is the meaning of history.

It is not easy to let go of things from the past. The older you are the harder it becomes. Yet the Bible introduces us to a God who is not only the Creator, but who is always busy re-creating. He is not trapped in the past, even though you might be.

As precious and lovely as the things of the past may be, as sacred and hallowed as the revered traditions may be, they are all in the process of being forgotten. God is busy creating a new earth and a new heaven – possibly even a new church, a new people just for Him. He is continuously moving beyond our field of vision, beyond even our wildest imaginings! When Jesus came to earth, His works were generally far beyond the capacity of the people's ability to understand.

> Hope is the faith that Jesus *will*, and belief is the certainty that He *can*.
>
> ~ MAX LUCADO

As you prepare yourself to move into the future, be grateful to God for what you can leave behind: much of it is evil and everything is transitory. Also, be grateful and happy for the prospect of a new Creation, for the new heaven and new earth that God is going to create. Pray and hope for a perfect new world and a perfect new heaven when Christ comes back to fetch His faithful children.

Protect me from clinging to the past, O Spirit of God, but let me instead look forward with hope to the new world You are going to create. **Amen.**

The sound of weeping and of crying will be heard in Jerusalem no more. (Isa. 65:19)

Read

Isa. 65:17-25

All of us cherish secret wishes for the future: whether it is to enjoy good health or to be healed of a disease; to find work again after a retrenchment; or to see a family rift repaired. However, we can be sure of one thing: the future will not bring us good luck only. It will bring success and failure, good health and bad health – as it has always done in the past.

Even so, you ought to be positive in your hope that God will keep His promises for the future. The prophet did not know what the future held in store for him. In spite of the fact that his nation knew disaster, defeat and slavery, these were always interspersed with times of restoration and prosperity. He dared to look forward to a restored Jerusalem. He firmly believed that the best still lay ahead and dreamt of a time when God would bring an end to suffering, pain and sorrow.

> If hope did not whisper in our ear that tomorrow will be better, how would anyone have the courage to endure today?
> ~ ROBERT BURNS

It is good to dream and to hope, and we do not have to limit our hope to Jerusalem. This theme is expanded in the book of Revelation. There is one striking aspect of the great gathering of the saints at the throne of God. The message is clear: on earth there will be sorrow and tears, but in heaven every tear will be dried! It is a glorious prospect that encourages us to carry on hoping.

Lord God Almighty, thank You for the hope that You will dry the tears from our eyes: let Your kingdom come. **Amen.**

"Do not be afraid of them, for I am with you and will rescue you," declares the LORD. (Jer. 1:8)

Many people suffer from emotional disturbances known as phobias. Fear causes people to make wrong decisions. It fills people's lives with horrors that haunt them at every step. Even people with a great deal of self-confidence feel a little nervous when they have to speak in front of a big crowd.

Jeremiah was hesitant in delivering God's message and he had good reason to fear. His message made him unpopular among the people and he was even accused of being unpatriotic. It demands courage to be an obedient child of God. The people one has to approach are usually angry (and guilty) about being confronted with God and they often attack the messenger.

> It is only our faith in God that is able to deliver us from the fear of other people.
>
> ~ JOHN WEATHERSPOON

Godly truth often brings the convictions of its hearers into question. It frequently reveals the shallowness of their culture. It might even threaten the vested interests of some of the people at whom it is directed. God's Word can sometimes be a Word of judgment, and no one enjoys being judged.

Today God is saying to you, "Don't be afraid of them." See, when you stand up for the truth and righteousness of God, you have a very high calling. It is a good thing to admit that you feel afraid. But just continue to hope in God and ask for His guidance and the courage to speak the right words. Always remember: when you are on God's side, He is on yours.

Gracious Father, remove all fear from the hearts of those who must witness for You and fill them with courage and hope. Amen.

"Do not be afraid of them, for I am with you and will rescue you," declares the LORD. (Jer. 1:8)

Read
Jer. 1:1-10

Most children are afraid of the dark, but when their fathers or mothers are with them in the darkness, they feel much braver. For the Christian disciple, Someone much stronger than any earthly mother or father is with you every step of the way and He encourages you by saying, "I am with you!" What powerful hope fills your heart at these words!

In spite of all Jeremiah's worries and fears, God promised to walk with him and protect him. There were many dangers and Jeremiah needed God's protection and security, because he had made enemies in high places.

God promises to be with you, too, however fraught with danger and difficulty your situation might seem. When you have to confront the possibility of physical danger, He is there

> We can easily forgive a child who is afraid of the dark; but the real tragedy of life is when men are afraid of the light.
> ~ PLATO

to protect you. It is probably much more likely that you will have to face economic dangers in the form of unemployment or the uncertainty of the share market. But God is with you in everything, taking care of you. When you have to endure emotional trauma, He is there. When you lose a life partner, when loved ones abandon you and leave you lonely, He is close to you and will never abandon you.

Maybe you are afraid that you are going to lose your health, or your mind; but always remember that He is keeping you safe in His strong hands. When political unrest breaks out and destroys everything you have worked for over a lifetime, He is still there to protect you and defend you. And when the thing that you fear most comes about and death knocks on your door, God in Jesus Christ is still there to lead you into His glory.

Savior, I pray that in whatever situation I may find myself, I will always cherish the hope that You will never let me fall. *Amen.*

Read

Jer. 1:11-19

The word of the LORD came to me: "What do you see, Jeremiah?" "I see the branch of an almond tree," I replied. (Jer. 1:11)

Different things have different meanings, depending on the way people look at them. For the artist an ancient oak tree is an object of beauty and he will bring this to light in a beautiful painting. In that same tree a carpenter will see precious wood for making furniture; a bird will see a place to make a nest. The prophets saw the same things that everyone else saw, but they perceived them differently. They viewed everyday things as message bearers from God, as signs of His omnipotence, control and creativity.

The almond tree was the first tree to blossom in the spring after the desolation of the winter months. When it flowered, it spoke of the newness of life, of revival. It indicated the end of winter, and the beginning of summer, new growth and warmth. It further held the promise of coming fruits. It was as if it was saying, "Something important is about to happen!"

Hope is a perennial fountain in the heart of everyone.

~ ALEXANDER POPE

Below the surface there is always something going on. Behind the scenes God is busy creating a new spring. He may allow winter to conceal His plans, but He will always call new life, new hope and new activity into being.

If you have struggled to survive after a spiritual winter, let the almond tree give you hope. Somewhere, and in some way, God is waiting to begin a new spring in your life. As cold and inaccessible as things may look at the moment, spring will break through with joy and there will once again be hope and love. Just be patient and wait hopefully for the Lord!

Lord Jesus, I pray that You will bring a new spring into the lives of those who have grown cold. Amen.

The LORD said to me, "You have seen correctly, for I am watching to see that My word is fulfilled." (Jer. 1:12)

Read
Jer. 1:11-19

People sometimes feel like God has abandoned them. They don't believe that He is listening to their prayers and as a result they stop praying. When something unpleasant occurs in their lives they feel that God has left them.

God showed Jeremiah the almond tree and used this image to say to the prophet, "However dark and cold the winter may be, I am still in control and spring will come again." People would watch the almond tree to see new life appearing.

In Hebrew the word for "almond tree" is *shaqed*, while the word for "watching" is *shoqed*. Jeremiah used a word play on the sounds. He said, "You think that God is sleeping, but He is ever watchful to see that His purposes for this world are carried out. His goal will be attained just as surely as the almond tree bursts into flower in the spring."

God is also watching you, however cold and dark your circumstances may seem. He is watching you and knows that you are struggling, and – without you even knowing it – He is giving you the strength to survive.

> Make no little plans. They have no magic to stir men's blood. Make big plans: aim high in hope and work.
> ~ DANIEL HUDSON BURNHAM

The almond tree draws strength from its inactivity in the winter and often we grow and learn more in the sad times of our lives than during the sunny days. God has not let you down, He has not even taken His eyes off you. Like a watchman protecting a military base, God is watching over you. You can safely hope for the dawning of spring – it will come!

Loving Lord Jesus, watch over everyone who is going through a spiritual winter. Amen.

Cisterns without Hope

"My people have committed two sins: they have forsaken Me, the spring of living water, and have dug their own broken cisterns that cannot hold water." (Jer. 2:13)

S toring water has always been a challenge. Today, due to great engineering achievements, we store our water in dams. In Bible times cisterns were chiseled out of porous sandstone rocks. These then had to be plastered to prevent the water from seeping out. When the plaster cracked, the cistern emptied quickly.

The problem that Jeremiah was facing was that the people of Judah had wandered away from worshiping the true God. In this way they had cut themselves off from the spring of Living Water. They worshiped other gods – those of the surrounding Canaanites – and these gods were spiritually empty. They could not give any spiritual comfort or cleanse people's sins. They were like burst cisterns.

> We are not cisterns made for hoarding, we are channels made for sharing.
> ~ BILLY GRAHAM

We may wonder why the people of that time were so foolish, but we are probably no better. The broken cisterns that we rely on are pleasure, gratification, sport, money, food and sex. Some people fill their every waking moment, besides work hours, with one or more of these pastimes. The tragedy is that they think that these are the only things life has to offer and that their lives are actually being enriched. They do not see how empty and meaningless it all is. Go to a casino and look at the way people use both hands to work two machines at once in the vain hope of winning more money – you will see the broken cisterns of our time.

The question that each one of us must ask ourselves is whether we are drinking from the Source of Living Water or whether we are depending on cracked cisterns?

Lord, help me to be able to distinguish between broken cisterns and Your fountain of Living Water. *Amen.*

At that time they will call Jerusalem The Throne of the LORD, and all nations will gather in Jerusalem to honor the name of the LORD. (Jer. 3:17)

Read
Jer. 3:6-18

There is a big difference between hope and optimism. Optimism weighs up advantages and disadvantages and lays a solid foundation for action when future opportunities come its way. It is usually a very personal and subjective matter. Hope sees all the negatives and believes that good will still triumph, in spite of the adverse circumstances.

Despite the unfaithfulness of the people and the threat of a military invasion, Jeremiah was not always a prophet of doom. His faith and hope were solidly grounded in God. In spite of everything that was going wrong, he dared to hope that God would allow the day to dawn when the Israelites would once again be united in worship in Jerusalem. Other nations would join in with them and also acknowledge the same God.

> Optimism means faith in *people* – that they will be able to help us in an emergency. But the Christian hope is the sure knowledge that the omnipotence of *God* is indeed able to meet our needs – or change us.
>
> ~ CARLO CARETTO

Jesus showed us that the latter hope was not entirely necessary because God really wanted people to "worship the Father in spirit and truth" (John 4:23), and not only in a particular place. The book of Revelation suggests the final vision – a new heavenly Jerusalem coming down from God with a new heaven and a new earth. The whole of Creation will be transformed and peace will reign supreme (see Rev. 21:22-23).

It is a courageous hope. But when it seems as if the whole world is disintegrating into chaos and confusion, you need the kind of faith that fervidly hopes and sees past the turmoil of the present. You can believe that after all the violence and evil of the present day, God will bring about truth, peace and perfection.

Lord of infinite hope, fill my heart with Your everlasting hope, grace and strength. Amen.

The stork knows her appointed seasons, and thrush observe the time of their migration. But my people do not know the requirements of the LORD. (Jer. 8:7)

In parts of Israel the nests of thrushes can be seen in chimneys and on telephone poles. Every year the birds appear after migrating from the southern parts of Africa. A few months later they vanish, only to return to the same nest the following year.

The same thing happened in Jeremiah's time too. He saw that these birds were clever enough to obey their instinct for migration that God placed within them. Many other birds did the same. God also created His people and called them to seek Him. He repeatedly called upon them to abandon their sinful ways and migrate back to Him. Unlike the birds, however, they stubbornly refused.

You and I have also been created to seek God. In your inmost being there is an inborn longing for God. Only God Himself can satisfy this longing. Unless God fulfills this inner need, you will be like a migrating bird that didn't leave on time and then finds itself on the wrong side of the earth in the wrong season.

> Order your soul; reduce your wants; live in charity; associate in Christian community; obey the laws; trust in Providence.
>
> ~ ST. AUGUSTINE

This does not have to happen. You can move according to the God-ordained plan for your life if you just open your heart and mind to the living Christ. When you give yourself to Him, He will reprogram your life to work itself out as He created it to do. Just like the clever birds, you can return to your original spiritual home – God! I know that this hope is burning in your heart – act now!

O Lord, my God and Father, I am coming home! *Amen.*

O my Comforter in sorrow, my heart is faint within me.
(Jer. 8:18)

Read
Jer. 8:14-22

Many things tend to get people down and drive them to despair. Conflict in the family is one of the main causes of sorrow. Yet there are many other causes, too, like problems at work, employers who are unreasonable and demanding, even fellow workers can cause trouble. Money is another source of pain: debt can paralyze you, government officials can make your life intolerable, and the exhaustion of working long hours can drive you to breaking point.

Jeremiah preached his heart out, but the people disregarded and ridiculed the serious messages that he brought them. This demoralized and frustrated him. He was afraid that the coming punishments of God would destroy his country and his people. He felt sick inside just thinking about the sins of the people and their rejection of God. Sorrowful and dejected, he turned to the only Source of help that he knew: God! He sobbed out, "O my Comforter in sorrow, my heart is faint within me." Jeremiah was honest before God. It was not in his nature to put on a brave front and try to cover up his true feelings.

> Hope is a passion for what is possible.
> ~ SØREN KIERKEGAARD

In our day of sorrow and pain we can also pour out our sorrow before God. If God is the sunshine of your life when things are going well, He is also your lamp in the darkness of midnight. When your heart is overwhelmed and many difficulties greatly upset you and it is all too much to share with other people, put your hope in God, your personal Comforter in sorrow.

Somewhere in the shadows of life we find You, Lord Jesus. And we recognize You by the nail marks in Your hands. Amen.

Balm in Gilead

Is there no balm in Gilead? Is there no physician there? Why then is there no healing for the wound of my people? (Jer. 8:22)

Many diseases and illnesses threaten humanity's well-being. A generation ago Polio was a serious illness for people. Now TB and HIV/Aids are the modern killers. Each disease challenges human ingenuity to find a cure. Enormous amounts of money are spent searching for effective cures.

In biblical times, Gilead stood on the eastern side of the Jordan River. Trading caravans traveled through this area from the east, moving south in the direction of Egypt. One of the products they brought with them was an aromatic substance used for healing, called balm. Thus "balm in Gilead" became a catch phrase for "cures" and "healing."

> As oxygen is to the lungs, so is hope the essence of life.
>
> ~ EMIL BRUNNER

Jeremiah saw the sickness of his people, but he knew that because their rebellion was against the living God, they could not be healed by the balm in Gilead – nor by any human doctor. Only God Himself could heal them. He had already indicated this in Exodus, "I am the LORD, who heals you" (Exod. 15:26). But they stubbornly refused to return to Him; their Source of health and life.

When you need healing, turn to God; give yourself over to Jesus and seek His help, whatever your illness may be. Remember also that God can use the skills and discoveries of the medical profession. Therefore use any prescription from your doctor. In the same way that Christ touched and healed the people in Galilee, He can do the same for you today. Millions are able to witness that their hope in Him was not in vain.

God of healing, give Your wisdom and blessing to researchers of healing remedies. Amen.

Therefore this is what the LORD Almighty says: "See, I will refine and test them." (Jer. 9:7)

Read
Jer. 9:3-16

A visit to a goldmine is an informative excursion. You go down deep into the earth and see thin ridges of space left behind after the goldbearing ore is removed, like a page torn from a book. You see how truckloads of rock are transported to the surface. There the rock is ground down and processed and eventually goes into a blast-furnace. At last, molten yellow liquid is cast into molds the size of a brick. Many tons of rock are needed to make one small brick of gold.

Jeremiah believed that God was dealing with His people in a similar way. Disaster was breaking loose all around them, adversity was at hand and tragedy struck them. Through this they would discover how it felt to be ground down and they would know the heat of the blast-furnace. In this way God would purify them.

> Hope is like the sun: when you look in its direction, it casts the shadows of your problems behind you.
> ~ SAMUEL SMILES

Life is a blend of successes and failures, joys and sorrows, triumphs and defeats. We all experience times of prosperity and success, but we all have setbacks too. Christians go through the same trials as everybody else.

See your problems and difficulties as a goldmine; God is calling on you to mine the pure gold of faith, hope and love. Many hard-hearted and bitter people have been broken by adversity, but they became sweeter, deeper and more creative souls because of the experience. They discovered that God was busy performing His work of purification in the midst of their pain and suffering. This gives us hope to work through our disappointments with courage.

Lord Jesus, purify me daily, more and more, through Your Spirit working in me. Amen.

Read
Jer. 14:19-22

Why have You afflicted us so that we cannot be healed? We hoped for peace but no good has come, for a time of healing but there is only terror. (Jer. 14:19)

A well-known sportsman who had come to the end of his career, said upon his retirement, "There is no fairytale ending in professional sport." He had hoped to go out in a blaze of glory, but he could no longer keep his place in the team. We all expect a dream future but reality is merciless and life is difficult.

Jeremiah's prayer to God gives us insight into how a man of deep faith and hope in God adapted himself to the merciless circumstances that surrounded him. "We" are the people of Israel. They hoped for peace so that they could build up their national life once again, be successful and prosper and grow. Instead they experienced terror, crime and threatening disaster all around them.

All human wisdom is summed up in two words – wait and hope.

~ ALEXANDRE DUMAS

There was sickness and pestilence and the dark times were made worse by poverty.

Yet, in spite of the darkness, Jeremiah kept hoping. He knew that God was still in control. He knew that the darker it was out there, the more he needed the light that only God can provide.

It is necessary for us to also fix our hope on God instead of on seeming good luck. We must acknowledge the darkness, but remember there is a Light that we can switch on. Jesus is still the Light of the world, even in our darkest hour.

Father God, help me to carry on hoping even when the world around me is falling apart. Amen.

Alas, my mother, that you gave me birth. (Jer. 15:10)

Read
Jer. 15:10

Do you envy those who move through life with cheerfulness, strength and optimism? You probably wonder how they manage it. They are truly a rare species. Most of us have our high and low points. Many of us go through times when we are at a very low ebb.

In our text for today, Jeremiah laments his day of birth and examines his trying life. He was obviously a very sensitive person, with deep feelings of loneliness and pain. The only reason he was able to keep his boat on course in the storm of life was because of his hope and faith in God and his ceaseless obedience to Him. A lesser person would have lost courage long before

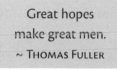

Great hopes
make great men.
~ THOMAS FULLER

and given up all hope. Yet all the trouble he was forced to face had taken its toll and he felt it badly. He would much rather have been popular, successful and cheerful. Instead, he was wishing he had never been born.

If you have ever thought that being a Christian means that you must always be cheerful and successful, think again. Remember the prophet Jeremiah. He was without a doubt one of the greatest figures of the Old Testament, if not of the entire Bible. He accepted the role that God ordained for him with hope and courage, then discovered just how difficult his path was. He paid the price for being a man of God. Yet, no amount of difficulty, criticism or opposition put him off. No suffering could deflect him from his walk with God. This was because Jeremiah knew that he always had the same God to hope in and cling to. If you ever find yourself in the depths of despair, remember that you share the same God as Jeremiah.

Almighty Savior, support me and give me hope, however desperate my situation may be. *Amen.*

The LORD said, "Surely I will deliver you for a good purpose; surely I will make your enemies plead with you in times of disaster and times of distress." (Jer. 15:11)

In moments of crisis, when children feel afraid and unable to cope, a mother will put her arms around her child and whisper, "Everything is going to be all right. I have asked the Lord to look after us." And He does!

Jeremiah was a target for his enemies, who loathed his political standpoint. They were also in danger of attack by a foreign army. Most of them perished when that army finally invaded Judah. Jeremiah was spared, however, and was exiled to Egypt. When Jeremiah poured out his heart in remorse before God, God did not take away the problem but He did promise to protect him. In life every disaster cannot be averted, but we can all seek the protection of God.

You worship a God who has promised to protect you, too. You need protection against criminals and you must take every possible precaution to ensure your physical safety. God also promises you His care and His defending hand. In today's world you are economically vulnerable, in danger of terrorist activity, political unrest, emotional trauma, danger on the roads, threats to your health and of natural disasters.

> Of all the forces that make for a better world, none is so indispensable, none so powerful, as hope. Without hope men are only half alive. With hope they dream and think and work.
>
> ~ CHARLES SAWYER

Don't become neurotic and worry yourself sick about all of it. Put yourself under God's control and protection and walk with Jesus, every minute of every day. You will not be safeguarded against all danger, but in the final instance God will be your haven of hope and security.

Almighty God, place Your wall of protection around me and guard me from all harm. Amen.

When Your words came, I ate them; they were my joy and my heart's delight, for I bear Your name, O LORD God Almighty. (Jer. 15:16)

Read
Jer. 15:15-21

Robert Louis Stevenson, an English author, emigrated to Samoa for health reasons. One night he was feeling sick and sat down in a chair. Just when he thought how pleasant it would be if he had a nice cup of coffee, his housekeeper walked in with a cup of steaming coffee. "How wonderful," Stevenson said, "you are very thoughtful." "No, Sir," answered the man, "I serve you with great love." Some people serve and obey out of a sense of duty. Others serve cheerfully and out of love.

Jeremiah, in spite of the burden that his surrender to God had placed upon him, nevertheless served God with joyous obedience. As tough as the requirements were, he accepted them gladly. He knew that it was a special privilege to belong to God and not a burden at all. To serve God was a joy for him.

Some of the demands that God makes on you will be pleasant to you. They will bring you joy when you carry them out. Others will be less pleasant. Through your obedience to Christ you will sometimes be able to satisfy God and yourself. On other occasions you will be able to please God only by denying yourself. A parent with a sick child may spend hours taking care of the child's needs and lose many hours of sleep in the process. But the parent does not count the cost and does not complain, because he or she serves and hopes in love.

> Hope is not the conviction that something will turn out well but the certainty that something makes sense, regardless of how it turns out.
> ~ VACLAV HAVEL

Do you serve the Lord joyfully? Or do you complain and hope for other, more pleasant things you can enjoy? If that is the case then it is time for self-examination and for defining your hope and your faith.

Merciful Master, make me delight in carrying out the tasks You give me to do. Amen.

O LORD, my strength and my fortress, my refuge in times of distress, to You the nations will come from the ends of the earth. (Jer. 16:19)

I know a lady who greets people in an unusual and rather unorthodox manner. When you say to her, "I am fine, thank you, and how are you?" she always answers, "Strong!" No one starts an unnecessary argument with that lady!

Most people are strong in one respect or another: in health, in intellect or in some other developed skill. Jeremiah was strong. He had a great deal of courage and hope. He challenged people: politicians and prophets, as well as the priests of his day. He was willing to obey God even when it meant persecution and suffering. He was lonely, sad and introverted. But he was tough! His greatest strength, however, was grounded in the knowledge that his strength was not his own. It came from God. He knew that he was not fighting a lone battle against the tyrants and rulers of his day. He possessed power that came from a source outside of himself – God!

> Hope against hope,
> and ask till ye receive.
> ~ JAMES MONTGOMERY

Do you know where your power comes from? If you are skillful in your professional capacity, acknowledge that your strength and your hope, your personality and your skills come from God, and that He has empowered you to develop them. If you have the gift of art, music, good communication, human relationships or spiritual strength, your abilities will be even greater when you profess that they come from God. You will be humbler and wiser, and that in itself is a mark of strength. You will use your abilities to the honor and glory of the One who gave them to you. Rely on God for your power and you will truly be strong.

Almighty God, You do not require us only to hope for holiness, but also to be strong. Help us in this through Your Holy Spirit. Amen.

Persevere in Hope

July 28

"My eyes are on all their ways; they are not hidden from Me, nor is their sin concealed from My eyes." (Jer. 16:17)

Read
Jer. 16:16-21

Perhaps there has been great sorrow in your life, difficulties, or disasters. You may have tried to give yourself a pep talk and reassure yourself that the worst will be over soon. You may have fervently prayed for the dawn of a new day. You may have eagerly hoped that God would bless you in one way or another to balance things out. You may possibly even have tried to bargain with the Lord. But sometimes the clouds do not roll away and the sun does not shine through. The darkness seems to last endlessly!

In his darkest hour, Jeremiah pleaded with God to destroy his enemies and save him. God usually answered when Jeremiah prayed. But now when the prophet prayed to God, there was no answer, only dead silence. God did not speak any words of comfort, or of hope; no promises of help, no hint of reassurance. There *was* no light at the end of the tunnel. None at all – only eternal darkness!

> We stand in life at midnight; we are always at the threshold of a new dawn.
> ~ MARTIN LUTHER KING, JR.

You may be familiar with this experience of Jeremiah. If not, don't think it will never happen to you. However devoted to God you may be, it can still happen. One disaster can follow another, and adverse and depressing circumstances can last for a long time. But God was with Jeremiah in the darkness, just as He was with many thousands of others. He will also be with you. Jesus promised, "And surely I am with you always, to the very end of the age" (Matt. 28:20). Persevere in hope and stay on course – the Lord is always with you.

Lord my God, when there is no light at the end of the tunnel, help me to carry on hoping and keep me safe in Your unfailing love. Amen.

Roots of Hope

Blessed is the man who trusts in the LORD. He will be like a tree planted by the water that sends out its roots by the stream. It does not fear when heat comes. (Jer. 17:7-8)

In the vast region of the Karoo, rain is scarce. The rain that does fall, quickly drains away or evaporates in the intense heat. Only small shrubs grow there and they provide food and nourishment for the sheep that are farmed in the area.

On the northern border of the Karoo flows the mighty Orange River. The water flows down from the mountains of Lesotho and the course of the river is banked on both sides by a green strip of fertile ground. A variety of trees, plants and flowers grow there. The trees grow strong and tall because their roots are watered by a constant flow of fresh water.

This is how Jeremiah understood the concept of hope and faith in God. In the text for today he does not compare the good person with the bad, but rather someone who has hope in the power and love of God, versus the person who trusts in human ability alone. Human strength is as unreliable as the rainfall in the Karoo. Hope in God draws its strength from a river that will never disappoint; a river that brings life wherever it flows and that fills the surrounding areas with hope and peace.

> Hope is the companion of power, and mother of success; for who so hopes strongly has within him the gift of miracles.
>
> ~ SAMUEL SMILES

Make sure that your hope is deeply and strongly rooted in God's grace and omnipotence. This will give you stability when stormy winds begin to blow, and the unsaved ones who stand in your shadow will also be able to draw strength from the hope and peace that emanates from you.

Grant, beloved Savior, that my roots of hope will be deeply anchored in Your omnipotence and love. Amen.

Do not be a terror to me; You are my refuge in the day of disaster. (Jer. 17:17)

Read
Jer. 17:14-18

Disaster can strike in different forms. Some people experience natural disasters: floods, hurricanes and earthquakes. For some a company shuts down and they lose their job and income. Others suffer break-ups in their family lives; or a fatal accident; or serious illness and premature death. Political unrest can also spell disaster. Most people experience some sort of disaster at one time or another in their lives.

Jeremiah found it difficult to bear the bitterness and hatred that he faced, simply because he chose to bring a message from God. He prayed to God that the bitterness against him would not escalate into terrorism. But his hope and faith in God were strong. He was indeed purified in the furnace of suffering and pain. He knew that the same God who had allowed him to be placed in the blasting-furnace was at the same time his only hope and refuge from difficulty.

> In any circumstance it is better to hope than to give yourself over to despair. Who knows what is possible for God and what isn't?
> ~ JOHANN WOLFGANG VON GOETHE

One of Jeremiah's messages was that a day of disaster was fast approaching. It would come in the form of a foreign army that would make a surprise attack on the land and capture it. In the face of this unbearable disaster, Jeremiah experienced both fear and hope; they co-existed, side by side, in his inmost being.

You and I can also be frightened sometimes. Jesus Christ Himself tried to avoid the cross at Gethsemane. But you do not have to be ruled by fear. You have the same God that Jeremiah had. However afraid you may be of the imminent disaster that lurks in the shadows, persevere in your hope in Jesus and trust in Him alone. He will always protect you and will never let you go!

We pray for everyone, merciful God, who has been affected by disaster today. May their hope never die. Amen.

Go to the Potter's House

This is the word that came to Jeremiah from the LORD: "Go down to the potter's house, and there I will give you My message." (Jer. 18:1-2)

At times we speak of or hear other people talking about "living close to God." It sounds like some sort of mystical achievement that elevates one to a higher spiritual status. It also sounds as if one needs to stir up a particular type of emotion.

The Bible presents a God who speaks to us, Someone who draws near to us in the most ordinary circumstances. It introduces us to a God who touches our everyday lives and gives us moments of special insight through our labors. God commanded Jeremiah to go to the potter's shop, not to buy a particular piece of pottery, but to receive a message from Him. God spoke to Amos while he was busy farming; to Moses while he was watching his father-in-law's sheep; and to Peter, Andrew, James and John while they were busy mending their fishing nets.

> These people who speak of hope when they themselves are walking under a dark cloud – they are our messengers of hope, the godly ones of our age.
>
> ~ HENRI J. NOUWEN

When you are walking in obedience to God, He will speak to you in everyday situations. A tree, a flower, a work situation, a domestic happening, a national event, can all contain a message from God. God can "appear" anywhere He wants to! In 1944 Alfred Delp wrote from a Nazi jail cell a few weeks before he was hanged, "Within my soul I am strongly connected to God. But one thing is certain and more tangible than ever before: the world is so full of God!"

Anywhere that people hope in Him, God reveals Himself and draws near to them. Are you drawing close to God?

Holy God, speak to the world every day through me, and help me to hope and trust in You. Amen.

AUGUST

If only for this life we have hope in Christ, we are to be pitied more than all men. But Christ has indeed been raised from the dead, the firstfruits of those who have fallen asleep.
~ 1 Corinthians 15:19-20

Loving and gracious Father God,
it stands so clearly in Your Word, "With God all things are possible!"
Jesus showed us the way when He prayed at Gethsemane
and surrendered Himself to Your perfect will.
Through this hope You raised Him from the dead.
I desire to feel the flame of that same hope in my heart.
God of the impossible, grant me, by Your grace,
an ample supply of hope.
Grant that I may hope for the impossible and
trust You unconditionally.
And when I ask for the impossible, O Father God,
I know that You are able to approve and to support me,
so that my hope does not weaken and die.
Almighty and all-knowing God, when I ask only for the possible,
I reduce You to my own size and limit You.
But, loving Father, You delight in giving me much more
than what my cup can hold.
Therefore, God, guide me with Your Holy Spirit and
according to Your will, to be courageous
and pray to You for lasting hope.
Grant me a fresh vision of Your inexhaustible omnipotence so that
there will always be an abundance – no matter how much I pray for.
Grant me the faith to understand Your will for me,
so that I will be able to do the impossible, according to Your will.
God of the impossible, grant me Your everlasting hope!
In Jesus' name and with thanksgiving.

Amen.

Hope is the golden thread that should
be woven into every experience of life.
~ Anonymous

If only for this life we have hope in Christ, we are to be pitied more than all men. But Christ has indeed been raised from the dead. (1 Cor. 15:19-20)

It is astonishing how many people view themselves as upright Christians, but have a vague understanding of eternal life. Some believe that it is their Christian duty to lead a good life on earth and to obey God's commands, but they also believe that when they die, life simply ends. They have absolutely nothing to look forward to.

This is pitiful, because those people are missing the whole point of the Christian faith: Jesus *was* not the Resurrection and the Life: He *is* the Life for everyone who believes in Him! Through the living Christ's death and resurrection, believers have the wonderful opportunity to live forever with God in His eternal kingdom, free from pain, tears, suffering or death.

> My salvation does not hinge on my emotions. I have an official record. I have the Word of God.
>
> ~ ADRIAN ROGERS

Life as we know it on earth is fleeting. It has moments of heartache and joy; pain and pleasure; anxiety and release. But at the same time it is unpredictable.

However, when you accept Jesus Christ as your Savior and Redeemer and dedicate your life completely to Him, you strive from that moment on towards eternal life in Christ. Your life becomes filled with joy, peace and hope. It is the Master's reward for everyone who is living a life dedicated to Him and to God the Father.

Resurrected and glorified Christ, I bring You my humble thanks and a song of praise for the hope You have given me through Your promise of eternal life. Amen.

"Take courage! It is I. Don't be afraid." (Mark 6:50)

Read
Mark 6:45-52

None of us know what lies ahead and, therefore, we cannot be prepared to deal with every situation that comes our way. In many instances we have no control over our circumstances or the events that crop up in our lives. These circumstances often cause fearful hearts.

Others, however, bring fear upon themselves, like when they hesitate to find the answer to a problem that has been troubling them for a long time. How many people are burdened by poor health and suffer terribly, more than what is necessary, because they refuse to seek medical advice out of fear that their condition is more serious than they thought?

> A life lived in fear
> is a life half lived.
> ~ SPANISH PROVERB

There are many instances where the debilitating consequences of anxiety can be prevented if people would only have the courage to confront their problems, or seek advice on how to manage their circumstances. Christ's disciples found themselves in a similar situation. They thought they were seeing a ghost walking towards them on the water. Their fear of the unknown compelled them to cry out until the familiar, calm voice of the Master banished their fear.

The answer to this dilemma is: lay your fear and anxiety at Jesus' feet and you will hear His compassionate voice saying, "Take courage! It is I. Don't be afraid." His love and assistance will always bring new hope to your situation.

Loving Lord Jesus, when my faith becomes fear, and when my joy changes to sorrow, let me hear You whisper, "Take courage! It is I." Amen.

Let Your hand rest on the man at Your right hand, the son of man You have raised up for Yourself. Then we will not turn away from You. (Ps. 80:17-18)

We live in troubled times and there are many people whose hearts are heavy like the psalmist's. Acts of violence shock people and there is evidence all around that the value of life is no longer respected. In these circumstances, only the most careless and uninvolved person can keep from pleading with God for the restoration of order, love and justice in the world.

What we must not lose sight of, however, is that people, and not God, are responsible for the current state of affairs. God made His Creation perfect and any imperfections have been born out of the deeds of disobedient man. God laid down the rules for a full and happy life. It was people who gave in to temptation and who were disobedient and unfaithful towards God.

> All that is necessary for the Evil One to gain the victory is for good people to do nothing.
> ~ EDMUND BURKE

There is a great need for people to confess their sins and turn to Christ with remorse in their hearts; and to resolve to live according to the standards of God. Until this happens, however; the situation of violence, chaos and confusion will continue.

Great responsibility rests on the shoulders of each person – a responsibility that begins with you and me and is motivated by the inextinguishable hope in our hearts.

Gracious Savior, forgive me if I have been uncaring. Help me to live each day according to the example Christ has set for me. **Amen.**

Many, O LORD, are the wonders You have done. Were I to tell of them, they would be too many to declare. (Ps. 40:5)

Read
Ps. 40:1-10

Things seldom go as planned. Standards are dropping, the moral behavior of people leaves much to be desired, and many people no longer respect each other. Sadly, there is a great deal of room for improvement.

But no matter how dark the future may seem, you dare not allow yourself to be driven to despair. Do not give up hope when you think there is no release or solution to your situation. That is exactly when you must focus on the majesty and omnipotence of God, revealed throughout the ages. He has always guided, controlled and led His creation: through conflict, confusion and difficulty, He has always brought us back to His safe harbor of hope and peace.

> A Christian will part with anything rather than his hope, he knows that hope is a beam of God, a spark of glory, and that nothing shall extinguish it till the soul be filled with glory.
> ~ THOMAS BROOKS

Therefore, you should put your hope and faith in your all-knowing and ever-present God in these uncertain times. Be faithful in His power to steer this world on the path of righteousness. Don't just lay the world's problems before God when you pray, offer your own efforts to make His world a better place. Hold fast to His promises and assurances and believe that He will once again bring about miracles of salvation, as He has done in the past. You will not be disappointed.

Creator God, with hope in my heart I place the future of my world in Your Almighty hands. Amen.

Read

Ps. 40:1-10

Many, O LORD, are the wonders You have done. Were I to tell of them, they would be too many to declare. (Ps. 40:5)

In times of financial difficulty, or when violence seems to reign supreme, it is easy to become disheartened. When you are living in an unhappy and uncertain environment, you can easily become overwhelmed by the negative circumstances. Once this happens it is easy to lose courage and succumb to the temptation to give up the battle against the seemingly overwhelming evil forces.

One surefire way to overcome your lack of strength is to keep your mind on the Almighty presence of God. Go back to the Scriptures. Read the story of Creation once more and notice again God's mighty deeds. Study the history of humanity and discern the hand of God in everything. Look around you and see the beauty of Creation and the miracle of progress and growth. Then listen to God Almighty whispering to you: "You dare not give up hope!"

> The future is as bright
> as the promises of God.
> ~ ADONIRAM JUDSON

Whenever things around you look dark and increasingly hopeless, turn to God. Pray for His Spirit to open your eyes so that you can look past the present circumstances and perceive the handiwork of God. See how He has protected humanity and the world over the past centuries. Look through Christ's eyes at the world.

Seek His light and your hope will once again be renewed. Your faith will continue to grow and you will *know* with certainty: However dismal it may be around you, God is still in control. He will overcome the world with love.

Holy Jesus, Lord of lords, through Your strength I can grow in faith and hope. I praise and thank You for this. Amen.

Those who hope in the LORD will renew their strength. They will soar on wings like eagles; they will run and not grow weary, they will walk and not be faint. (Isa. 40:31)

Read
Isa. 40:25-31

Weakness and depression often dawn on us and cause us to forget the rich spiritual experiences of the past. Then the conviction is born that we are the worst sinners on earth.

It could be that you are having a similar experience in your spiritual life at the moment. If so, it is imperative for you to remember that it is not permanent. God does not want you to remain weak and spiritually ineffectual. Your spiritual depression could be the result of sin, or of disobedience. A time of confession and repentance will once again let you experience the joy of powerful and dynamic faith and hope.

It is definitely not the will of your loving Father for your relationship with Him to be miserable and pointless. A proven way of regaining and maintaining your spiritual strength is to live consciously in the presence of God's love. This may sound like a pointless spiritual exercise to some, but nothing could be further from the truth. To faithfully wait and hope upon the Master at all times, you need to open up your mind and your spirit to His love and grace. In the same way that you absorb His presence in your morning quiet time and carry the feeling with you throughout your busy working day, so godly qualities become yours through God's grace.

> In God alone is there faithfulness. To hold to God is to rely on the fact that God is there for me, and to live in this certainty.
> ~ KARL BARTH

Lord my God, the knowledge of Your loving, indwelling presence continues to renew me. I humbly thank You for this. Amen.

Read
2 Cor. 4:16-5:10

Therefore we do not lose heart. Though outwardly we are wasting away, yet inwardly we are being renewed day by day. (2 Cor. 4:16)

Your first encounter with Jesus Christ was probably a miraculous moment that surpassed your highest expectations. Your new faith was dynamic, meaningful and alive, and you felt completely secure in God's eternal love for you. But as time went by, things may have changed radically. Your love and enthusiasm began to fade and your zeal for Him evaporated; like mist in the morning sun.

When your faith becomes prescriptive, instead of a way of life, something very valuable is lost. If you long for your faith to remain dynamic and meaningful, you need to grow spiritually. Without this growth, those essential qualities that are necessary for a more intimate walk with God, cannot be developed.

> Mere change is not growth. Growth is the synthesis of change and perseverance, for where there is no perseverance, there can be no growth.
>
> ~ C. S. Lewis

Every disciple of Christ acknowledges the value of prayer, but how many of us strive for a mature, more intimate prayer life? Scripture readings and Bible study inspire the weary spirit, but few of Christ's followers make the most of this privilege.

It is not enough to merely be aware of our privileges; we have to make them an integral part of our spiritual lives. We must constantly be renewed by growing under guidance of the Holy Spirit. Then the hope in our lives will never weaken or die.

God of new life and hope, save me from spiritual stagnation and grant me constant renewal born from intimate fellowship with You. *Amen.*

We rejoice in the hope of the glory of God. (Rom. 5:2)

Read
Rom. 5:1-11

You probably often wonder what the future has in store for you. You ponder over the amount of time you have left on earth. You hope for many things: that you and your spouse will spend many years together; that you will never be left alone; that you will not be plagued by illnesses and ailments; and most of all that you will be able to enjoy life for a long time to come. But in spite of everything, uncertainty and anxiety still catch you unawares.

As a Christian, however, you always have much to rejoice over. From the moment you gave your life to your Savior and Redeemer, you were able to rejoice in your freedom in God. As His disciple you learn many exciting things. When you become a member of God's family, your old life is irrevocably over, and a spiritual kaleidoscope opens before you. Hope takes the place of your prior despair and confusion. Rejoice in this hope every day of your life!

> All earthly delights are sweeter in expectation than in enjoyment; all spiritual pleasures, more in fruition than in expectation.
> ~ OWEN FELTHAM

You can joyfully look forward to the future, with God's hope in your heart, because you have the eternal promise of His continuous presence. This will enable you to rise above the difficulties and anxieties of your earthly life. You have been created for the sole purpose of sharing in the glory of God in heaven. Nothing less should be good enough for you.

In His presence you will know complete happiness and everlasting love. This joy and hope is yours because Christ loves you. Delight yourself in His hope: the best is yet to come!

Glorified Lord Jesus, here and now, make me a hopeful bearer of good cheer, so that I may taste Your joy – on earth and in the life to come. *Amen.*

Read
Eph. 1:3-14

To the praise of His glorious grace, which He has freely given us in the One He loves. In Him we have redemption through His blood, the forgiveness of sins. (Eph. 1:6-7)

How deep is the deepest part of the ocean? How far is the farthest star? As impossible as it is to answer these questions, it is just as impossible to determine the extent of God's grace.

The writer of the well-known song, *Amazing Grace*, made a courageous effort to do this, but he quickly realized how hard this was. And so he wrote, "When we've been here ten thousand years, bright shining as the sun, we've no less days to sing Your praise than when we'd first begun."

If you think about the Lord accepting you just as you are, that He died in your place so that you could receive forgiveness, that He assures you of your salvation and promises you eternal life, that He gives you life abundantly and enfolds you in His eternal love, that everything you are and everything you have comes from your merciful God – then you will have some notion of the full extent of His grace.

> Grace is when God gives us what we don't deserve and mercy is when God doesn't give us what we do deserve.
>
> ~ ANONYMOUS

When you start complaining about your lot in life, or when you feel that the world is not treating you fairly, be still before God for a moment and count all your blessings that flow out of His merciful heart. Is there any more reason in all creation for blazing hope?

Until now, God of Grace, You have led me safely through every danger and temptation. Therefore hope blazes in my heart that You will also lead me safely home. Amen.

When anxiety was great within me, Your consolation brought joy to my soul. (Ps. 94:19)

In this information age, great pressure is placed on both young and old to achieve more, work harder and acquire more money. A result of this pressure is that many people suffer from stress and "burnout." So people turn to medication and professional help in order to seek relief. In some instances the pressure becomes too much and people take refuge in drastic methods of escape, which are detrimental to their mental and physical well-being.

During His earthly ministry, Jesus Christ radiated a calm everywhere He went and whenever He came into contact with people. The fear, anxiety and worry that haunted them evaporated under His liberating influence. He drove out evil spirits and approached people in love. He filled those who had no hope left with new hope and trust.

> We are all healers who can bring about recovery; we are all patients needing a cure.
> ~ HENRI J. NOUWEN

The living Christ also accompanies you through life, through His Holy Spirit, from start to finish. His love will banish your anxiety and help you to hold your own in every situation. Open your heart and your ears, listen to His loving voice and take hope anew. Feel how you are filled with hope in the presence of Christ.

By placing your hope in God, you will not only find a new sense of meaning in life, but God will comfort you in every circumstance and strengthen you to live for the honor and glory of His name.

Merciful Lord Jesus, simply by touching the hem of Your robe I find healing for my soul. Thank You for making me whole every time I kneel, broken, before You. Amen.

Find Your Hope in Christ

I pray that you may be active in sharing your faith, so that you will have a full understanding of every good thing we have in Christ. (Philem. 6)

Many Christians want the assurance that their faith will always make them feel happy; that it will inspire and uplift them with promises of success at all times. They expect God to always be available and prepared to forgive all their sins without being judgmental about their shortcomings.

Experience shows that this concept of God, created by people for their own convenience, is completely inadequate against the demands of everyday life. God does not exist just to make life comfortable for human beings.

If you want to derive the full benefit of your faith in God, you must be obedient to His commands. You need to remember that God has never disappointed you, but that it is you who disappoints Him. God asks you to have unconditional faith in Him and accept Him as the only Lord of your life. Without this faith and acceptance God remains unreal and ineffectual to you. God needs to be a personal and intimate experience for you. And this is possible only through the living Christ. Refusing to accept Christ into your life simply spells failure and ruin. It is tantamount to cutting yourself off from God and trying to live without Him.

> God does not require you to follow His leadings on blind trust. Behold the evidence of an invisible intelligence pervading everything, even your own mind and body.
> ~ RAYMOND HOLLIWELL

Faith in Him, however, guarantees a fulfilling and satisfying life. Turn back, therefore, to the only true Source who can bring sense and meaning to your life: the same God who fills you with hope in this life and in the life to come.

Guide and Master, save me from the stubbornness and pride that prevents me from acknowledging Your authority in my life. Amen.

"I am coming soon. Hold on to what you have, so that no one will take your crown." (Rev. 3:11)

Read
Rev. 3:7-13

There comes times in your life when you feel like you are not in control. Everything goes wrong. Monotony makes every day meaningless, resulting in life losing its purpose and sparkle. Consequently you might take on a couldn't-care-less attitude. Along with this unfortunate state of affairs, your spiritual life loses the intimacy you previously experienced with the Holy Father. You no longer sense the presence of the living Christ in your life as you did before.

When you lose your sense of unity with the living God, you also lose your grip on life. It is impossible, though, to stray from life's path if you are living in harmony with your heavenly Father. Reaffirm your faith in Him and acknowledge the value of your faith. For when your faith is restored to its rightful place in your life, you will find that everything else falls back into place too.

Giving your faith in God its rightful place also means that you are emphasizing the true importance of prayer. Prayer brings you into a more intimate relationship with the living Christ. A relationship of this kind is

> The only limit to our realization of tomorrow will be our doubts of today. Let us move forward with strong and active faith.
> ~ FRANKLIN D. ROOSEVELT

far more than just an emotional experience. It is an act of faith that acknowledges that the Spirit of Christ lives in you and He assures you that your life will never fall apart again. You will know without a doubt that God loves you and, therefore, you have all the hope you need for the future.

Lord and Master, I thank You that I can face the challenges of life through the power of Your Holy Spirit that dwells in me. *Amen.*

Read
Jonah 2:1-10

In my distress I called to the LORD, and He answered me. From the depths of the grave I called for help, and You listened to my cry. (Jonah 2:2)

One of the most common complaints of people who are disillusioned with life, is that God does not answer their prayers. They claim that they have laid all their difficulties and anxieties in faith before the Lord, but without any results. Eventually they become convinced that prayer serves no purpose.

These people are so terribly wrong. They do not understand the basic principles of prayer.

We need to understand that prayer is not a battering ram that we can use to force God to accede to our demands and give us everything we desire. True prayer means laying your prayer requests and concerns before the throne of grace, handing them over in faith and hope to the Lord and then waiting patiently for Him until He gives you the right answer – in His time and His way.

> Prayer doesn't change God; it changes the one who prays.
> ~ SØREN KIERKEGAARD

God's answers to your prayers will not necessarily be what you expect, but you can be sure that they will always contribute to your ultimate well-being. God knows what is in your best interests.

The Holy Spirit will assist you and help you to pray correctly. Open your heart up to God and allow Him to speak to you through His Spirit. You will quickly come to realize that His love is leading you on the right path – to hope.

Lord my God, You call weary and heavily-laden people to come to You. Therefore, I approach You with the certainty in my heart that You are listening to me. Amen.

Blessed is he whose help is the God of Jacob, whose hope is in the LORD his God. (Ps. 146:5)

Read
Ps. 146:1-10

Whenever you start something new, you experience moments of doubt and fear that can make you hesitate. Because human nature is so fallible, these feelings may overwhelm you so much that you do not want to go ahead with your new project. Your feelings and doubts lead you to failure even before you have started.

The greatest adventure of all is of course life itself. We are challenged by the prospect of an exciting future and the promise of everything it might hold for us. The worrying questions still remain, however: How will I cope with the future? Will I be able to move ahead in faith and zealously pursue my goals? Or will I give in to fear of the unknown and consequently have to be satisfied with second best – a monotonous, mediocre life?

> Even if I knew that the world was going to end tomorrow, I would still plant my apple tree today.
> ~ MARTIN LUTHER

Listen to what God is lovingly whispering to you! He invites you to make Him a partner in all your undertakings. He assures you of His presence at all times. He assures you in Hebrews 13:5, "Never will I leave you; never will I forsake you."

With this loving assurance, you can move forward and *live* in the strength of the Holy Spirit! Allow Him to take complete control of your life. Then your life will be fulfilling, meaningful and successful, and all your hopes will be realized.

Almighty Father, when I try to stand alone, I sink. Enfold me in Your loving arms and enable me to move forward in hope. Amen.

Hope for Good Things

Read
1 Sam. 7:2-12

He named it Ebenezer, saying, "Thus far has the LORD helped us." (1 Sam. 7:12)

There are times in life when we need to become still and take stock of everything that has happened to us. Too often, people only remember the bad things that have happened, rather than all the good times they have enjoyed. How often do we hear people say, "I am so grateful that period of my life is over. I never want to go through that again."

It is at such times that we need to be still in God's presence and reflect upon all the good things that have happened in our lives. Consider all the events in the lives of the people you have been in some kind of a relationship with. Think about the better side of life – those incidents that have had a beneficial influence on you, and even on the whole of humanity.

A single thought of thankfulness that rises up to heaven is a perfect prayer.
~ GOTTHOLD LESSING

Your attitude towards life – and particularly towards the future – is determined largely by your thoughts and emotions. If you are pessimistic, you will find that your life is controlled by negative thoughts that leave you unhappy, restless and dissatisfied. To enable yourself to meet the future with faith and hope in your heart, you need to remind yourself every day how God has provided and taken care of you in the past.

Put your hope in the living Christ and believe that He will also take care of your future. God's giving is endless. Pray that He will also give you a thankful heart, filled with hope. Make time to thank Him for all His kindnesses and blessings, and you will have little time left to complain.

Savior and Master, for all Your blessings and mercies that carry me so faithfully through life, I sing a song of thanks in Your honor. *Amen.*

Those who had been scattered preached the word wherever they went. (Acts 8:4)

Read
Acts 8:4-13

Violent and bloody persecution broke out against the early church of Christ. The apostles could have sunk into self-pity as a result of these brutal events. They could have asked, "Why is God allowing this?" Instead, they seized every opportunity to spread the gospel and to proclaim that the Messiah had risen from the dead. Their life-changing message helped them to rise above the difficulties of the times they were living in. They submitted themselves with joy to the will of Christ – in spite of the danger of persecution and death.

The gift of mercy that turns hope- lessness into hope and defeat into victory, stems from a firm belief in the God who is bigger than any disaster that can strike you. When you believe that all things work together for good for those who love the Lord (see Rom.

> Faith is a living, daring confidence in God's grace, so sure and certain that a man could stake his life on it a thousand times.
> ~ MARTIN LUTHER

8:28) and that everything takes place according to His perfect plan, nothing will be able to get you down. You will become more than a conqueror through Him who loves you (see Rom. 8:37). Life will still have its times of failure and disappointment, but you are assured of the ultimate victory.

When Christ is in complete control of your life, you are able to look beyond the present with all its failures. On the other side of failure God is whispering to you promises of success. And you have the ability to turn defeat into victory: through the love and mercy of the God of hope.

In Your power and through Your wisdom, trustworthy Master, I can turn defeat into victory. **Amen.**

Blessed is the man who trusts in the LORD. He will be like a tree planted by the water that sends out its roots by the stream. It never fails to bear fruit. (Jer. 17:7-8)

It is unfortunately a sad truth that many Christians lead a superficial spiritual life. That is why, in times of stress, their faith is not enough to help them hold their own in a crisis.

It is essential to know that the resources Christ makes available to you are because He loves you. They are: a positive faith that becomes stronger the more you practice it; the consciousness of God's presence, not only when you keep company with Him one on one, but also during the busyness of everyday life; the knowledge that you can go to God for inspiration; and knowledge of the Scriptures to help strengthen you in times of trials and temptations. However, these sources of faith and hope can be effective only if you apply them rigorously. The more you apply them, the more effective they will become in your life.

> The word that God has written on the forehead of every one is hope.
>
> ~ VICTOR HUGO

When your faith has a strong foundation, you will be able to stand firm in times of crisis and stress. In times of spiritual drought, when your spirit level is at a low, your hope and faith will stand you in good stead. In spite of the outward circumstances, you will triumph over the storms of life.

I thank You, my loving God, that my faith in You is greater than all the emotional conflict in my deepest being. **Amen.**

This is the day the LORD has made; let us rejoice and be glad in it. (Ps. 118:24)

Read
Ps. 118:19-29

Do you sometimes wake up in the morning and wonder what the day will bring? Do you ever feel anxious about what may happen? This is unfortunately the case for many believers. They plod through their days and timidly accept everything that comes their way. They completely forget that it is not necessary to live a dull life. As children of God we can plan our days through prayer and Bible study in such a way that we can live constructively and creatively.

Your first thoughts when you wake up in the morning are of the greatest importance. They determine how the rest of your day will develop. As a child of God, your first thoughts should be of thankfulness towards God for the privilege of entering a new day in His presence. If you do wake up depressed, purposefully offer thanks to God until a thankful spirit overcomes your depression. Remember, your emotions must not rule you – you are the master of your thoughts. It is completely up to you whether you are going to feel miserable or happy.

> And I smiled to think God's greatness flowed around our incompleteness; round our restlessness, His rest.
> ~ ELIZABETH BARRETT BROWNING

If you fall asleep at peace with God, you will definitely wake up the next morning with joy and faith in your heart. With the power of the living Christ who lives in you, you can awaken in the morning with His loving voice of hope in your heart. There is no better way to begin each new day.

Lord, my loving Father, in Your Almighty power I find the strength to go out to meet each new day in faith and with inner peace. Amen.

The Hope of Eternal Life (1)

Brothers, we do not want you to be ignorant about those who fall asleep, or to grieve like the rest of men, who have no hope. (1 Thess. 4:13)

Although black is a fashionable color today, it is still associated with death. This color adds an extra heaviness to the sorrow that hangs like a dark cloud over those who have lost a loved one.

While mourning over the loss of someone who was dear to you is natural and understandable, the crucifixion and resurrection of Jesus Christ should dispel all doubt about what happens to our dear departed ones. It should bring an end to inconsolable suffering. On the cross Jesus took everyone's sins upon Himself and triumphed over death. He gave us the gift of salvation, and His resurrection ensured that we would have eternal life. The portal to this eternal joy and salvation is inevitably physical death.

> On this side of the grave are our outcasts, on the other side are our citizens; on this side are our orphans, on the other side our children; on this side prisoners, on the other side those who have been set free.
>
> ~ HENRY WARD BEECHER

Do not allow death to disturb you so much. Eternal life in Christ Jesus is the reward that He offers to everyone who dies in faith. We also have the assurance that we will be reunited with our loved ones. We should actually view death as a friend – although a feared friend. It is indeed only through death that we can enter into the eternal life that Jesus has prepared for us. What a sacred hope to cherish.

Lord of Life, when the dark night is over and the new dawn breaks, I will walk forever in the Light. I praise and thank You for this. Amen.

Brothers, we do not want you to be ignorant about those who fall asleep, or to grieve like the rest of men, who have no hope. (1 Thess. 4:13)

Read
1 Thess. 4:13-18

The death of a loved one always has a huge impact on those who one left behind. Even when we see death as a release from pain and suffering, the feeling of final separation and the resulting emptiness that it leaves behind, fills us with sorrow and pain. Bereaved people are often inconsolable in their sorrow.

Although heartache is a natural consequence of parting, one of the most important and comforting aspects of our Christian faith is this assurance: for everyone who believes in God and hopes in Him, the death of the body is not the end, but a new beginning. It is the beginning of a glorious and eternal life with the Lord in His perfect kingdom.

Jesus, the living Christ, has given to all believers the absolute assurance that in His perfect time we will return to Him and be with Him forever. We will be in the Father's house, together with our loved ones.

> It is not darkness where we move, for God is light. It is not loneliness, for Christ is with us. It is also not unknown territory, for Christ is already there.
> ~ CHARLES KINGSLEY

Even though the passing away of a dear one brings sorrow, we must not allow our grief to strip us of all hope. Hold on to the hope and the assurance of Christ, who has gone to prepare a place for us and will come again to fetch us. Keep this hope burning in your heart – even in the face of death.

Forever with You, Lord! This is the earnest cry of our hearts. Lord of life, let it be so. Amen.

God Is the Caring Father

(In the desert) you saw how the LORD your God carried you, as a father carries his son, all the way you went until you reached this place. (Deut. 1:31)

Life does not always go smoothly. Times of happiness and peace are intertwined with times of frustration, irritation, disappointment, sorrow and setbacks, which threaten to cast a dark cloud over life.

If you give in to the temptation to crack under such circumstances, you can be sure that your daily life will soon become empty and barren. You will allow melancholy and despair to take control of your emotions. You will develop a pessimistic outlook on life and, in doing so, you will rob yourself of the dynamism, meaning and purpose of life. But now the question remains: How do you overcome this type of adversity?

> Trials are just
> the shadow of God's
> protective wings.
> ~ GEORGE MACDONALD

Closely examine the lives of believers in the Bible. Then look at your own life and the lives of the people around you. You will find enough proof to convince you that no one can withstand the setbacks of life. Life is more difficult for some than for others and the consequences of some events are far-reaching. Your study of the Scripture, however, will reveal to you that people who place their hope and faith in God always discover that God is there to help them and see them through their trials.

The next time you find yourself in a crisis, seek refuge in God; cast your anxieties and concerns on Him and experience His care for you. Listen to His voice calling out to you, "Keep your hope alive. I will carry you through this!"

I praise and thank You, loving Father, for continually being at my side, for helping me over all the stumbling blocks of life. Amen.

God has chosen to make known among the Gentiles the glorious riches of this mystery, which is Christ in you, the hope of glory. (Col. 1:27)

Read
Col. 1:14-29

God expects His people to be loving, good, peaceful and trustworthy. We have to admit, however, that a person can be "good" without being committed to Jesus Christ. There are many agnostics and even atheists who lead commendable lives. They do not swear or steal, and they treat other people with love and respect. It is unfortunately true that they are better than many Christians in these respects.

However, even a "good" life without Christ has no eternal meaning. The purpose of a Christian's life should not just be to live a "good" life. We must strive to become more Christlike every day.

This may sound to you like an unattainable goal, yet it is the clarion call of Christianity. And you can master this challenge by making a study of the life of Jesus Christ and endeavoring to follow Him. Grow daily in love, joy, peace, patience, kindness, forgiveness, humility and self-control. These are all characteristics of the Master that you can cultivate and nurture in your life as you become more and more like Him.

> Nearness to God brings likeness to God. The more you see God the more of God will be seen in you.
>
> ~ CHARLES H. SPURGEON

Ask God for the gift of the fruit of the Holy Spirit and try every day and to the best of your ability to live according to the example that Jesus has given us.

Lord Jesus, help me through Your Spirit to reflect Your glory so that others may come to believe in You. Amen.

Read
Phil. 1:12-26

Because of my chains, most of the brothers in the Lord have been encouraged to speak the word of God more courageously and fearlessly. (Phil. 1:14)

There are unfortunately many Christians who are slow to witness. It is not that their experience with Christ is not genuine, they just find it difficult to confess or to defend their faith in Him to others. Then they feel embarrassed and guilty because they know that they are denying the Master. If you lack the courage or faith to witness for Christ, you must set matters right as soon as possible. It is indeed Jesus' Great Commission that we will bear witness to Him.

To be able to witness properly, Jesus Christ must be the most important person in your life. You cannot speak about Him with conviction if you do not have a personal and intimate relationship with Him and are always striving to know Him better. Build on your relationship with Him by communicating in prayer and Bible study.

> We are called to witness, not to advocate.
> ~ DONNA MADDOX

It is also essential to be part of a Christian community. Your fellow believers will help you overcome your reserve and they will strengthen your faith so that you become a powerful witness for the Master. You will no longer be able to keep your Christian experience a secret. Your love for Christ will become visible in your life and will be clearly discerned in your conversation. With the Holy Spirit living inside you, you will not be able to keep the miraculous message of Christ to yourself. You will want to share it with everyone, in the hope that they, too, will come to know Him as their Savior and Redeemer.

Holy and merciful Lord, forgive me for being so slow to witness about Your miracles in my life. Make me courageous so that I will be a trustworthy witness for You at all times. Amen.

Should not your piety be your confidence and your blameless ways your hope? (Job 4:6)

Read
Job 4:1-11

One day you suddenly realize that the old foundations that have served you so well in the past are crumbling. You do not feel safe any more. The things that you placed your trust in have let you down. A feeling of panic bordering on despair starts to take over.

In your growing fear and uncertainty, you need to be wise enough to steer your thoughts away from the mire that surrounds you and focus on the living Christ. This may sound idealistic to you in the midst of the storm you are in, but it is the best and only thing to do. Giving in to fear means exposing yourself to even greater calamity. Putting your faith in God, however, means hearing the language of His love and finding rest and calm in the middle of the raging storm.

> Never be afraid to trust
> an unknown future
> to a known God.
> ~ CORRIE TEN BOOM

Perhaps you are asking how it is possible to focus on God when it seems as if everything in your life has gone awry. Have you forgotten, then, those encouraging times when you were so deeply conscious of the presence of the Master? Look back over your life and see how He has led you. He has never disappointed you. Why should He disappoint you now? Even though the foundations of your life have been shaken, never doubt the Father's love for you.

Even if it is pitch dark around you right now, look past the darkness and see the bright promise of dawn. We look at events in terms of time – but God sees them from an eternal perspective. Keep on hoping and trusting in God's continuous deliverance.

Father God, I place my hope and trust in You and I do not fear the future. Amen.

Failure Is Not the End

He who was seated on the throne said, "I am making everything new!" (Rev. 21:5)

Your dreams are shattered, your hopes are lost, your pride is offended – it looks as if it is not worth carrying on. Does this describe your life right now? When you have failed, it feels as if your world is collapsing around you and you start to believe that the future will always look so bleak.

The great danger at such a time in your life is that self-pity can overwhelm you. You may want to blame others or claim that circumstances have led you to failure. It would, however, benefit you to make time for serious self-examination. Look honestly at your life and search for the real reasons why you failed.

Also remember this very important fact: however badly you failed, never take your failure as final. If there is something in your life that you must confess to God, do so immediately. Ask God for a new and fresh vision for your life, as well as the determination to accomplish what you need to do. Also pray for more courage

> Failure doesn't mean that God has abandoned you; it means He has a better way.
>
> ~ Anonymous

and hope. Remember, whatever your needs are at this moment, you will remain a failure as long as you see yourself as one.

There is no person on earth who has not failed at one time or another. You are no exception. However, as a Christian disciple you have enormous power for renewal and revival at your disposal. Listen to how God speaks to you in love at this time and promises you that He will make all things new; that He will lead you from failure to success. Just remain faithful and obedient to Him and continue to hope for His salvation.

Thank You, my Father God, that You give me the victory through Jesus Christ. Amen.

Is Believing Enough?

In the same way, faith by itself, if it is not accompanied by action, is dead. (James 2:17)

Read
James 2:14-26

We cannot divide our lives into secular and spiritual areas. Work without spiritual inspiration usually becomes slavery. In the same way, a spiritual life without a practical side becomes an emotional outlet without reason and balance. The secular forms a large part of our lives and therefore cannot be ignored, yet the spiritual side cannot be pushed aside as if it is of no importance either. Both aspects are crucial for a balanced life.

In Christ we see the perfect example of how our spiritual lives can find expression in our day-to-day existence. Jesus was spiritually oriented, yet He made His radiant spirituality an earthly reality through simple stories and works which made God and His ways meaningful to ordinary people. For Christ, the ordinary things in life became the instruments He could use to honor God.

> Faith is the root
> of all good works.
> A root that produces
> nothing is dead.
> ~ THOMAS WILSON

Spirituality without any practical expression is of little value. You may be very active in your religious sector, but if you cheat on your income tax, or you are dishonest in your business dealings, what use is your religion then?

Therefore, James says to us in our text for today: If your faith is not accompanied by action, it is useless and dead. Good works that are borne out of love are, however, a strong witness of your faith in God.

Holy Spirit of God, teach me to express my faith in good works, so that my life can reflect God's glory and love. Amen.

Hope Will Triumph

Read
Joel 2:21-32

"You will have plenty to eat, until you are full, and you will praise the name of the LORD, who has worked wonders for you." (Joel 2:26)

Daily we hear of the distress, disaster and crime that happens all around us. Media reports are filled with violence, poverty, natural disasters and incurable diseases. We wonder where it is all going to end.

When we are touched personally by these things, there is the danger of allowing it to lead to a negative attitude towards life. The troubles that you experience in your own life play havoc with your emotions, and your spiritual well-being goes into reverse gear. Eventually the stress and tension can become too much for you to bear.

If this is how you are experiencing life right now, it is high time you turned away from these adversities and focused instead on the loving acts of God. Read in the Scriptures how He miraculously saved people. See how often He turned defeat into victory. Look anew at the greatest and most glorious example of the omnipotence of God – the triumph of Christ Jesus over sin, the Evil One, and death on the cross of Golgotha.

> God, who foresaw your tribulation, has specially armed you to go through it, not without pain, but without stain.
>
> ~ C. S. LEWIS

When the situation in the world seems to be at its most dire, it is time to contemplate the miracles of God. Focus on His love and on how much He cares for His people. You will have no option but to realize that God is all-powerful; supreme in all things. He will never disappoint you when you place your hope in Him.

Almighty Father, even in the darkest hour I will fix my hope on You. I know that Your love will lead me to victory. Amen.

Let Christ Take Control

I pray that out of His glorious riches He may strengthen you with power through His Spirit in your inner being. (Eph. 3:16)

Read
Eph. 3:14-21

There are many occasions when people feel weak, vulnerable and hopeless. This leaves them with the sense that they are not good enough. Then they hesitate to take the lead or express an opinion. The outcome is always a feeling of frustration and inadequacy.

If you are feeling this way, don't think that you are the only one. This is not at all a unique experience, but rather a common occurrence for countless people who withdraw as a result of their reserve. Therefore, they run the risk of being pushed to one side and written off by the more dynamic, self-confident people who feel that they are a match for any situation or challenge.

> Optimism is the faith that leads us to accomplishment. We are powerless without hope and faith.
>
> ~ HELEN KELLER

It is of the greatest importance to remember that, as a child of God, the Holy Spirit provides you with sufficient capability to cope with every facet of life. Accept that He is a holy force who enables you to behave with a measure of authority. Grow daily in your understanding of the grace of God and work on an attitude of humility. Presumptuous, domineering ways are not part of the power of God. Rather, He will help you to speak and behave as Jesus did.

If you are striving to overcome your feelings of inadequacy, persevere in your fellowship with the living Christ. Give Him dominion over your thoughts. In this way you will develop a surprising gift of self-confidence and the Spirit will think, speak and act through you. Just put your hope fully in Christ and not in your own abilities.

Living Lord Jesus, take control of my whole being so that I can live trusting You. Amen.

Read
1 Kings 19:1-10

And the word of the LORD came to him: "What are you doing here, Elijah?" (1 Kings 19:9)

Sometimes people wonder how they ended up in a particular situation. Perhaps it is because they ran away from a heavy obligation or tried to shirk their responsibilities. Perhaps they gave in to temptation and now find themselves in a dilemma. Whatever the reason may be for ending up in that particular situation, the consequences are usually feelings of embarrassment, shame and guilt.

There are many obstructions in life, and if you don't stay on your guard you can very easily find yourself in trouble. Even if you lose your concentration for just a brief moment, you may find that you have become entangled in an undesirable situation. Satan thrives in circumstances like these and sows his seeds of despair and feelings of guilt.

> If you are tempted into one or other act of iniquity, flee from it. Falling into the water is normal but to remain face down in it will cause you to drown.
> ~ MATTHEW HENRY

It is essential that you keep your prayer life strong and alive. Ask God to keep your mind and your spirit clear and at the ready, so that you will be receptive to His still, small voice when He speaks to you in love. When you are tempted in any way, make absolutely sure that your mind is focused on Christ and that you remember what He expects of you.

If you have perhaps strayed a long way on the path of temptation, it is never too late to turn back to the path of safety and God's loving forgiveness. Find your hope in the Most High and find rest for your restless soul.

Savior and Friend, grant me the grace to stay close to You. Thank You for allowing me to know that You will save me from the temptations that Satan brings across my path. You give me new hope. Amen.

Whether you turn to the right or to the left, your ears will hear a voice behind you, saying, "This is the way; walk in it." (Isa. 30:21)

Read
Isa. 30:19-26

The average person faces the future with either hesitation or expectation. Because we do not know what lies ahead, we feel unsure and even a little afraid of what the future might bring. This extends further than our own, private realm: we do not know what the future holds for the world either. These feelings of uncertainty and anxiety are not unique to our time. Over the past centuries, people have entered the future with caution and have tried to see into its mists – yet without any success.

Whatever the future may hold for you, and however uncertain you are about it, there is one fact you can be absolutely sure of: God is with you, always and everywhere! Listen very carefully and you will hear His voice every step of the way. He is always there to lead you through each stage of your life's path, into the future that He planned for you. Take the experience of the psalmist as your own: "The LORD will keep you from all harm – He will watch over your life; the LORD will watch over your coming and going both now and forevermore" (Ps. 121:7-8).

> The great thing as a child of God is to be found at your post, living each day as if it is your last, but planning ahead as if you are going to be living in the world for a hundred more years.
>
> ~ C. S. LEWIS

Take the outstretched hand that the Lord is offering you. With Him as your Guide and Leader you can move into the future with hope in your heart and faith in the eternal love of God the Father.

Eternal Father of Compassion, as Your child I can always hide under the safety of Your wings. Your Omnipotence is my guarantee that my future is safe. For this I thank and praise You. Amen.

As a Christian you have so many things to rejoice and delight over. Because you have given your life to the Lord, you have first-hand knowledge of the love and peace of God. You are able to share in so many exciting truths that are revealed to you in the Word of God. When you become a child in God's family, you are accepted into a unique fellowship with others who share your faith. Your old life is gone forever. Your new life has begun. Praise the Lord!

It is said that hope is our faith for the future. What do you think the future has in store for you? Do you just think of all the bad things that might happen to you? Or do you think of all the blessings God still has planned for you?

> There is no medicine like hope, no incentive so great, no tonic so powerful as expectation of something better tomorrow.
>
> ~ ORISON SWETT MARDEN

As a Christian, you can truly look forward to the future with hope, because you have the glorious and trustworthy promises of God that you will know His glory and experience His love. These promises will help you rise above the anxieties and difficulties of this earthly life. In the midst of turmoil you can hold on to the promise of Christ that He will return to earth; this time to fetch us and allow us to share in the glory of God.

What a wonderful prospect and hope of glorious joy! What mercy to be able to live forever in the presence of God. Thank and praise Him for this and allow the unfailing promise of God to impel you to never stop hoping!

Holy Spirit of God, teach me to persevere in hope so that I may taste the joy of the hereafter with You. Amen.

May the God of hope fill you with all joy and peace as you trust in Him, so that you may overflow with hope by the power of the Holy Spirit.

~ ROMANS 15:13

Gracious God of everlasting hope,
Thank You for assuring us that our hope will endure;
that Your Spirit will always allow our hope to rise up again;
that Your children are not destined to despair but to hope!
Because, without hope we cannot live or die.
Give us the hope that keeps our expectations alive,
because without hope we would all have broken hearts.
Sanctify our hope, Lord Jesus,
so that we may be clothed with Your righteousness.
Grant that we will not rely on hope itself, but only in You,
the Source of our purest hope.
Your birth, life, suffering, death and resurrection
have brought the message of hope to our sin-torn world:
Hope of forgiveness, hope for peace with God,
and hope of eternal glory with God in the house of the Father.
Holy Spirit of God, we know that our future is rosy
because our hope for the future is unstoppable.
Guard us from any other futile hope
that may stealthily invade our lives.
We pray this in Jesus' name and with thanksgiving.

Amen.

Everything that is done in the world is done by hope.
~ MARTIN LUTHER

Read
John 4:19-26

"God is Spirit, and His worshipers must worship in spirit and in truth." (John 4:24)

People worship different kinds of idols. The early Egyptians took an animal or bird and made a god of it. Others built idols out of wood and stone and bowed before them and worshiped them. There are people whose ancestors have become their idols. For many, the heroes of "pop culture" and sports take on the stature of idols. Political freedom fighters are also elevated to a godlike status sometimes.

All of these man-made idols are merely false representations of the true God. The fact that there are so many idols proves how easy it is to follow the wrong god. People are most inclined to put a false god in place of the true God. Where it concerns God there are many ways to err, but only one way to make right; you must subject yourself to the Holy Spirit's guidance.

> Worship that pleases God comes from an obedient heart.
>
> ~ JOHN CALVIN

One of the functions of the Holy Spirit is to point people to Jesus, the living Christ. The Holy Spirit comes from God the Father and God the Son. When we worship God, we worship Him through the inspiration of the Holy Spirit. If we do not do this, we will quickly go astray. It also means that we are not just worshiping a Higher Being – we are searching for and responding to the One who has come to us in the name of Jesus Christ. Only His Spirit enables us to worship as we should.

Worship is far more than what we do in church on Sundays. Our entire lives become worship when we do these things with the help of the Holy Spirit. The Spirit is our hope of true, devout worship.

Lord Jesus, help me to worship in spirit and in truth. *Amen.*

I know that Messiah (called Christ) is coming. When He comes, He will explain everything to us. (John 4:25)

Read
John 4:19-26

Life is never easy or straightforward. We struggle to make sense of things and many of our problems remain unresolved. There are so many questions that confuse us and many of the answers we have do not seem to apply to the question. Most of us learn to live with these frustrations, tensions and issues.

The Jewish people's hope of a Messiah was borne out of their pain and suffering as a nation. They were selected by God to be His chosen people, but century after century they were oppressed by other nations. It did not make sense to them that their Almighty God would allow their suffering. But they knew Him as the God who keeps His promises and because of this they held out hope for the future. Even though He did not intervene in their trials at that particular time, He could still appear at any future point, banish their enemies, heal their diseases and give them good harvests and food in abundance. When that glorious future arrived, He would solve all their problems for them, answer all their questions and set everything right that had gone wrong. It was a delightful hope and it carried them through all the centuries of suffering and oppression.

> Hope is born right in the place where a person rises above his own despair by becoming involved in the joy and pain of others. Hope grows in communication with one's fellow man.
> ~ JURGEN MOLTMANN

Christians all over the world today look forward to the messianic era; because we know that Jesus Christ, the true Messiah, will come and mend all that is broken in our world, realize all our dreams, and solve all of our confusing dilemmas. Until then we must work and pray and hope.

Messiah, come quickly to this chaotic world and let Your kingdom of hope, love and peace become a reality. *Amen.*

Read
John 4:43-54

Jesus replied, "You may go. Your son will live." The man took Jesus at His word and departed. (John 4:50)

The greatest of all mysteries in life is death. A healthy fear of death determines many of the things we do and believe. When an animal is seriously hurt, the vet will put it down. We do not hesitate to act in this way with an animal, but when it comes to human beings we cannot bring ourselves to do the same thing. When death threatens us we prefer to take the attitude of, "As long as there is life, there is hope!"

The Bible makes it clear that we live under an ever-present threat of death. It is the eventuality that we fear most, both for ourselves and for our loved ones. Paul said, "The last enemy to be destroyed is death" (1 Cor. 15:26). Jesus Christ affirmed life. Through Him life conquered death. That is why so many incidents in His earthly sojourn speak of healing. Every miracle of healing is a preparation and an indication of that final miracle – the resurrection.

> Life is a mystery to be lived, not a problem to be solved.
> ~ ADRIAN VAN KAAM

In this story of the healing of the royal official's son, the declaration that the son was alive and would live is repeated three times. This was done to emphasize the victory and the power of Jesus over death. Jesus is life in abundance.

Life and death are engaged in a bitter struggle within every person – young or old, healthy or ill. The same struggle is taking place in you at this very moment. When you invite Jesus into your life in faith, you have Someone living inside you who is alive forever – and who is able to bring you the kind of life that God planned for you to enjoy and that you can look forward to in faith.

Living Lord Jesus, live triumphantly in me now and forever. *Amen.*

"The fever left (your son) yesterday at the seventh hour." The father realized that this was the exact time at which Jesus had said to him, "Your son will live." (John 4:52-53)

Read
John 4:43-54

When you receive a letter telling you that you have won a big prize, you do not take it seriously because you know there is a catch involved. However, when you receive a letter with a lawyer's letterhead informing you that an aunt has left you a few million rand, you immediately start planning how you are going to spend the money.

The power and authority of any message depends on the credibility of the person who sends it. Salesmen, particularly those who sell through the mail, have a low credibility rating. Lawyers, on the other hand, are held in high esteem. Jesus spoke with the authority of God. The wind and the waves were obedient to Him. The multitudes believed in Him. Demons fled when He spoke. At His call fishermen left their nets and followed Him. In answer to the plea of a royal official, Jesus healed his son. When Jesus spoke, sickness and pestilence left the body.

> The Word is the face of God, the image of God. He was brought into the Light and made known to us.
> ~ CLEMENT OF ALEXANDRIA

The Bible tells us that through the word of God the universe was called into being. On His orders the Ten Commandments were delivered into the hands of Moses. Through the mouths of the prophets He spoke in judgment over the ungodly nations.

God is continually speaking, and His Word carries great authority and power. He also speaks to you daily from the Word. He speaks of hope, comfort, wisdom, healing and mercy. Can you hear God's Word of life, and is it bringing you hope?

Let me hear Your Word and respond accordingly, my Lord and my God. Amen.

Crossing Over into Life

"Whoever hears My word and believes Him who sent Me has eternal life and will not be condemned; he has crossed over from death to life." (John 5:24)

Are you truly living, or are you simply existing? For some people, life means living every day to the fullest. For others, it means accumulating money and possessions. There are people who believe that the purpose of life is to avoid work, problems and stress. There are those who live empty, monotonous lives. Some people don't really know who they are, why they are here or what they want for the future.

When you come to the point of accepting Jesus Christ as your Savior and Redeemer, you cross over from death into life. You no longer live for yourself. The things that you valued so much before no longer hold any attraction for you. Your former goals now seem meaningless. Instead of blaming other people for your problems, you now do everything in your power to help them with theirs.

> Make sure that what you are living for is worth dying for.
> ~ CHARLES MAYES

Instead of grabbing everything you can lay your hands on, you find enjoyment in giving. Where previously you complained at the slightest irritation, you now accept hardship and suffering as a means of glorifying God and sharing in the sufferings of Christ. Before you "crossed over," you were number one in your own small world, but now you put the triune God first and see yourself in relationship to Him. Previously your body was a source of pleasure or delight, but now it is the temple of the Holy Spirit. Before you crossed over, you tried to make God do what you wanted, but now you find joy and new meaning in doing what He expects of you.

The burning hope of every Christian disciple must be crossing over from death into life.

God of life, help me to live every day to the full and not merely exist. **Amen.**

"A time is coming and has now come when the dead will hear the voice of the Son of God and those who hear will live." (John 5:25)

Read
John 5:18-29

Some people claim that when you die everything is over and that's all there is to it. Others believe that the spirit leaves the body and lives forever. You therefore continue to live after death as a spirit. Then there are those who refuse to think about death at all because it is just too frightening. For them, life is tough enough and they don't want to upset themselves by thinking about death and the afterlife.

The New Testament teaches us that Jesus rose from the dead and that everyone who believes in Him will also rise. In our reading for today, Jesus predicts His own Second Coming and how all who believe in Him will be resurrected and will enjoy a fuller and richer life with Him for eternity.

> There are better things ahead than any we leave behind in this life.
> ~ C. S. Lewis

Because Jesus Christ is the Resurrection and the Life, death is no longer a sad portal. It is also not the end of life. It is simply the end of the beginning. For Jesus' followers, this life is just a place of learning and preparation for the glorious life we will live with Him in heaven.

What is more, this life determines much of the quality of the life to come. Whatever you do or permit to be done, whatever you believe or refuse to believe, whether you grow in love or allow your love to ebb away, whether you share in His praise, practice compassion and help to build up the community – these choices will shape your life beyond the grave. The choice is yours. Choose well!

Lord Jesus, help me to be ready when I die. *Amen.*

The Truth Will Set You Free

"If you hold to My teaching, you are really My disciples. Then you will know the truth, and the truth will set you free." (John 8:31-32)

Our text for today is often used to convince someone to tell the truth. If the truth were to be known about many offences, it would not set everyone free – in fact, it would lead to a life in prison for many!

The truth that is borne out of your knowledge of Jesus and out of your discipleship, however, does indeed set you free. And this is the truth that Jesus is talking about. Discipleship leads to freedom. When you become a follower of Jesus, He frees you from fear. You know that your life is now in the hands of the One who is able to calm the wind and the waves. You don't have to be afraid of what is going to happen to you – you are safe in His loving arms, in life and in death. You are in fellowship with Him and He will hold you tight.

> We find freedom when we find God; we lose it when we lose Him.
> ~ PAUL E. SCHERER

Christ also frees you from your self-centeredness. This is one of the characteristics of the Christian life. You no longer need to push yourself into the foreground of everything that you think and do. You can now put Jesus first and other people second, before yourself.

Knowing Jesus also sets you free from sin. Paul said, "For sin shall not be your master, because you are not under law, but under grace" (Rom. 6:14). When you are serving Jesus in a ministry, you experience a new freedom. Truth means that you are completely free when you are surrendered to the Master in love and service.

If you are searching for true freedom, Jesus Christ is the place to begin.

Lord my God, lead me in the truth that sets me free. Amen.

"I know you are Abraham's descendants. Yet you are ready to kill Me, because you have no room for My word." (John 8:37)

Read
John 8:31-47

Some people believe that their status in their community guarantees them a privileged position before God. They think that if they are able to pull some strings in human society, then they can use the same methods in the spiritual world.

In our text for today, Jesus is speaking to the Jewish people who had gathered for a religious festival in Jerusalem. When He spoke of freedom they became upset, because they thought they were already free and that they had no need of God's help. Abraham's status before God was so great that they thought, because they were descendants of Abraham, acceptance by God was guaranteed. Yet this is a foolish assumption. Everyone is of equal value in God's eyes. Soon after, when the gospel was extended to the Gentiles, anyone could have access to God through faith in Jesus Christ. Faith in Christ is the only way to find God's acceptance.

> None are more hopelessly enslaved than those who falsely believe they are free.
> ~ JOHANN WOLFGANG VON GOETHE

Don't rely solely on your ancestors' heritage. Even if your father was the Archbishop of Canterbury, that is not enough – you personally must come to know Jesus and believe in Him. Even if your parents built the church where you now worship, you must first put your faith in Jesus Christ. You may be the mayor of your town or the captain of your football team, a member of Parliament, a millionaire, or the director of a dozen companies, but you still need a personal belief in Jesus Christ. Otherwise you cannot hope for freedom and you will never know the truth of God in Jesus.

Help those, Lord Jesus, who rely on their status in this world to be humble and come to You in faith. **Amen.**

Hope in God

And who is equal to such a task? (2 Cor. 2:16)

Have you ever wondered where people find the strength to fulfill the responsibilities they carry on their shoulders? Statesmen and women control the destinies of their countries; business magnates are called upon to make decisions for giant corporations – decisions that will affect their own future, the welfare of their employees and, in many cases, the business world in general. The pace that these people work and live at is unimaginable and we wonder how they manage to do it.

You can be sure that those leaders who live stable lives and whose efforts are exerted in the interests of humanity, are devoted Christians with unshakable faith in God. Those who have little or no faith in the Lord will be self-centered, shallow and relatively unconcerned about the welfare of the people who are dependent on them.

> Size is not a measure of success. Faithfulness is the measure of success. Biblical fidelity is the measure of success.
> ~ CHUCK COLSON

Whatever the task that has been entrusted to you, whether large or small, you can give of your best only if you dedicate your task to the Lord and lay it before Him in prayer. If your aim is to obey His will, you will be empowered by the strength of the living Christ, who will give you guidance and physical strength. Without Him there is no hope of achievement and all your efforts will be in vain. In Jesus you have the hope of achieving much.

I thank You, heavenly Father, that I am able to do everything I undertake in Your power and through hope in You. Amen.

Let us fix our eyes on Jesus, the author and perfecter of our faith. (Heb. 12:2)

Read
Heb. 12:1-13

The Christian experience is not always a happy one and can sometimes be hampered by inaction or lack of interest. Spiritual growth is seldom easy but it can be achieved through an ever-deepening prayer life and a steadily growing awareness of the presence of the living Christ. Spiritual growth takes time, dedication and the realization that there can be no delay on the path of discipleship.

If your Christian walk is not as real and dynamic now as it was at the time of your conversion, or when you pledged your faith to Jesus for the first time, you need to realize that the fault lies with you and not with the Master. His love for you is strong and steadfast, but your weakened faith is the result of letting other interests take precedence in your life. You still respect Jesus but your hope and faith are not in Him alone.

> Spiritual growth consists most in the growth of the root, which is out of sight.
> ~ MATTHEW HENRY

If you long for a dynamic and meaningful Christian walk, you must be willing to measure up to the highest standards that Christ has set for all His disciples. Without absolute obedience to the Master there can be no dynamic and meaningful spiritual experience. The responsibility to experience this deeper relationship lies with you. The Lord has stood by His promises: now it is your responsibility to allow this to become a working proposition in your life. It is where your hope must lead you.

Give to me, Lord Jesus, the inspiration of the Holy Spirit so that I may lead an active, strong spiritual life. Amen.

Hope Preserved in Heaven

Read

Col. 1:1-14

The faith and love that spring from the hope that is stored up for you in heaven and that you have already heard about in the word of truth, the gospel. (Col. 1:5)

During the Second World War a doctor in a Nazi concentration camp wondered why some people died from suffering while others survived. He discovered that those who survived had one thing in common. They each cherished a dream of what they would do when they were free again. Each one of them had a different hope, but they all looked to the future. While there was hope, there was life.

Hope is one of the most powerful human motivators. The early Christians went to the stake or to the arena, praying to be united with Jesus in heaven. All Christians hope for something special after death. They know that it is not death, non-existence and an end that awaits them, but a fuller and richer life with God. It is a life filled with glory, joy and love. By looking past the sufferings and trials that are their earthly lot, Christians can endure hardship and even death. They are inspired to live courageously, calmly and trustingly, because the hope that is "preserved in heaven" empowers them to hold on to an eternal perspective when faced with defeats and disappointments.

> Hope is a thing with feathers that perches in the soul, and sings the tune – without the words, and never stops at all.
>
> ~ EMILY DICKINSON

Looking to the future with hope is not escapism. It is realism. Hope in Christ deepens and strengthens your faith. It increases your love and makes you truly compassionate. It broadens your horizons and makes your actions dynamic. It brings sense and meaning to every moment of your life.

Gracious Father God, grant that I will never lose hope. Amen.

All over the world this gospel is bearing fruit and growing, just as it has been doing among you since the day you heard it and understood God's grace. (Col. 1:6)

Read
Col. 1:1-14

We often use the word *gospel* together with the word *truth* to emphasize the truth of what we are saying. We especially do this when someone questions something that we said, "I'm telling you, it is the gospel truth." In one way or another the "gospel truth" is viewed as more certain than the usual truth!

The gospel that the Bible refers to is the Good News that Jesus, the Son of God, has come, that He lived, ministered and died, that He was raised from the dead and now sits at the right hand of God making intercession for us. These events are the foundation of a new life of fulfillment for everyone who believes and wants to entrust himself or herself to Jesus.

> Where I found the Truth, there found I my God, the Truth itself.
> ~ St. Augustine

But is the gospel really the truth? Either these events really happened and it is all true, or they didn't happen and therefore it is not true. They *did* happen, because they brought about true change and gave us a way of seeing the truth and making sense of it. The gospel is true because it brings sense and meaning to ordinary, everyday life. It is true because it inspires people to hope and persevere in the face of adversity. It is true because it moves ordinary people to come to their senses and see the truth about themselves, the world around them and God. It is true because it brings courage, love and sacrifice to everyone who accepts it. It is true because it comes from God and because it works perfectly!

Help me, heavenly Father, to hear, see and believe the truth about the living Christ. Amen.

Buried and Resurrected

Read
Col. 2:6-15

Having been buried with Him in baptism and raised with Him through your faith in the power of God, who raised Him from the dead. (Col. 2:12)

Some people, especially those who suffer from an addiction of some sort, try to forget the past so they can make a new beginning. This is usually a traumatic experience for them. There are also people who do this after a painful experience like a divorce, or because they feel they need to move in a new direction in their lives.

The people Paul addressed in our text for today put their heathen past behind them, were baptized and began a new life with and in Christ. Paul told them that their old way of life was dead. Descending into the waters of baptism was symbolic of the death and burial of their old lives and the beginning of a new life with Christ. Christ died and was buried but He rose from the grave.

> Without the Resurrection, Christianity would not exist – Christianity stands or falls on the Resurrection, and this single factor makes Christianity one of a kind.
> ~ STEVE KUMAR

Their act of baptism was therefore a spiritual parallel with Christ's death and Resurrection. Paul told them that they were taking part in Christ's death and Resurrection through their faith and that they would receive the new qualities of the resurrection life that Christ brought them.

All who call themselves Christians ought to recognize this resurrection power. If you need it or want it, you can get it first by acknowledging the worthlessness of your past and laying it down. Die to it and bury it. Then move into the future with your trust in the resurrected Christ and allow His resurrection life to touch and transform your own life. Allow Him to fulfill your life and then move into the future that He has prepared for you with hope in your heart.

Lead me, risen Lord, through Your power to a true resurrection life. Amen.

> When you were dead in your sins and in the uncircumcision of your sinful nature, God made you alive with Christ. He forgave us all our sins. (Col. 2:13)

Read
Col. 2:6-15

During the persecution of early Christians some believers were thrown to the lions. It was a quick death. Others were not so fortunate. They were sent to mines in North Africa where they were branded on the forehead with hot irons and then sent underground. Many of them never returned. Their chains were shortened so that they could not stand up straight. They were the scum of the earth. Their slave-drivers often killed the Christians just for the fun of it.

Some believers tried to write letters on the inside of the tunnels to loved ones or friends. With charcoal they wrote names, prayers and praises. One piece of writing that repeatedly appeared was the Latin word: *Vita, Vita, Vita!* (*Life, Life, Life!*). After human death they would live on in Christ, and they knew it.

> God is the author of who we are and where we are to go.
> ~ ANONYMOUS

Paul described life without Christ as a spiritual death. It was an existence of a completely lower order. When the Colossians came to know Christ, confessed their sins, changed their direction and entered into a new life with Christ, He gave them a measure of His post-resurrection power. Then they truly began to live.

When He forgave their sins they were saved from the clutches of their guilty feelings and they came to know true freedom, joy and hope. They lived with greater depth, with a new feeling of peace and were motivated by powerful love and hope. You can also truly live if you live in Christ and He lives in you!

Living Lord Jesus, fill me with Your new life each day. *Amen.*

And having disarmed the powers and authorities, He made a public spectacle of them, triumphing over them by the cross. (Col. 2:15)

The evil forces of the world seem so powerful that they threaten to drive us to despair. Sickness and pestilence, poverty and crime, war and terrorism – these and other things like greed, lust and violence, create the impression that the world is dominated by evil.

Against this formidable spectacle, the Christian faith places a Man on a cross, apparently weak and helpless. He is hardly a symbol of victory, in fact, He is just the opposite. The nature of the kingdom of God and His omnipotence is such, however, that the faithful ones know that Christ is the victor over the Evil One. The cross proclaims it. The empty grave affirms it.

> Faith is a reasoning trust, a trust which reckons thoughtfully and confidently upon the trustworthiness of God.
>
> ~ JOHN R. STOTT

Paul draws an effective and well-known picture of the triumph of a Roman general. Whenever a Roman general attained a noteworthy victory, He would march his triumphant armies through the streets of Rome while the miserable leaders and the people of the conquered armies walked behind them in chains. They were openly branded as his conquered enemies. Paul thinks of Jesus as a triumphant Victor. And in His triumph the power of the Evil One was defeated forever and one day everyone will see it.

Do not allow yourself to be deceived. The evil that you see all around you just disguises a hidden truth. Every enemy will eventually be brought to submission by Christ and He will reign in glory for all to see. Our hope is focused on that happy day.

Lord Jesus, help me in the most oppressive circumstances to have hope in Your final triumph. Amen.

These are a shadow of the things that were to come; the reality, however, is found in Christ. (Col. 2:17)

Read
Col. 2:16-23

The difference between a substitute and the real thing is often very difficult to see. A fake Christmas tree can be very lovely and do what it was made for, but it is not a real tree: it is plastic.

You can also mistakenly regard a number of Christian practices to be the true worship of God. The teachers who misled the Christians in Colosse, did exactly that. They got the people to accept various festivals, that had nothing to do with Jesus, as Christian festivals. It is easy to draw up a set of rules and regulations and think that if you obey them you are a Christian. This is the fault that Jesus found with the religious leaders of His time. They had not grasped the real meaning of being a Christian.

The true reality is love for Jesus the living Christ, because Christ Himself is a reality. The problem with putting your faith in a substitute, is that you are misleading yourself (and probably other people too) into believing that it is the real thing. In this way you rob yourself of knowing Jesus personally.

> Every religion is false which, as to its faith, does not worship one God as the origin of everything and which, as to its morality, does not love only one God as the object of everything.
> ~ BLAISE PASCAL

In your decision as to what true faith in Jesus is, always ask if it puts Jesus Christ first, focuses on Him, glorifies Him or helps you to conform to Him. Be careful of rules and regulations. Be careful that you do not "water down" the person of Christ by thinking that goodness, honesty and good intentions are what it is all about. It is all about Christ and not about anyone else. He alone is the reality and our only hope. *Soli Deo Gloria*!

Gracious Father, help me to focus so strongly on Jesus Christ that all illusions fade away. **Amen.**

Read
Col. 2:16-23

The whole body, supported and held together by its ligaments and sinews, grows as God causes it to grow. (Col. 2:19)

There are many different kinds of strength. A balanced diet will give you energy to work and play and will build your body up properly. You also need strength of mind, which involves a positive self-image, motivation to achieve, and the perseverance to see things through. Courage is another form of strength.

Paul, who wrote this letter, knew of the necessity of also having spiritual strength. He discovered in his own life that only Christ can give us that power. He tried to please God in his own strength but he came up short. Christ, however, provided him with the strength he lacked, both for himself and for the whole church – called the "body" here.

You also need spiritual strength, regardless of how strong you may be physically or mentally. Christ can give you that strength, and He is the only One you can hope to receive it from. It is necessary to first acknowledge your own weakness in this respect. Then accept the offer of Christ and rely on the power that He promises you. Practice your faith and prove the trustworthiness of Christ for those who hope in Him. Always acknowledge that the power He provides is not your own, and recognize your complete dependence on Him.

> In order to be strong in the Lord you must be weak in yourself.
> ~ CHARLES H. SPURGEON

Feed your faith by living in the presence and glory of God and in the incomparable power of Christ. Go to the Source of spiritual strength daily. Jesus Himself will renew your strength and your hope in Him every day.

I come in weakness, Lord Jesus, to draw my strength every day from You. Amen.

We rejoice in the hope of the glory of God. (Rom. 5:2)

In the Christian life there is much to rejoice over. Because you have given your life to Christ, you should know the joy of peace with God. When you become a disciple of Christ, you learn many exciting truths. Because you have been accepted into the family of God, you join a community of likeminded people. Your old life is behind you and a new spiritual awareness opens up for you. In the place of despair and confusion, you now have inextinguishable hope. Rejoice in it!

Someone once said: Faith is our hope for the future. When you think about the future, what do you expect? Perhaps you think about all the years you still have left to live. Some have the prospect of loneliness if they outlive their partners. If they still have a life partner, they hope for many more happy years together. You hope to enjoy life and escape serious illness. Good health

> The next moment is as much beyond our grasp, and as much in God's care, as that a hundred years away.
> ~ C. S. Lewis

and having enough money to live on are of the utmost importance to the elderly.

As a Christian you can look to the future with hope because you have the promise of the ongoing presence and glory of God beyond your earthly problems. You were created to eventually share in God's glory. Nothing less is good enough. You are destined to know abundant joy and never-ending love. Not because you have done anything good, but because Christ loves you and through His love you can be made perfect. Rejoice therefore: the best is yet to come!

Grant that in the here and now I will persevere in hope, Lord Jesus, and will rejoice in it so I can share in the glory of the hereafter. Amen.

Read
Rom. 12:9-21

Be joyful in hope, patient in affliction, faithful in prayer.
(Rom. 12:12)

Most people are subject to moods. In good times our spirits are high, but when things go wrong we become depressed and lose hope. Our behavior patterns are dictated by our emotions at any specific moment.

One of the qualities that distinguishes the dedicated Christian from others is faith. Without faith in the triune God we cannot lead a Christian life, but with faith we can overcome all things in the strength that the living Christ gives us.

Regardless of your circumstances, it is essential that you cling to your faith in the all-embracing, victorious love of Christ. Place your complete hope and trust in Him to lead you through every experience and situation in life. Lay before Him your fears, your worries and your decisions, with thanksgiving. Submit yourself entirely to God's protection and grace.

> We hold onto our hope in the Lord, because we belong to the Lord of our hope.
> ~ ANONYMOUS

After you have done this, rest in God in the knowledge that He will protect you and take care of you in the best way possible, because He alone knows your every desire and need, as well as the best way to protect you. Jesus invites you, "Come to Me, all you who are weary and burdened, and I will give you rest" (Matt. 11:28).

Holy Spirit of God, grant me strength and faith so that I will always hope in the promises of God. Amen.

One thing I do: Forgetting what is behind and straining toward what is ahead. (Phil. 3:13)

Read
Phil. 3:10-21

It is possible to reach a point in life where you feel you just cannot go any further. The road that you have walked so far is covered with the ashes of failure. Only you and God know how hard you have tried, but now you have reached the end of your tether.

At such times sweet words of comfort help little and you are convinced that you are fighting a lone battle and that no one cares about what happens to you. You are wrong! God cares! He did not create you to be a failure, but His will for you is that you will attain what He has planned for your life. Forget the past, with all its defeats and failures, and give God the throne position in your life and live as He expects you to do.

> Every new blade of grass, every blossom, every tree that buds, carries the inscription: Hope.
> ~ RICHARD JEFFRIES

Show your courage to make a new beginning. On God's road you will not always experience frustration and failure. He will give you a full and satisfying life and enable you to develop and grow through prayer and studying the Word.

To make your prayer life truly effective, you must accept Jesus Christ as your Savior and Redeemer – as Lord of your life. Focus your whole life and hope on Him. Ask Him humbly to lead you, and as you come to trust Him more and more, you will discover that you really matter to Him.

I praise You, Lord Jesus, that my sins and failures of the past are forgiven and that I can become a new person in Your power and strength. Amen.

I press on toward the goal to win the prize for which God has called me heavenward in Christ Jesus. (Phil. 3:14)

There is no doubt that the past influences the present and impacts the future. You are today what you have chosen to become. Your heritage may leave much to be desired and the odds may be against you – to such a degree that you feel that it is pointless resisting – and consequently you give up without fighting back.

The glorious truth is that it is never too late to take stock of the past and extract from it everything that was good. Once you have done this, you can turn to the future with the determination to make something worthwhile of it, something that is pleasing to God. If you have become discouraged about doing precisely this, and what you once hoped would become a wonderful future has become a miserable and discouraging effort, it is time to take stock of your life.

> Those who move mountains begin by removing small stones.
> ~ CHINESE PROVERB

Ask yourself how serious you are about a rosy future. Ask God to increase your hope and faith and use what you already have. It is only when you really want a better future and are willing to accept discipline, hard work and sacrifice, that such a future can become possible for you.

God expects your help in making your future what it ought to be. With Him you can reach your true life-goal, but without your cooperation He cannot do it for you.

Living Master, I dedicate my life humbly to You and accept with thankfulness the good things that You have in store for me. *Amen.*

I can do everything through Him who gives me strength.
(Phil. 4:13)

There are moments in life when you wonder how you are going to get through your current situation; when you wonder how exactly you are going to solve a difficult matter and where you are going to find the strength to do what needs to be done.

Your problem may have originated from a serious illness or death; it may have to do with a setback in your business career; you may be confronted by a radical change of lifestyle; or you may have been asked to make a serious decision or to undertake a difficult task.

Often, in such circumstances, people become so anxious that they are rendered completely powerless to act and are in no condition to make a well-thought-out decision, with the result that they put themselves in danger of behaving irrationally and failing in their task.

> Men create real miracles when they use their God-given courage and intelligence.
> ~ JEAN ANOUILH

Make Jesus Christ your mentor and partner in every area of your life. Take your anxieties, whatever they may be, to Him in prayer; open yourself to His guidance and be obedient to the movement of the Holy Spirit.

He will not disappoint you and He will empower you to handle any crisis with authority.

Grant, gracious Lord, that in matters big and small, Your will and not my own, will lead me and give me strength and wisdom. **Amen.**

Read
1 John 2:7-17

I write to you, dear children, because your sins have been forgiven on account of His name. (1 John 2:12)

Your name is your identity. There is something very personal and exclusively yours, something special in your name that becomes lost in the number in an identity book.

The name of Jesus is important. It means "Redeemer" or "Savior". Its full importance does not arise only out of its meaning, however. Its importance comes mainly from the identity of the Person behind the name – who He was and is. It also comes from what He has done and continues to do.

In Christ's time there were many people called Jesus. But only one Jesus is worshiped, remembered and revered by millions of His followers. This is because He was God in human form. By becoming a human being, and intervening in human life, He changed life on earth as we knew it forever. He was the only One who was able to forgive people's sins against God. Other people, such as priests, teachers and counselors may declare that our sins are forgiven. But only Jesus can forgive those sins you have committed against God.

> The deadliest sin is the consciousness of no sin.
> ~ THOMAS CARLYLE

Your sins are forgiven only when *Jesus* forgives them. You are not forgiven because you have confessed your sins or because you have done enough good to balance out the books. The fact is that the only thing that you can present for the forgiveness of your sins, is the very sin for which you need to receive forgiveness for! Jesus does the rest for you. Through trusting in Him, and in no one else, you receive forgiveness, life, hope, joy and peace.

Gracious God, let me find sense and joy, hope and peace in everything that Jesus has done and continues to do. Amen.

And this is the testimony: God has given us eternal life, and this life is in His Son. (1 John 5:11)

Read
1 John 5:6-17

People today expect to live well into their seventies. Due to the development of medicines and the growth of the medical profession, people are living longer than ever before. The average life expectancy has risen considerably over the years. In biblical times only a handful of people reached old age. Because of this there was a much greater awareness of the brevity of life.

In an effort to gratify the longings of the human heart, many religions promised eternal life. If you believed, you were allowed to live the life of the gods. But only Jesus Christ was able to fulfill that kind of promise. Eternal life really means living in God, because only God is eternal. Only God can offer eternal life, because He shares His own life with those who believe in Him.

> Fear not that thy life shall come to an end, but rather that it shall never have a beginning.
> ~ JOHN HENRY NEWMAN

Because God is peace, eternal life encompasses peace of mind and tranquility, rather than the stress and pressure of the world. Eternal life gives you the victory over everyday frustrations, because you draw strength from the life that God shares with you. Because God is holy, He offers you His holiness – and this means that you are able to live on a high moral level and are therefore better equipped to withstand temptation and sin.

God is also love and He fills your heart with His love that banishes hate and bitterness. Because God is eternal, you possess a quality of life that overcomes death. The life that God offers you is indestructible. What more can anyone hope for?

Lord Jesus, fill the years of my life with the eternity that belongs to You alone. Amen.

Read
1 John 5:6-17

He who has the Son has life; he who does not have the Son of God does not have life. (1 John 5:12)

What is life really about? For some people it is all about the attainment of material things – cars, houses and other earthly valuables. For others it means money and more money – the greater the amount the better life is, and for others it is about pleasure. Some people want achievements, others go for power and others search for self-fulfillment.

The message of the Bible is simple and direct. Life is about Jesus Christ. If you have Jesus, you have life, and if you don't have Jesus, you do not have life. Knowing Jesus may bring you success – and it might not. Following Jesus brought status to a small number of people. For many others it led to long years of humble service without any obvious status and very little sign of reward.

> For those who do
> not know God,
> hope is their only hope.
> ~ JOHN MONTGOMERY

When Jesus comes into your life, He brings completion. He Himself said, "I have come that they may have life, and have it to the full" (John 10:10). He gives you priorities that you would never have set for yourself, but which are fulfilling and often exciting. Because He has forgiven your sins He creates a feeling of peace within yourself and towards the world. The poet, John Masefield, said, "The deep peace burnt my me alive." When you welcome Jesus into your life, your eyes are opened. Now you see yourself as you really are; you see God as He really is; and you see the world for what it is. You have a new perspective on life that is real and liberating.

These things will happen to you when you have Jesus in your life. Do you have Him? If you don't, today is the day to find Him.

Lord of life, I have only one short life to live. Grant that I will make the best use of it that I possibly can. *Amen.*

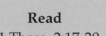

What is our hope, our joy, or the crown in which we will glory in the presence of our Lord Jesus when He comes? Indeed, You are our glory and joy. (1 Thess. 2:19-20)

Read
1 Thess. 2:17-20

Parents often try to relive their own childhood through their children. They want to see their children succeed where they themselves failed. Sometimes parents experience deep disappointment in the reluctance of their children to fulfill their most cherished expectations for them.

There is a similar dynamic between teachers and pupils, and even more so between ministers, pastors and priests and their congregations. Ministers have a special relationship with those congregants whom they personally led to faith or encouraged to become more serious disciples of Christ.

> Don't go through life,
> grow through life.
> ~ ERIC BUTTERWORTH

Paul puts it well in our text for today. He sees the heathen converts who came to Christ through his ministry as prize winners that he will one day present before Christ as evidence of his servanthood. Notice that Paul is not glorying in his own achievements, only in the faith, holiness and maturity of those disciples who have sat under his ministry.

You are probably in the same sense the hope, joy and crown of someone in your life; perhaps a catechist, youth leader, parent or teacher who introduced you to Christ. They take joy in seeing you grow in grace and spiritual maturity. Thank God for what they have done in your life and delight yourself in their spiritual investment in you.

Holy God, I thank You today for those who have helped to build me up in Christ. Amen.

Read
1 Thess. 4:13-18

We do not want you to be ignorant about those who fall asleep, or to grieve like the rest of men, who have no hope. (1 Thess. 4:13)

For some people the mention of the word *death* is too scary. The thought of it conjures up somber visions of darkness, while the loved ones who remain behind are bewildered in their sorrow and face a future that seems colorless, empty and hopeless.

We can't deny that death brings sorrow and separation. But the Christian faith teaches us that, through the resurrection of Jesus Christ, there is hope even in death – not despair. With His victory over the grave, the Son of God banished all fear of death and gave new meaning to the statement He made just a few days before His own death, "I am the resurrection and the life. He who believes in Me will live, even though he dies; and whoever lives and believes in Me will never die" (John 11:25).

> The valley of the shadow of death holds no darkness for the child of God. There must be light, else there could be no shadow. Jesus is our light. He has overcome death.
>
> ~ Dwight L. Moody

When a loved one dies, look in the strength of the Master past the limitations of physical life. Even though the light of life has gone out, the purpose is not to cast you into the darkness of despair, but to herald a new dawn for the one who has been called: the dawn of a new, glorious life that has been promised by the living Christ to all who believe in Him. The hopelessness of death is transformed into life in Christ on the other side of the grave.

Where, O death, is your victory? Where, O death, is your sting? (1 Corinthians 15:55). *Amen.*

God has given us new birth into a living hope through the resurrection of Jesus Christ, and into an inheritance that can never perish – kept in heaven for you. (1 Pet. 1:3-4)

Read
1 Pet. 1:1-9

Not all hope is ongoing. Some fades and dies. It is a sad moment when someone gives up hope. "I used to hope that my husband would stop drinking," an elderly lady said, "but now I have lost all hope."

Undoubtedly many people followed popular religions in New Testament times and put their faith in false gods. They brought sacrifices to them, but eventually gave up all hope that the promises that had been made to them would ever be fulfilled. In contrast to this, the hope that Jesus gave to His people was fulfilled on an ongoing basis. This would continue even though many people who adopted Christianity were killed during the persecution of Christians at that time.

Today, two thousand years later, hope in Christ still lives on. Because this living hope has its origins in the resurrection of Jesus, it outlived the stagnation of a seemingly endless cycle of years. Because Jesus died and rose again, people had a realistic hope of a new life in Him after death. They knew that all the imperfections and unresolved matters of this life would be sorted out on the other side of the

> Hope is the best possession. None are completely wretched but those who are without hope, and few are reduced so low as that.
>
> ~ WILLIAM HAZLITT

grave. They were able to believe that God would finally triumph over the Evil One.

Today people can continue to believe, because the hope that originated in Jesus lives on. Whatever opposition might confront Christians, however bad world circumstances may seem, however confused people may be about Jesus, however far the moral standards of today may sink, Jesus is still alive! So, too, are those who have put their faith and hope in Him.

Protect me, O Holy Spirit, from ever despairing. Amen.

Prepare your minds for action; be self-controlled; set your hope fully on the grace to be given you when Jesus Christ is revealed. (1 Pet. 1:13)

Human beings are inclined to look toward the future with caution and fear. We often say with a foreboding feeling, "Who knows what tomorrow will bring?"

Even when death was staring them in the face, the early Christians knew no fear. They looked to the future in faith with cheerful expectancy, certain that Christ was coming soon. They knew that they did not have to fear His Second Coming. Through His birth in Bethlehem, Christ stepped upon the human scene, full of grace and truth. When He comes again it will be in glory, love and kindness. The early Christians looked to the future in the knowledge that God in His great mercy would be good to them.

> Many of us crucify ourselves between two thieves – regret for the past and fear for the future.
>
> ~ ANONYMOUS

The future will hold the same blend of adversity and glorious new possibilities for us as it has done in the past. There will be crime, injustices and disorder, yes. But God will intersperse it all with miraculous new discoveries, medicines and solutions to major problems. Because Christians have a God, they do not have to be depressed over the future. They know that God is going to be just as good to them next week as He was last week; as much next year as He was last year.

They know that the future is in God's hands: both their own and the world's. They also know that Christ will eventually return in glory and might. Then all evil will come to an end and God will be everything, and in everyone.

Lord who is coming back, I place all my hope in You. *Amen.*

Always be prepared to give an answer to everyone who asks you to give the reason for the hope that you have. But do this with gentleness and respect. (1 Pet. 3:15)

Read
1 Pet. 3:13-22

Perhaps you feel that you don't know enough about the Bible to get involved in religious arguments. It is a broad subject with many pitfalls to avoid. Very few unbelievers can be brought to faith with clever arguments.

Even so, Paul told believers to prepare themselves to offer their clear and sensible witness if anyone should ask why they believed in Jesus. He did not expect them to obtain their degrees in theology. He knew, however, that there were genuine seekers; people who would be curious to know about the faith they had embraced and why they could trust in their own futures.

Remember: concern for the future was an actual reality for Paul's believers, because they could face death for their faith at any moment. Some people were amazed that Christians could stare death in the face with such courage and that they could be so sure that they would be with Christ when they died.

> I am to become a Christ to my neighbor and be for him what Christ is for me.
> ~ MARTIN LUTHER

You and I also need to know the reason for the hope we have. You do not have to be clever or educated to provide a simple, honest answer if you are questioned about your hope.

It is enough to say: I hope and believe in Him because He has helped me over the years. Some knowledge of the Bible would take you a step further. Always be prepared to take the opportunity to share your hope and faith with others – it might just be the turning point in someone else's life.

Grant, gracious Lord Jesus, that I will be Your trustworthy and fearless witness. Amen.

OCTOBER

Dear friends, let us love one another, for love comes from God.
Everyone who loves has been born of God and knows God.
Whoever does not love does not know God, because God is love.

~ 1 JOHN 4:7-8

Love

Eternal God, You are Love!
Teach me to love truly, Father.
You are the source of all lasting and true love:
Teach me then, Heavenly Source of love:
that there is no problem that enough love cannot solve;
that there is no spiritual disturbance that cannot be healed by love;
that there is no alienation that enough love cannot overcome;
that there is no misunderstanding that enough love cannot resolve;
that there is no wall of silence that enough love cannot break down;
that there is no trespass that enough love cannot forgive.
Holy Father, through Your grace we now know:
however hopeless the outlook may seem;
however deep the separation may be;
however shocking the transgression –
genuine godly love can resolve it all!
Teach me, loving Lord, to love as You do –
unconditionally, enduring to the end.
Refine and purify my love, even if I must go through the fire.
Let my love always burn bright and pure so that I may be
a reflection of Your godly love.
In the name of Jesus who loves His people to the end.

Amen.

Love is a force more formidable than any other.
It is invisible, it cannot be seen or measured, yet it is
powerful enough to transform you in a moment,
and offer you more joy than any material possession could.
~ BARBARA DE ANGELIS

Read

Gen. 22:1-14

"Now I know that you fear God, because you have not withheld from Me your son, your only son." (Gen. 22:12)

A study of the lives of the people of Israel in the Old Testament will reflect their fear of God. The Scriptures tell of those who tried to flee or hide from the Great Jehovah. They lived in the consciousness of His wrath. Abraham was willing to sacrifice his only son, Isaac, not out of obedience but because he feared God.

To establish that God must be revered, but also that He is essentially a God of love, God Himself, in the form of Jesus Christ, came to live on earth as an ordinary person. Through His life and sacrificial death, He brought the love of God to humankind so that their fear could be wiped out and their way could be opened to come into a new relationship of godly love with Almighty God.

> The fact that Jesus came to save us is final and irrefutable proof that God loves sinners.
>
> ~ WILLIAM BARCLAY

There are still many people who find it difficult to accept the fact that God is not only a righteous Judge who frowns upon people's wrong paths and punishes them accordingly, depending on the extent of the transgression. As a result, their spiritual lives are handicapped and stunted and their worship is motivated by fear, instead of a genuine desire to worship.

Never lose sight of the fact that, while you will be called to account for the way you have lived, Jesus Christ came to bring you the love of God and lead you into a personal relationship with Him. Live continually in His love and experience the fullness and abundance of life in Jesus, the living and loving Christ.

Holy Lord Jesus, it is in Your love that I find the fulfillment of all my hopes. Amen.

"For God so loved the world that He gave His one and only Son, that whoever believes in Him shall not perish but have eternal life." (John 3:16)

Read
John 3:16-21

If you really want to get to know someone, you have to meet the person, share conversations, and spend some time together. Some people enjoy corresponding with pen pals. If you have one, you have probably told that person a good deal about yourself and sent a photo of yourself so that he can get to know you better. If you talk to each other on the phone, you can probably recognize each other's voices. When someone you know visits nearby to where your pen pal lives, you will probably ask this person to pay your pen pal a visit or even deliver a gift from you. Throughout your correspondence your pen pal's knowledge of you will grow. You might even meet each other in person one day and come to know each other even better.

When Jesus was born in Bethlehem, God Himself came into the world. Mes-

Genuine love can be so blindingly bright that it casts a shadow across the sun.
~ CHARLES DICKENS

sages were no longer necessary. A personal relationship became possible. Jesus did not come to earth only for Peter, James and John, but for everyone – including you and me!

When Neil Armstrong landed on the moon, he left this message, "We came in peace for all of mankind." When Jesus Christ arrived on Earth, His message was, "I have come in love for the entire human race!" That made an overwhelming truth evident: God is abundant, pure, self-sacrificing love and His coming is the most important event that the world has ever experienced.

God and Father of our Lord Jesus Christ, also our Father, may the whole world hear of Your love. Amen.

Read
John 15:9-17

"Greater love has no one than this, that he lay down his life for his friends." (John 15:13)

Every year a Remembrance Day is held all over the world. People commemorate acts of bravery, heroism and self-sacrifice of those men and women who, without consideration for their own safety, have laid down their lives for others for the sake of a better world to come.

Many centuries before the institution of Remembrance Day as we know it, the lone figure of Jesus Christ signified another valiant sacrifice on the cross at Golgotha. Jesus, who gave His life for the whole of humanity, performed the greatest act of sacrificial love that we have ever known. It was a deed of bravery that overshadowed anything that humanity has witnessed. The Son of God also gave His life to make the world a better place, and a sacrifice of this kind is immeasurable in material terms.

> The cross is God's truth about us, and therefore it is the only power which can make us truthful. When we know the cross, we are no longer afraid of the truth.
> ~ DIETRICH BONHOEFFER

The only way that we can try to repay our debt to Him is to witness His coming to others and reveal the same love that was the reason why the Son of God, and other believers after Him, were compelled to make the highest sacrifice on behalf of us all.

Our hostile world also demands a certain degree of sacrifice on our side. Let your own act of remembrance be the moment that you choose to walk the same road as the Lord when the opportunity presents itself.

Living Savior, grant that I may honor You by taking the road that You have ordained for me. *Amen.*

While Jesus was in Bethany, a woman came with an alabaster jar of very expensive perfume. She broke the jar and poured the perfume on His head. (Mark 14:3)

Read
Mark 14:3-9

People have different ways of showing their love. Some will spend as much time as possible with their loved one; some will speak the language of love through poetry; some will come up with pleasant little surprises and some will shower their loved ones with many gifts.

The woman in our text for today demonstrated her love for Jesus by giving Him a particularly expensive gift. It is possible that Jesus had done something for her that has not been recorded in the Scriptures and she wanted to show her extreme gratefulness and love. Therefore, in one impulsive gesture of devotion and thankfulness, she poured out the precious oil over Him. Her conduct was in sharp contrast to the opposition Jesus was experiencing from the religious authorities. They were intent on killing Him; this woman was intent on showering Him with her love. The religious leaders should have supported and encouraged Him.

> He loved us not because we were lovable, but because He is love.
> ~ C. S. Lewis

In what way do you show your love and thankfulness to Jesus? You can do it with prayer and other religious activities; you can give your energies to a particular ministry in His kingdom; you can spend time in acts of charity – like Mother Teresa. You can tell others of your faith and aim to lead people to Jesus and a new life in Him. You can join movements that are trying to stop crime and violence. Do as much good as you can, for as many people as you can, for as long as you can. Let us do something today that will make our love for Jesus a glorious reality.

Crucified Lord Jesus, I want to prove my love for You in a specific way. Grant that Your Holy Spirit will help me to do this. Amen.

Read
Mark 10:35-45

"For even the Son of Man did not come to be served, but to serve, and to give His life as a ransom for many." (Mark 10:45)

People are often willing to pay exorbitant prices for an object that they really want to have. An affluent Iranian, whose hobby was collecting antique furniture, traveled to London to bid on a beautiful eighteenth-century French wooden table. There were many other bidders and the Iranian had to go much higher than anyone had expected. When asked if he did not think he had paid too much, he answered with a smile, "Love has no price tag!"

Jesus saw His crucifixion as the price He needed to pay to save us from the bondage of sin. In the ancient world slaves were bought and sold in the same way as ordinary goods. But a slave could be redeemed from bondage if someone was willing to pay the price, which was known as "ransom money." Some slaves accumulated savings and paid the ransom themselves. The best thing that could happen to a slave was to be set free, but unfortunately this didn't happen often as the price was simply too high.

> The cross is proof of both the immense love of God and the profound wickedness of sin.
>
> ~ JOHN MACARTHUR

Jesus ransomed you and me and He paid the highest price possible in order to achieve this. His love for us is so great that He was willing to pay for our freedom with His own life. He cherishes you in love. You mean more to Jesus than that antique French table meant to the wealthy Iranian. Therefore, repeat Paul's words to yourself, "The life I live in the body, I live by faith in the Son of God, who loved me and gave Himself for me" (Gal. 2:20). Say this over and over to yourself until the miracle of it all fills your whole life with thankfulness and joy.

Lord Jesus, let me live with thankfulness and love for You in return for the freedom that Your death has brought me. *Amen.*

He who pursues righteousness and love finds life, prosperity and honor. (Prov. 21:21)

Read
Prov. 21:21-31

When people make a success of life by being dubious and underhanded, we often doubt the old saying that says honesty is the best policy. How frequently do we find people living in luxury who have made their fortunes unethically, while some honest people of integrity seem to struggle just to make a simple living.

In spite of the modern-day emphasis on luxury, wealth and possessions, the fact remains that integrity, a clean conscience and peace of mind are valuable assets that money cannot buy.

Inevitably you will come across those people who have acquired their wealth at the expense of honesty and integrity, and they will always remain dissatisfied and unfulfilled. Motivated by greed, they are always searching for more wealth. Spurred on by a burning sense of competition, they are always looking to be one better than the opposition and even their own colleagues. They always seem to be greedily striving for more, and as a result they are never satisfied with life.

> Let it be your business to keep your mind in the presence of the Lord.
> ~ BROTHER LAWRENCE

When you follow the teachings and example of the living Christ, if you place Him first, above all else, as your most precious possession, you will experience a life of abundant spiritual wealth that far exceeds any of the riches that this world has to offer. Where does your wealth lie: in earthly luxury or in the riches of the love of Christ?

Lord Jesus, for me there is no other name above Yours. In You I find love, life and true joy. Amen.

Read
Isa. 12:1-6

Surely God is my salvation; I will trust and not be afraid.
(Isa. 12:2)

In times of great danger our human instincts compel us to focus on survival and self-preservation. Very often our minds become confused when fear takes over and we find it difficult to think clearly. It is in circumstances like these that we run the risk of being overwhelmed by the difficulties that confront us.

It is important to know that God's love is all-embracing and encompasses every facet of your life. He constantly watches over you; He is always ready to listen to your cry of distress; and He is with you at all times. When you do feel that God is far away, it could be that you have distanced yourself from Him in some way – not He from you.

In spite of anything that may happen to you, always remember that Jesus the living Christ offers you salvation. He died so that you could be saved, and He gave you His Holy Spirit to carry you through all the difficulties and distresses of life – especially those issues that you cannot resolve in your own strength.

> Though our feelings come and go, God's love for us does not.
> ~ C. S. LEWIS

When trials are staring you in the face, do not give in to the human temptation to give in because of fear. Open your heart to Jesus; He has overcome the Evil One. Put your trust in the Lord and remember, "There is no fear in love. But perfect love drives out fear" (1 John 4:18).

Holy Master, I place my complete faith in Your ability to drive out all my fear. Amen.

Rejoice greatly, O Daughter of Zion! See, your King comes to you, righteous and having salvation, gentle and riding on a donkey, on a colt, the foal of a donkey. (Zech. 9:9)

Read
Zech. 9:1-10

Many people feel we are living in a time of aggression. There is definitely sufficient evidence to support this viewpoint when we consider the international and national conflict all around us. We can take this even further when we look with concern at the competitive aggression between opponents in the business world and on the sports field. The number of incidents of road rage and aggression amongst motorists is on the increase. There is also heightened inter-personal aggression and all of this contributes to an unsatisfactory state of affairs.

> Humility is not a grace that can be acquired in a few months: it is the work of a lifetime.
> ~ FRANÇOIS FÈNELON

When Jesus entered Jerusalem on the first Palm Sunday, the people were aggressive. They were expecting the promised Messiah to arrive in the person of a great warrior who would lead them in a revolution against their Roman oppressors. Instead they saw someone riding into the city on the back of a donkey – the usual mount for a peace-loving leader of the time.

In that time the Lord Jesus' love won the battle against aggression. Through His followers He must and can achieve the same outcome in this day and age. Ask yourself: Am I contributing to His gentleness and love? Or am I on the side of senseless aggression?

Humble but exalted Savior, thank You that Your Spirit is helping me to be more and more like You. Amen.

Read
Jer. 24:1-10

"I will give them a heart to know Me, that I am the LORD. They will be My people, and I will be their God, for they will return to Me with all their heart." (Jer. 24:7)

The brain is the part of your body that deals with knowledge. It is the rational organ that absorbs data, stores information, connects the various parts of the body and makes decisions. If you need to increase your knowledge about something or someone, you simply store away the relevant information in your brain and use it whenever you need it.

Knowing God is somewhat different. You know Him with your heart. You can take in many facts and ideas about Him in your mind, but it is in your heart that you come to know Him as a Person. God promised that the exiles in Babylon would know Him in a new way after they had repented and confessed, knelt before Him in humility and sought His forgiveness. As a result of their change of heart, deep self-examination and a new yearning for God they would attain a new knowledge of Him.

> The God of the Christians is a God of love and consolation, a God who fills the soul and hearts of His own.
>
> ~ BLAISE PASCAL

If your heart is hardened, bitter, or inclined to wrongdoing, you will never come to know God. If you are judgmental, nurse grievances, or are involved in anything that is in direct opposition to the will of God, then your heart will be separated from Him and it will become impossible to know Him. You learn to know Him only when you place Him first in everything. Christ spelt it out for us, "Love the Lord your God with all your heart and with all your soul and with all your mind and with all your strength" (Mark 12:30). The question is: do you love God in this way?

Help me, Merciful Father, to love You more each day so that every day I may learn to know You better. *Amen.*

> If a wicked man turns away from all the sins he has committed and keeps all My decrees and does what is just and right, he will surely live. (Ezek. 18:21)

Read
Ezek. 18:14-23

The issue of sin and punishment has been a matter of concern over the centuries. There are those who think that evildoers should never be allowed to forget their transgressions. On the other hand, social reformers plead for forgiveness and rehabilitation. In human relationships people tend to judge and nurse grievances as a result of their reluctance to forgive and forget and this often leads to great unhappiness in the lives of both the evildoer and the victim.

The glorious miracle of our Christian faith is that, in spite of our fickle nature, our couldn't-care-less attitude and our disobedience, God still loves us with a love that is both forgiving and cleansing. It makes no difference who we are or what we have done: if we are willing to renounce our sins and take refuge in God in true repentance, He will receive us with the loving forgiveness of a Father.

> We are certain that there is forgiveness, because there is a gospel, and the very essence of the gospel lies in the proclamation of the pardon of sin.
> ~ CHARLES H. SPURGEON

Perhaps you are plagued by feelings of remorse and self-recrimination for an action that you feel particularly guilty about. Or maybe you feel hurt and condemned because of someone else's wrong actions against you.

Remind yourself once again of the extent of God's forgiving love and take refuge in Him as your Source of strength to forgive those who have hurt you. Do this and you will know the freedom of reconciliation in the Lord.

Allow me, O Holy Spirit, to live with You in the love of God. *Amen.*

Reflect God's Love

Who is a God like You, who forgives the transgression of the remnant of His inheritance? You do not stay angry forever but delight to show mercy. (Mic. 7:18)

In your circle of friends, companions and acquaintances, you perhaps know someone who always forgives, regardless of what happened; someone who never holds a grudge or remains angry; someone who always maintains a loving attitude. Can we honestly say that we possess these characteristics?

If we want to be completely honest and sincere, our answer will be "No." We are fallible and our human nature is vulnerable. Consequently we allow our dispositions, feelings and reactions to dominate our thoughts in certain circumstances.

> The hero is one who kindles a great light in the world, who sets up blazing torches in the dark streets of life for men to see by. The saint is the man who walks through the dark paths of the world, himself a light.
> ~ FELIX ADLER

In spite of our weaknesses, however, we can delight ourselves in the knowledge that our God is a God of love, a God who cares and forgives and a Father who loves us with an eternal love.

Such a love can never be paid back, but it can be paid forward through our witness and behavior, and this is our Christian duty. With the help of the Holy Spirit we must allow the love of God and the living Christ to be reflected in our lives in every circumstance, to the glory of the triune God.

My most loving Lord Jesus Christ, in whose life I see everything I fail to be, through Your grace let the light of Your love shine out of my life. Amen.

The lips of the righteous know what is fitting, but the mouth of the wicked only what is perverse. (Prov. 10:32)

Read
Prov. 10:20-32

Some people are careless in their use of words. They do not consider whether it is the right moment to say something or if they might offend or hurt someone. They always boast that they are "straight talkers" while in reality they are just downright rude. These people usually walk a lonely road and wherever possible are avoided by others.

How you present the truth is always important. Sometimes you have to speak a truth that the recipient would rather not hear. However it is expressed, it will cause pain. When this is the case you need to choose your words extremely carefully. The spirit in which you express yourself is also of great importance. People who understand the impact of words use them to help, encourage, comfort and heal others. Unpleasant things have to be said sometimes, but let them always be expressed firmly, kindly and sympathetically. This will reduce the pain that will inevitably be caused.

> The tongue is but three inches long, yet it can kill a man six feet high.
> ~ JAPANESE PROVERB

When you must speak out directly, as a Christian it is advisable to spend quiet time in the presence of the Lord beforehand and seek the leading of the Holy Spirit. By doing so you can execute your unpleasant task with grace, dignity and love. As a "righteous person" who needs to say "the right thing" in a difficult situation, you can trust in the Holy Spirit to lead you in this.

Holy Spirit of God, I humbly request that You anoint my tongue and my words when I have to speak out in truth. Amen.

Read
Prov. 24:14-22

Do not gloat when your enemy falls; when he stumbles, do not let your heart rejoice. (Prov. 24:17)

All too often, people take delight in the disasters that befall others. When someone who stands in high repute in the community makes an unfortunate mistake, some people rejoice in his embarrassment and humiliation. When an adversary or enemy suffers a setback, it brings great joy and satisfaction to his rival. How often do people nod their heads sympathetically and smile knowingly when the world of a successful person collapses like a house of cards.

The foundation of the Christian faith is love! You have been commanded by the living Christ to love God first and to love your neighbor as yourself. John puts it very clearly, "If anyone says, 'I love God,' yet hates his brother, he is a liar. For anyone who does not love his brother, whom he has seen, cannot love God, whom he has not seen" (1 John 4:20).

> Love is an act of faith, and whoever is of little faith is also of little love.
>
> ~ ERICH FROMM

It is not at all easy to love someone you don't like and for whom you have no respect. This is normally far beyond our human capabilities and the requirement is usually too much for us. It is therefore essential to submit and devote ourselves to Christ and invoke the indwelling power and influence of the Holy Spirit.

Allow Him to take control of your thoughts and emotions and lead you so that you will see all people through the eyes of Jesus and be able to love them with a Christian love. When you do this, you will find that your life will take on new meaning and as a result you will become a better person and Christian.

Holy Lord Jesus, help me to love as You love and do what You would do. Amen.

"I have loved you with an everlasting love; I have drawn you with loving-kindness." (Jer. 31:3)

Read
Jer. 31:1-9

How many young people who have been smitten by first love promise to love each other forever. A day or two later there is a small disagreement and it is all over. And soon afterwards they promise the same thing to someone else.

Conflict is one of the characteristics of romantic love, but steadfastness is the benchmark of God's love. He made a covenant on Mount Sinai concerning this. God carried on loving His people. However fickle their love for Him, He never wavered. However weak their faith in Him, His love for them never lessened.

God loves you and me in the same way. He loved your ancestors and He will love your descendants. He loved you when you were ill and when you were glowingly healthy. He loved you in the prime of your youth and He will

> The love of Christ is like an azure sky that enables you to see clearly, but you can never measure its true extent.
> ~ ROBERT MURRAY MCCHEYNE

still love you in your old age. He loves you now and He will love you when you are at death's door. And when this life is over His love will unfold in all its glory.

God will love you when the sun shines and life smiles at you. He will also love you when you bite the dust. He loves you when everyone around you does, and He will still love you when you are feeling lonely and sad. In Jesus Christ He gave expression to that eternal love in the flesh and blood of another person. God expects you to love in the same way, and the more you do, the better and more complete a person you will become. Keep a watchful eye on the quality of your love: Jesus is your example and your standard.

Lord Jesus, who is love, fill my life with Your kind of love. *Amen.*

Not Even Death ...

My heart is glad and my tongue rejoices; my body also will rest secure, because You will not abandon me to the grave. (Ps. 16:9-10)

There are three aspects of death that cause people to approach the subject with trepidation and fear. The first is physical pain and suffering. Some people die in peace, but many do not. We fear that we will be tormented by illness like many other people. Our next fear is that we will descend into a bottomless pit where there is only darkness – forever.

Our greatest fear, however, is being separated from our loved ones. The loss of these relationships is too awful to contemplate. Just the thought of the loneliness is unnerving and we cannot even think about being separated from them. They are our inspiration and warmth and make life on earth pleasant and worth living.

> Death is as the foreshadowing of life. We die that we may die no more.
> ~ HERMAN HOOKER

Christians who follow Jesus Christ do not have to fear this isolation. His resurrection from the dead reassures us that He is in control of the life hereafter. The one thing, above all else, that should dominate your thoughts when you think about death is that Jesus will be there. He will never abandon you or forsake you (see Heb. 13:5).

He will ensure that you cope with this period in your life to the best of your ability. He will accompany you through the experience of death. He will keep you safe and love you forever. He will lead you into the glory of the Kingdom of the Father, where there is only light and love and where you will be reunited with the ones you loved so much on earth – and who loved you.

Loving Lord Jesus, be with me every step of the way when it is my time to die. Amen.

Here is a boy with five small barley loaves and two small fish, but how far will they go among so many? (John 6:9)

Read
John 6:1-15

Everyone who prepares food, especially mothers, knows how to make a little go a long way. People develop this art through sheer necessity. Food is costly and every crumb must be put to good use.

The boy in our text for today had a miraculous experience. It was an amazing miracle for everyone, but for him it was a day he would remember for the rest of his life. Each time that the story was told, he most probably said, "Yes, it was my lunch that He used!" He gave what he had to Jesus. And children can be hungry and eat a great deal! Although needy in his own hunger, he nevertheless placed his bread and fish in the Lord's hands.

> God is more anxious to bestow His blessings on us than we are to receive them.
> ~ St. Augustine

Bring whatever you have and offer it to Jesus. However trifling your gift may be, give it to Jesus. Bring Him your personal gifts and allow Him to multiply them and use them to bring hope and meaning into the lives of many others. Bring your financial resources and allow Him to bless them and also the people who will be helped by your gift of love. Bring your professional skills and knowledge. Bring your abilities, your family relationships, your home, your capacity for caring, your faith, your position in the community, your day job, your leadership and influence, your intellect and your enthusiasm – however modest, humble or undeveloped they may be. Put them in the hands of the Master and you will become a fellow worker of miracles.

It is just possible that Jesus is waiting to perform a glorious miracle through you today. Are you willing to cooperate?

Holy Spirit of mercy, make my today a blessing to others. *Amen.*

Humility Is a Fruit of Love

Read

John 13:1-15

After that, He poured water into a basin and began to wash His disciples' feet, drying them with the towel that was wrapped around Him. (John 13:5)

We will never fully grasp what the atmosphere in the Upper Room must have been like on the eve of Jesus' crucifixion. There were disciples who must have irritated Him endlessly with their self-centeredness. Others were to speedily flee from Him when He needed their support most. One of them would betray Him to the authorities, opening the door to His barbaric torture and crucifixion.

Jesus knew exactly what was going to happen and He also knew how each disciple was going to react and behave. He knew that He would soon have to endure the bitter hatred of His enemies – completely alone!

It was in the tension of this moment that Jesus taught one of His greatest and most moving lessons on humility and love. He humbled Himself and performed the servile task of washing the disciples' feet. He took on the role of a domestic servant and served these fickle people – one of whom was to betray Him.

> Humility is a grace in the soul. It is indescribable wealth, a name and a gift from God.
>
> ~ JOHN CLIMACUS

There are occasions when you will feel imposed upon, hurt or wrongly judged. When this happens, you should not retaliate with revenge, but rather follow the example of the Master. As it happened in the past, so it will come about again today: Christian love and humility will be triumphant!

Help me, O Spirit of mercy, to follow the example of the Master every day and in all circumstances. Amen.

"If anyone loves Me, he will obey My teaching. My Father will love him, and We will come to him and make Our home with him." (John 14:23)

Read
John 14:15-31

Most people want the best out of life, but very few people are prepared to put their best into it. This is not because of selfish motives, but purely because they have never taken the trouble to discover what is best for them. They simply accept what life has to offer and never ask: What is the best that life can offer me, personally? Or at least: What more can life offer me?

What you see as the best for yourself is determined by the standards you set, because you will never be able to reach higher than that. If you have a low threshold of expectation, your life will be unproductive. But if you have faith, energy and concentration, you will be blessed and enriched in every way imaginable.

> Whoso loves believes the impossible.
> ~ ELIZABETH BARRETT BROWNING

Most people are satisfied with limited objectives because their intellectual horizons are limited. They reduce their goals to personal ambition and fail to realize that the Person and teachings of Jesus Christ can offer them the best of all – a relationship with God Himself!

When you experience the power of God in your life through the indwelling Christ, you attain the best that life offers. He leads those who are confused; gives strength to those who are weak; brings comfort to those who are sad; faith to the unsure; and satisfaction in everyday life. He also brings an awareness of eternal life – the perception that the story of human life is not a brief tale but an integral part of God's eternity. When you know God and His love, you have the very best.

Eternal God and Father, it is breathtaking to realize that You live in me – I give You all the glory. Amen.

Read

John 13:1-8

Having loved His own who were in the world, He now showed them the full extent of His love. (John 13:1)

It is very easy to lose your self-confidence. Sometimes everything goes well and you feel a rising of faith in what you are able to achieve. In times like these, life is a special experience. But suddenly, for no apparent reason, you begin to lose your self-confidence and start to experience a shattering feeling of incompetence. You convince yourself that you will never again be successful in anything you attempt. To add to your dejection, you start thinking that God doesn't care about you anymore, or even that He has lost faith in you.

One of the amazing truths that Scripture reveals is that, even though Jesus knew that His disciples were going to let Him down, He still continued to love them and have faith in them. Christ saw past their failures and incompetence and knew what they could become through the power and anointing of the Holy Spirit. He persevered in His love for them in spite of their weaknesses and imperfections.

> In our life there is a single color, as on an artist's palette, which provides the meaning of life and art. It is the color of love.
>
> ~ MARC CHAGALL

The principle that was laid down then, long ago, remains true and applicable today. God knows you for what you are; nothing can be hidden from Him. But He does not stop loving you and leading you on to a richer and more purposeful life. You may have lost confidence in yourself, but the living Christ still believes that you can become a channel for His love and mercy in the world around you.

Through my love for You, Lord Jesus, I grow daily in self-confidence. Amen.

"If you love Me, you will obey what I command." (John 14:15)

Christianity is presently going through a difficult time. The existence of countless sects that all claim scriptural authority; the displacement in certain regions of the world of Christian thought; the transition of a life-changing gospel into one that is socially and politically correct; the infiltration into the church of forces that aim to bring about its downfall: all these things conspire to confuse disciples who already find it difficult to know what to believe and accept.

Thank the King of the church that in the midst of all the prevailing religious confusion, there is a healthy core of believers who place the living Christ first. They may differ greatly in doctrine and their traditions may be divergent and even irreconcilable, but in their hearts there is a great love for Jesus. It is this love that constitutes the core of the true church of Christ.

> When evening comes, you will be examined in love. Learn to love as God desires to be loved and abandon your own ways of acting.
>
> ~ JOHN OF THE CROSS

Christian love should be expressed in practical ways. The term "social love" is a contradiction, because true Christian love is concerned about the lonely, the afflicted and the underprivileged. It is an attitude that is inspired by the love of Christ and distinguishes Christian ministry from purely humanitarian assistance.

If you are in the company of those who sincerely love Christ, you will find you have the ability to rise above differences and your vision will become so broad that you will be free of narrow-mindedness. You will no longer judge fellow Christians by their dogmatic statements, but by the depth and quality of their love for Christ and their fellow man.

Lord of love, let my life be under the control of the Holy Spirit and Your law of love. Amen.

October 21 | The Meaning of Love

Read
John 13:1-17

"Now that I have washed your feet, you also should wash one another's feet. I have set you an example that you should do as I have done for you." (John 13:14-15)

Throughout the period of His earthly ministry, Jesus showed people by word and deed how God expected them to live their lives. Each lesson was based on love in the highest sense of the word: love that was willing to make sacrifices to reveal its sincerity.

One of the most exceptional and touching examples of this took place on the night before Jesus' crucifixion, in the Upper Room where He and His disciples had come together for the Last Supper before the sacrifice at Golgotha. On this occasion He took on the role of a domestic servant and performed the humble task of washing the disciples' feet – including Judas, who was to betray Him just a short while later.

Love means to
love the unlovable,
or it is no virtue at all.

~ G. K. Chesterton

Certain people try to pass off this act of the Master as a sign of slavery. On the contrary, however, this humble deed is a demonstration of the gracious charity that is a very real mark of the Christian faith. It ought to be the aim and purpose of every follower of Jesus to imitate Him in this.

Learn from this what the true meaning of love is; follow the example of Jesus and, in so doing, you will be a true ambassador of Christ in a world that desperately needs to understand this kind of Christian love.

Grant, merciful Lord Jesus, that by example we will show ourselves worthy of Your love. **Amen.**

Those who passed by hurled insults at Him, saying, "Come down from the cross, if You are the Son of God!" (Matt. 27:39-40)

Read
Matt. 27:32-44

When we read the story of the first Easter Sunday in the Bible, we are inclined to leave Good Friday and the anxiety it evokes behind us as quickly as we can. We would much rather relive the ecstasy of the Resurrection. By doing this, we often lose sight of the fact that our duty as Christians is to commemorate not only our faith in the Resurrection, but also in the death of Jesus. These are the truths that the church commemorates.

Throughout the centuries, since the founding of the church of Jesus Christ, there have always been people intent on sabotaging the work of the Lord by belittling the efforts of those trying to sow the seeds of true faith. Their intention is to create doubt in the minds of those whose faith, for whatever reason, has declined and grown weak.

> No one understands the Scriptures, unless he be acquainted with the cross.
> ~ MARTIN LUTHER

Those undermining influences are still at work in the church itself. Today, just as much as any other time in the course of history, the Christian faith is under fire through the modern equivalent of passers-by in the streets around Golgotha. They still insult Jesus and shake their heads in disapproval in an effort to drive a wedge between the crucified Christ and His faithful followers.

Our duty is to show the love of God to all people. This is difficult, if not impossible, when we are acting without love. Jesus led by example. Once and for all He proved beyond doubt the triumphant power of love. Accept the challenge: Jesus trusts you to follow His example.

Holy Spirit of Truth, help me to prove that I am not afraid to confess Jesus and defend His cause by showing true love. *Amen.*

"Because of the increase of wickedness, the love of most will grow cold." (Matt. 24:12)

The world is full of nice people who call themselves Christians, but they would be just as pleasant if they called themselves something else. They have received the Christian tradition as their heritage and they accept the teachings of Jesus Christ when it is convenient to them, or when it makes no real demands upon their time. They travel through life on the periphery of faith and contribute little to the work of the Master. They rob themselves of the opportunity for true repentance, the forgiveness of sins and indwelling of the Holy Spirit, as well as the presence of Christ in their lives.

God does not acknowledge "pretend" Christians. Accepting Christ as your Savior and Redeemer entails a positive confirmation of your faith that identifies you closely with Him. It is essential in turn to put Him first in your thoughts and deeds; that you allow yourself to be formed and reformed by the gracious influence of His Holy Spirit. Without this surrender and dedication you are just pleasing yourself instead of pleasing God – and then it doesn't help to call yourself a Christian at all.

> There is no human power that can replace the power of the Spirit.
> ~ LEWI PETHRUS

The difference between a "pretend" Christian and a true Christian is that the former lacks the Spirit of Jesus but the latter possesses it. The Scriptures teach us, "No one can enter the Kingdom of God unless he is born of water and the Spirit" (John 3:5). Everyone who affirms a genuine faith in Christ and confesses it is able to experience the joy and love that comes with being a child of God.

Resurrected Lord Jesus, at my rebirth I accept You into my life so that I may have a living and sincere faith. Amen.

He took bread, gave thanks, broke it and began to give it to them. Then their eyes were opened and they recognized Him. (Luke 24:30-31)

Read
Luke 24:25-35

It is true that God comes to us at particular times. He comes to some people during a worship service or at a spiritual gathering. He has appeared to many young people at youth camps and claimed their love and service. Others have met Him during adult baptism, or when they were taking Communion.

He came to a house in Emmaus when He was invited one night to stay over. It had been a memorable day and a very long walk home. The Stranger led the men into truths they had not known before. After the long walk they were probably hungry, so He spoke the blessing and broke the bread, and suddenly they all knew: It was Jesus! It was just a simple meal. There was nothing special about the food, as they had been away for several days. But it did not matter. Jesus made Himself completely at home in their house! They came to know Him while they were enjoying a very ordinary meal.

> When Christ reveals Himself there is satisfaction in the slenderest portion, and without Christ there is emptiness in the greatest fullness.
> ~ ALEXANDER GROSSE

God can come to you at any time and at any opportunity. It does not have to be a special time. It does not even have to be a religious or spiritual occasion. God comes to touch your everyday life with His love. He comes to share everything with you: food, conversation, joy and the cross that you bear. He comes to bless your ordinary daily life with love. All you have to do is invite Him in to stay.

Lord of life and love, touch my daily life with Your presence and love. Amen.

But they rested on the Sabbath in obedience to the commandment. (Luke 23:56)

The crucifixion was over and the threat for the temple leaders had been eliminated. Jesus' body was taken down from the cross, according to the requirements of the Law, while the bodies of the other two men were left as prey for the vultures. All the formalities had been taken into consideration and now, because it was the Sabbath, the people rested according to the demands of the Law and their religious practices. God had commanded that the Sabbath should be a day of rest and in the eyes of the Jewish leaders, nothing could be permitted to break this command; not even love, empathy or mercy.

In their hypocritical approach to life, they found it permissible, however, to disregard all the other commands when they conspired against Jesus to bring about His death. Once again love, empathy and mercy were completely disregarded in their efforts to uphold the Law at the cost of the life of the very One who had come from God to reveal the true meaning of God's Word to humanity.

> If the Spirit of grace is absent, the law is present only to convict and kill.
>
> ~ St. Augustine

In your Christian walk it is critical that you do not become enslaved to form and ritual, rules and regulations, foregoing the love of Christ. While order in every area of life is essential, it must always be established in love. This is the way of our living Master and it must also be our way.

Lord Jesus, teach us the art of living in submission to love. *Amen.*

But they rested on the Sabbath in obedience to the commandment. (Luke 23:56)

Read
Luke 23:44-56

The matter had been dealt with successfully! This Jesus of Nazareth, whose ministry of love, compassion and forgiveness that was such a threat to the religious leaders was now over; He had been crucified with two common criminals. Now He was dead and His body was safely buried in a grave. Their task was complete. Their lifestyle was no longer under threat by this Man for whom love had meant a great deal more than just ritual and religious form. Now that everything was complete and they had disposed of Christ's body before the arrival of the Sabbath, these so-called religious people could rest "according to the Law."

> The man who loves because he is made free by the truth of God is the most revolutionary person on earth.
> ~ DIETRICH BONHOEFFER

Every Christian can learn an important lesson from the events that followed after the crucifixion. While there is a need for rules and regulations to ensure proper order in the affairs of the church, it should never be the case that the love of Jesus Christ is overshadowed or even eliminated altogether.

All too often the letter of the Law takes precedence over compassion, mercy and forgiveness; all too often the rigidity of church law is blindly applied, excluding any spontaneous display of the love of Christ that is so absolutely essential.

Justice should always be tempered by mercy to ensure that the mistakes of the religious leaders in the time of Jesus are never repeated. Then the love that Jesus died for will be freely available to everyone and will never again be relegated to second place in the church of Christ.

Lord Jesus, Your love is greater than the human mind can conceive. Grant that it will never be lost to us. *Amen.*

Read
Luke 23:44-56

But they rested on the Sabbath in obedience to the commandment. (Luke 23:56)

After the crucifixion, the Evil One had taken over the hearts of the people and brought about the death of the One God had sent to earth to demonstrate His love. The threat to their hypocritical way of life was silenced. They were not concerned about the blood on their hands and in their false piety they rested on the Sabbath, as the Law required.

These people, who adhered fanatically to the letter of the Law of Moses, could not (or would not) see that they had disobeyed the true Law of the love that was manifest in Jesus, the living Christ.

The Gospels offer examples of incidents where the temple leaders were critical and strongly judgmental of love, mercy, healing and forgiveness brought about in any way other than the manner in which they had interpreted the scope of the Law.

The Lord does not look so much to the grandeur of our works as to the love with which they are done.
~ TERESA OF AVILA

Christians must learn from this and ensure that nothing is ever allowed, under the guise of religious legalism, to predominate over the compassionate love of God, as demonstrated in the life and ministry of Jesus. Jesus' liberating love can also set us free from the letter of the Law and from empty religious form.

Heavenly Father, grant that nothing will ever cause me to ignore the Law of love. Amen.

> Without wood a fire goes out; without gossip a quarrel dies down. (Prov. 26:20)

Read
Prov. 26:18-28

Idle words and gossip are probably the main causes of broken relationships. In certain instances these are mean or vindictive, while in others they are just plain inconsiderate. Whatever the case may be, the end result is always painful. The damage has been done and it is almost impossible to undo.

The Scriptures warn us to be careful about what we say so that we will be able to avoid the consequent difficulty and pain of unguarded statements and assumptions. People often justify their remarks by saying they are innocent, or that they did not mean any harm, but the fact remains that we need to be extremely careful about what we say and the way we say it.

One of the best ways to hold your tongue is to obey Jesus' command to love others as He has loved us. Remember that by hurting your fellow man, you also hurt Christ. If you take His command to love seriously, you will realize that you have been called to share His attitudes in your approach to and behavior towards other people.

> God has given us two ears but one tongue, to show that we should be swift to listen, but slow to speak. God has set a double fence before the tongue, the teeth and the lips, to teach us to be wary that we offend not with our tongue.
>
> ~ THOMAS WATSON

This leaves no room for anything that can hurt or harm anyone.

Earnestly seek the help of the Holy Spirit in your efforts to conform your life to Christ. Faithfully follow the example of Jesus and become a channel of His love in all your relationships with other people.

Jesus, Source of love, grant me the grace to control my tongue by offering myself as a channel for Your love. **Amen.**

Love Has No Place for the Ego

The LORD said, "You have been concerned about this vine, though you did not tend it or make it grow. Should I not be concerned about Nineveh?" (Jonah 4:10-11)

The Holy Spirit of God is effectively at work and moves on every level of society. There are increasing numbers of people in search of a deeper knowledge of the living Christ. More people are becoming involved in prayer groups, Bible study groups and care groups. The establishment of house churches, at one time regarded as somewhat strange, is regarded as normal and essential by the general public today. People for whom the Christian faith used to mean attending a service on Sundays, are now very involved in mid-week church activities such as Bible schools, seminars, retreats and so on. All of this allows the focus to fall on the Lord Jesus Christ with greater clarity.

This kind of zeal is admirable and must definitely be encouraged. However, there is a danger to avoid if you are truly seeking a life of fulfillment in Jesus Christ. The enthusiastic Christian disciple has a tendency to feel sorry for those who are not involved in these kinds of activities. Your duty as a Christian is to go much further than compassion. Discipleship means showing the love of Jesus to all people. Your responsibility is winning souls for Jesus through the witness of your life.

> A Christians' life
> is the world's Bible.
> ~ ANONYMOUS

Draw strength from your meeting with the Master in your group context so that you can go out among other people and extend charity and mercy to them in the midst of the rush of everyday life. You need to love them right into the Kingdom of God!

Holy Lord Jesus, grant that I will never be so busy searching for You that I neglect to introduce You to others. Amen.

All the ways of the LORD are loving and faithful for those who keep the demands of His covenant. (Ps. 25:10)

Read
Ps. 25:1-11

There are a large number of people who look at the Christian faith in God with a great measure of skepticism. Some people call themselves fatalists and place their trust in their own capabilities. For them faith and trust in God's omnipotence over our lives is of little interest. They have little appreciation for the miraculous works of God's creation and His influence over the destinies of people. When something goes wrong in the life of a Christian, these people are quick to say that Christianity has little value.

No one – especially not Jesus Christ – has ever maintained that the life of a Christian is a euphoric or Utopian experience. Surrender to Christ does not mean you are immune to the hardships, difficulties and problems of life. It also doesn't bring you freedom from suffering.

Nevertheless, those who remain faithful to God are assured of God's constant presence and love in every circumstance of life. He will be with you to share in your joys and sorrows; to prevent you from struggling; or to help you when you fall. He will support you and help you along the way.

> The greatest happiness of life is the conviction that we are loved – loved for ourselves, or rather, loved in spite of ourselves.
> ~ VICTOR HUGO

If you will boldly believe and cherish the conviction in your heart that God is faithful, it will bring you peace of mind and calmness of spirit. You can rest safely in Christ's love.

Dear Lord Jesus, I thank You for Your unfailing love and care in my life. Amen.

Come and see what God has done, how awesome His works in man's behalf! (Ps. 66:5)

Our thoughts and emotions can be very inconsistent. Sudden changes of mood can make us feel happy the one moment, and down in the dumps the next. It is remarkable that in a second hope can change to despair; strength to weakness; or positive, faithful self-confidence to negativity, indecisiveness and a complete lack of trust. Our entire approach to life can be influenced by world events, personal success or a crisis – even weather conditions. Who has not been reduced to melancholy on a rainy winter's day?

Throughout your whole life and in any situation you may find yourself in, it is essential to strive to be as even-tempered and level-headed as possible, so that you can cope with the demands of everyday life. In the face of an uncertain world, you need to hold on to the kind of hope that will give you peace of mind.

We look forward to the time when the power of love will replace the love of power. Then will our world know the blessing of peace.

~ WILLIAM GLADSTONE

To achieve this, be still for a while and think about God's miraculous creation all around you. Absorb the beauty of nature, music, art, books and admire the achievements of science.

But above all – always remember God's love for you! It was very powerfully demonstrated by Jesus Christ on the cross at Golgotha. Hold on to this love and live in peace.

Loving Lord Jesus, You are pure, unconditional Love. Visit my fearful heart with Your love. Amen.

NOVEMBER

"Love the Lord your God with all your heart and
with all your soul and with all your mind.
This is the first and greatest commandment."
~ MATTHEW 22:37-38

Holy God, our loving Father, through Jesus Christ
I come before You to plead for my urgent need:
Help me to love You. Kindle my love and let it grow every day.
Thank You that Your love casts out all fear
and that You are able to draw love from my wicked heart.
Rule over my emotions, Lord, despite my disloyalty to Your love.
Purge in the fire of Your love every wrong desire in me.
You are the perfect Source of love.
Grant me the grace to love You fearlessly;
with a love that will stand the test of eternity.
I often rebel against Your love, but without it I am nothing.
God of love, have mercy on me, a poor sinner.
Grant me a new vision of Your love so that I will know
and be able to obey Your will for my life.
Open my heart and protect Your love in me.
Grant that I will live up to the full measure of Your love.
Grant that I will love through my will, my words,
my thoughts and my deeds.
Thank You that Your love has not left me alone,
but reached out to me and brought me home to Your love.
God of love, come into my life and ignite me with Your love,
so that I can love You and my fellow man the same way You do.
God of love, I pray in Your name!

Amen.

Every Christian would agree that man's spiritual health
is exactly in proportion to his love for God.
~ C. S. LEWIS

Read
1 Cor. 13:1-13

Now I will show you the most excellent way. (1 Cor. 13:1)

There is only one thing that can bind the church together in perfect unity, and that is love. After Paul said this, he continued with a song of praise and love. Our reading for today is one of the most wonderful chapters in the whole of the New Testament when we grasp its full meaning.

Paul maintains that a person can possess all the spiritual gifts mentioned in the previous chapter, but if a gift is not given in love, it is worthless. One may speak "in the tongues of men and of angels" and be as articulate as one can, but without love this is nothing more than the sound of a clanging cymbal. One may "have the gift of prophecy" and understand its deepest mysteries, but without love this means nothing. Paul's words can be compared to a modern sermon with two kinds of speakers: the prophet of doom and the pastor who is concerned about the immortal souls of the congregation and aims to draw them back to God in love.

> What does love look like? It has the hands to help others. It has the feet to hasten to the poor and needy. It has eyes to see misery and want. It has the ears to hear the sighs and sorrows of men. That is what love looks like.
>
> ~ St. Augustine

Paul goes on to say, "If I have all knowledge ... " Only the kind of knowledge that can be brought to life by an ardent love can lead people to a true knowledge of God. You may have "a faith that can move mountains", but without love, you are nothing.

There is barely any other portion of Scripture that demands as deep an examination of the Christian faith as this passage does. Let us go forward in prayerful admiration to the God of love.

Father of love, give me the grace to examine honestly the quality of my love for You and my fellow man. Amen.

Love is patient. (1 Cor. 13:4)

The Greek word *makrothumein* is used in the New Testament to mean "patience with people" and not patience with circumstances. It applies to a person who has suffered an injury and has the power to avenge, but chooses not to do so. It describes someone who is slow to anger. It is used for God Himself, and His relationships with humanity.

In our dealings with people, however vindictive or unkind they may be, we are called to practice the same patience that God exercises with us. It is true that patience is not a sign of weakness, but of strength; it is not the way of defeat, but the only road to victory.

> Patience with others is love; patience with yourself is hope; patience with God is faith.
> ~ ADEL BESTAVROS

No one treated President Abraham Lincoln with more disdain than Edwin Stanton. He called Lincoln "a vulgar, common clown". He gave him the nickname "Original Gorilla". But Lincoln did not react to this. He made Stanton his Minister of Defense because he considered him to be the best man for the job. Through all the years he treated Stanton with respect. The night that Lincoln died and his body lay in its coffin, Stanton looked at him with teary eyes, and said, "Here lies the greatest ruler of men that this world has ever known." Lincoln's patience and love had triumphed in the end.

When Jesus Christ was jeered and mocked, when a crown of thorns was placed on His head, when He hung on the cross and died in the company of criminals, the world was seeing the greatest Man who ever lived. His patience with and love for us is still unchanging today.

Thank You, Savior and Lord, that Your patience with me is never-ending because You love me. *Amen.*

Kindness and Love

Love is kind. (1 Cor. 13:4)

Origen described this kind of love as "kind-hearted to everyone". Jerome called it "the gentleness of love". There are many Christians who are good, but not kind. A little girl once prayed, "Lord Jesus, make all the bad people good and all the good people kind."

There was no man more devout than Philip II of Spain and yet he instigated the Spanish Inquisition and thought that he was serving God by torturing and murdering people of different religious persuasions.

According to Paul, there are spiritual cannibals among Christians who devour each other, "If you keep on biting and devouring each other, watch out or you will be destroyed by each other" (Gal. 5:15). Love that is not tempered by kindness is not truly love. Christ attracted people to Him not only through His love, but also through kindness – even towards tax collectors and prostitutes.

> The greatest thing a man can do for his heavenly Father is to be kind to some of His other children.
>
> ~ HENRY DRUMMOND

Most modern-day Christians would probably have chosen the side of the scribes and the church authorities, rather than support Jesus in the case of the woman caught in adultery.

Love is convincing only when it is accompanied by genuine kindness.

Kind Lord Jesus, teach me the virtue of kindness as I emulate Your way of life. Amen.

Love does not envy. (1 Cor. 13:4)

Noël Coward claims, "There are really only two types of people in the world: those who are millionaires, and those who want to be." There are also two kinds of envy. First there is the kind that covets the possessions of others, simply because of human weakness. The other kind is much more serious: people become jealous because someone else has something that they do not have. It is not so much that they want to have it, but rather that they resent the other person for having it.

Such meanness and lovelessness can hardly sink lower than this. Envy eats at the soul. It ruins your health and robs you of your peace of mind. Finally, it completely destroys you.

Chaucer, in his *Canterbury Tales*, identifies two types of envy: "People who are distressed over the goodness of others" and "people who rejoice over the sorrow of others." Envy means begrudging another person anything good. These people will do everything to undermine others, without having the faintest idea that they are actually undermining themselves at the same time.

> Love looks through a telescope; envy looks through a microscope.
> ~ JOSH BILLINGS

The Pharisees and the scribes in Jesus' time were filled with envy because the people were following Jesus and listened to Him. They would have done anything to destroy Him. They thought they had achieved their goal when they nailed Him to the cross. But love triumphed once again.

Let this be a lesson of confirmation for us – to never allow envy to prosper at the expense of love.

Humble Savior, grant that I will learn by Your example never to be envious of the good things others have. Amen.

Boastful Pride

Love does not boast, it is not proud. (1 Cor. 13:4)

The Chinese have a proverb that goes: "If you want to know how important you really are, draw a bucket of water, clench your fist, push your arm into the water and take it out again. The hole you leave behind in the water is a symbol of your greatness." There is definitely an aspect of humility in love.

Real love never blows its own horn. Loving people are filled with discretion even when they have achieved great things. It was St. Augustine who observed, "Do you wish to rise? Begin by descending. You plan a tower that will pierce the clouds? Lay first the foundation of humility." Christian humility is based on an accurate image of oneself, a vision of Christ and an understanding of God's greatness. Just as proud angels were reduced to demons, so humility can restore bad human behavior.

> Meekness is love at school, at the school of Christ.
> ~ JAMES HAMILTON

Some people give their love as if they are doing the recipient a huge favor. This makes a mockery of love, reducing it to something cold and unreal. Real love knows how to say, "I was wrong and I'm sorry." Arrogance refuses to accept the blame. Many love relationships have been wrecked on this very rock: people are too proud to admit their faults.

In the spiritual realm pride is an enemy of grace. This was amply demonstrated by Satan's rebellion against God and Judas's refusal to acknowledge his mistake in time. Judas preferred to commit suicide rather than accept the grace of his Lord. Peter, on the other hand, was able to confess, "You know that I love You!"

Pride expects and demands the love of others. Genuine love is always in awe of unconditional love.

God of the humble, grant that I may follow the example of the Master and wash the feet of others. Amen.

Love is not rude, it is not self-seeking. (1 Cor. 13:5)

Read
1 Cor. 13:1-13

There is a certain type of Christian who takes delight in being abrupt, almost brutal. There is power in this behavior, but no kindness. These people usually act grim, proper and come across as loveless. It seems as if they are scared to be friendly or kind for fear of undermining their Christianity.

John B. Lightfoot said of one of his students, "No matter where he goes, his face will always be a sermon." Christian love shows kindness that never forgets that politeness, tact and friendliness are excellent virtues. The underlying strength they reveal is gracious love and kindness.

Loving behavior is always seemly and well-mannered. Paul wrote to the Corinthians, "Everything should be done in a fitting and orderly way" (1 Cor. 14:40).

It is possible for a Christian to be strong-principled and firm, and yet be compelled by love to be kind. You will be a much better witness for Jesus Christ if you always behave in a kind way towards people.

> If kindness does not distinguish us from other people, it is not the same grace that He bestows upon His chosen ones.
> ~ CHARLES H. SPURGEON

Holy and gentle Lord Jesus, may I always be a true witness of Your love. Amen.

Love Is Not Angered

Love is not easily angered. (1 Cor. 13:5)

The Christian with real love in his heart is never impatient or bad-tempered with others, because not being able to control your temper is a sign of failure and defeat. When you become bitter and lose your temper, you lose everything: your authority, your self-respect, your respect for others, your argument, and above all, your friend.

Rudyard Kipling calls this the measure of a man: If you can keep your head when all about you are losing theirs and blaming it on you, you'll be a man. When you are treated unfairly, do not allow any room for revenge and bitterness. Christ set the example for us: on the cross He prayed for the very ones who had crucified Him.

With a calm and restrained attitude we can overcome the world. Anger and a quick temper bring about sad endings to the good relationships in our lives.

> To rule one's anger is well; to prevent it is still better.
> ~ TRYON EDWARDS

A young boy made his mother very angry. They were both enraged because they were both quick-tempered. The mother sent him to his room, saying he should pray that Jesus would take his bad temper away. She listened at the door while he prayed, "Lord Jesus, please take away my bad temper. And while You are at it, please take my mother's away too."

We are extremely offended when someone hurts our self-esteem and tend to brood over it. The result is hatred and bitter thoughts. Remaining angry with someone is just a waste of time and emotional energy.

Father of mercy, please grant me the grace not to become unnecessarily angry. Amen.

Love is not self-seeking. (1 Cor. 13:5)

Read
1 Cor. 13:1-3

There are two types of people in this world: those who only think about their rights, and those who think only of their duties; those who are always laying claim to these rights, and those who think only of their responsibilities; those who always think about what life owes them, and those who are never able to forget what they owe life. If people thought less about their rights and more about their duties, most of the world's problems would be solved.

In life there are the "takers" who grab everything they can out of life and relationships to their own selfish advantage, and never give anything back. Then, there are also the "givers" who always offer generously of their best for the enrichment and benefit of humanity. Kahlil Gibran described them as the people who are like a myrtle bush in the valley, perfuming the air without expecting anything in return.

> For a small reward, a man will hurry away on a long journey; while for eternal life, many will hardly take a single step.
> ~ THOMAS Á KEMPIS

We should be asking what we can contribute to life through love and ministry, rather than asking what we can take out of life for ourselves. The Jordan River flows through Israel. Three subsidiary streams join together and a concrete canal was constructed to channel this water. Because the water was no longer purified by filtering through the soil, deadly salts were left behind and caused the fish to die. There is no shortcut to success. When the elevator is out of order, you will have to take the stairs.

Good Master, protect me always against selfishness, through Your Holy Spirit. **Amen.**

Read
1 Cor. 13:1-13

Love keeps no record of wrongs. (1 Cor. 13:5)

Some people keep a balance sheet of wrong and right things done to them. But one of the greatest Christian virtues is learning the art of forgiveness.

Many people nurse their anger and keep it aflame, despite the fact that they are hurting themselves. Christian love teaches the important lesson of forgiving and forgetting. C. S. Lewis speaks of this as "surprised by joy!" He was always astounded by the fact that God had forgiven him.

Jesus did not just command us to forgive and forget: He Himself demonstrated this when He forgave His murderers on the cross. My love for God is demonstrated and confirmed through my love for my neighbor, "If anyone says, 'I love God,' yet hates his brother, he is a liar. For anyone who does not love his brother, whom he has seen, cannot love God, whom he has not seen" (1 John 4:20).

> We must go to Golgotha if we want to understand how much it cost to forgive us; and then remain with the One who was crucified to learn how to forgive.
>
> ~ CHARLES H. SPURGEON

One day some children were playing in the park. A young boy came down a slope on his skateboard, the picture of sheer joy. At the bottom of the hill he lost control, crashed into the sidewalk and landed head-over-heels on the grassy verge. He was not hurt but when he stood up, he was furious. He walked back to the sidewalk and kicked it with all his might. Naturally he hurt himself more and started to cry. We don't like accidents, especially when they are offensive to our self-respect. But it is a waste of our time and energy to refuse to forgive and forget.

Lord Jesus, help me to follow Your example of how to truly forgive and forget. Amen.

Love does not delight in evil but rejoices with the truth. (1 Cor. 13:6)

Read
1 Cor. 13:1-13

Wwill probably understand this verse better if we take it to mean that love finds no pleasure in anything wrong. It is not so much taking delight in doing wrong deeds, but rather the malicious pleasure that causes us to enjoy hearing about someone else's misfortunes rather than their successes. This is one of the peculiar and sinful characteristics of human nature.

We find it much easier to weep with those who are weeping than to delight in someone else's joy. It is generally so much more pleasurable for us to hear a juicy story of someone else's fall than to listen to the wonderful story of their success or victory.

Love delights itself in the truth. But this is easier said than done. There are times when we definitely do not want the truth to triumph and other times when the truth is the last thing we want to hear. Christian love has no desire to conceal the truth, because it has nothing to hide. It is grateful and happy when truth triumphs.

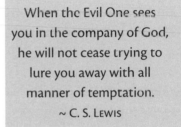

> When the Evil One sees you in the company of God, he will not cease trying to lure you away with all manner of temptation.
> ~ C. S. Lewis

"So if the Son sets you free, you will be free indeed" (John 8:36). Christian love has none of that jealous rivalry that worldly people seem to thrive on so much.

God of love, please let my love be honest and without any ulterior motives. **Amen.**

Love Endures

Love always protects. (1 Cor. 13:7)

This aspect of love shows that Christian love can cover anything. This love will never bring another's mistake out in the open. It will make an effort to quietly and without fuss make things right, rather than shout from the rooftops and denounce the culprit publicly.

The text for today also mean that Christian love can endure insults, trauma and disappointments. It describes the kind of love that was in Jesus' heart: His enemies hated, despised, and insulted Him. But He never stopped forgiving them and loving them.

In the world we live in, everyone is chasing after excitement and if someone's feelings, reputation, integrity and humanity are destroyed in the process, it doesn't really matter.

> Forgiveness forms
> the basis of the church.
> ~ JOHN CALVIN

Johan Cilliers describes it well, "Here is something to think about: Every morning you faithfully put out the garbage bag for the municipal workers to remove it. But just before the trucks arrive, you run outside, bring the bag back into the house and add it to the growing pile in your kitchen. It stinks, the neighbors are moaning, your circle of friends has noticeably grown smaller, your family are all looking for reasons to move out ... but, undisturbed, you carry on bringing the garbage in, going back on your promise ... Absurd? Yet many people do just that! Of course not literally, but in their unwillingness to forgive.

We continually rake up the misdeeds of others; we allow the trash of other people's sins to permeate our houses, our churches and our spirits. We don't want Christ's forgiveness to take away the misdeeds of others, and our own, once and for all. We would rather transform ourselves into a black bag of unforgiveness. We choose garbage over forgiveness."

God of grace and forgiveness, let Your Spirit cultivate in me the gift of forgiveness. *Amen.*

Love always trusts. (1 Cor. 13:7)

Read
1 Cor. 13:1-13

This characteristic of love has two aspects: In our relationship with God it means that love trusts in God's Word; it believes in His promises without reservation; and every promise that begins with "They who ..." becomes personal and is actually saying, "This is for me!" This love has its origin in the kind of faith that will lay its life on the line to affirm that there is a God.

In our relationships with our fellow men, Christian love always believes the best of others. It is true, however, that we judge people according to what we think they are.

When Thomas Arnold became the principal of Rugby School in England, he adopted a completely new way of doing things. Before him, terror and tyranny reigned at the school. Arnold called the boys together and explained that in future, they were going to have much more freedom and see much less of the cane. "You are free," he said, "but you are also responsible. My intention is to leave you mainly to yourselves and your honor. I believe that as long as your every move is

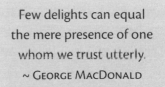

Few delights can equal the mere presence of one whom we trust utterly.
~ GEORGE MACDONALD

monitored you will grow up to know only submissive fear. When you are eventually given freedom, you won't know what to do with it."

The boys found it difficult to believe. When they were summoned to own up to their misdeeds, they still offered all the old excuses and told all the old lies. "Boys, if you say so then it must be true – I'll take your word for it," was Arnold's only response. The day dawned in Rugby School when the boys said to each other, "It's scandalous to lie to Arnold – he always believes us." Arnold believed in them and he made them what he believed they could be. Love improves individuals by believing the best of them.

Lord Jesus, make my faith in the triune God unshakeable. Amen.

Read
1 Cor. 13:1-13

Love always hopes. (1 Cor. 13:7)

Jesus Christ believes that no one is a hopeless case: He proved this in His behavior towards one of the criminals who had been crucified with Him. This is great encouragement for all sinners. Love that hopes is a virtue that surpasses all others. No situation is so hopeless that you have to give yourself over to despair. When you do this you belittle the grace of God.

Christian hope is not the same thing as "positive thinking". A Christian's hope lies in this knowledge that even in my utmost need God is still there; even in my deepest loneliness I am not alone, because the Good Shepherd is with me. Those who believe in God expect eternal hope, but those who do not believe will meet a hopeless end.

> Hope is not the conviction that everything will go well, but the certainty that it will all make sense, regardless of how things turn out.
>
> ~ VACLAV HAVEL

Adam Clarke was one of the greatest theologians of his time, but at school he was a slow learner. A respected guest once visited the school. The teacher pointed to Clarke and said, "He is the dumbest pupil in this school." Before he left, the visitor went up to Clarke and said softly to him, "You may be an important student one day, son. Don't be discouraged, just try hard and keep on trying." The teacher had no hope but the visitor was hopeful. Eternity may one day reveal what those few words of hope meant for Clarke and for the kingdom of God.

Loving Master, thank You for the hope that is aflame in my heart. Grant that it will never die. Amen.

Love never fails. (1 Cor. 13:8)

Read
1 Cor. 13:8-13

In the reading for today, Paul says three final things about Christian love: Firstly he emphasizes the importance of the permanence of love. When all the earthly things that people like to boast about have passed away, love will still endure.

In Song of Songs there is one of the most wonderful truths about love, "For love is as strong as death, its jealousy unyielding as the grave. It burns like blazing fire, like a mighty flame. Many waters cannot quench love; rivers cannot wash it away" (Song of Songs 8:6-7). The one unconquerable thing in life is love. When love comes into someone's life a relationship is established that time cannot destroy and that outlasts death.

Secondly, Paul emphasizes the absolute perfection of love. We are looking into a dim mirror. The Corinthians understood this comparison even better than we can. Corinthian mirrors were made of highly polished metal and at best gave only a dim reflection. Much of what we know about God is still a riddle and a mystery to us. Our knowledge is like that of a child. But our love will lead us to the day when the veil will be removed and we will see God face-to-face. We cannot reach that day without love, because God is love and only those who love will see God.

> We can do no great things – only small things with great love.
> ~ MOTHER TERESA

Thirdly, Paul emphasizes the absolute supremacy of love. Faith and hope are important, but love is so much greater. Faith without love is cold and heartless, and hope without love is rigid and grim. Love is the fire that ignites and kindles faith and transforms hope into certainty.

God of love, help me never to lose my focus on love.   *Amen.*

Love and Obedience

If anyone obeys His word, God's love is truly made complete in him. (1 John 2:5)

We often find it difficult to submit our will to the will of God. We want to tell God what His will should be and attempt to bring His will into line with ours. The problem is that we are too full of ourselves and our own dreams and schemes. Even though we know that we need to open ourselves up and allow God's love to fill our hearts, we still find it difficult to let go and let God do His will in our lives.

The love of God comes into our lives completely. It is not a reward for carefully obeying every command of God. It is an undeserved gift that we are not entitled to. We can try as hard as we like but we will never be worthy of it in any way. All we can do is open ourselves to His love and allow Him to take complete control of our lives. When we do this, God fills us to the brim with His love. When God's love attains its perfect purpose in us, we find ourselves able to obey His every command. Obeying Him is pure joy for His willing subjects.

> Every virtue is a form of obedience to God. Every evil word or act is a form of rebellion against Him.
> ~ STEPHEN NEILL

With His love perfected in us, we are able to love Him in return, and also our fellow man whom He sends across our paths.

We love in obedience to God's Word, not through any strength of our own, but rather in and through His love. The question is: Has His love reached its fulfillment in you?

God of love, fill me with Your love that it will be a joy to me to obey Your commands. Amen.

Whoever loves his brother lives in the light, and there is nothing in him to make him stumble. (1 John 2:10)

Read
1 John 2:1-11

In the business world there are certain products with added value. If you are willing to pay extra, you get them as a luxury. You buy an economy-class ticket on an airplane, and if you pay more, you can travel business class. For a first-class ticket you will have to dig even deeper in your pocket.

There are many people who think that the Christian faith works in a similar way. You live a respectable life, you don't do anything seriously wrong, and you go to church regularly on a Sunday. Doing a good deed for the church or for someone else is an "optional extra".

It actually doesn't work like that. Loving other people is not an extra option – it is the essence of being a Christian. Walking in the light of Christ means spreading His light across the whole world. It means loving the important people as well as the less important ones.

> Everyone really has two faces. You show one to the world and the other to the one you love.
> ~ ROBERT BROWNING

Living in the light means showing kindness not only to church members, but also to people of other religions. We should treat them politely, considerately, with dignity, and help all the weak and powerless people to feel that they are valuable to God.

It means treating troublemakers as children of God too; and dealing with them patiently and carefully, in the same way that you would relate to the "pleasant" people. When you love all people in this way, your love can reach out to "the unreachable" through them.

Lord Jesus, grant that the measure of my love for You will be evident in my love for my fellow man. Amen.

Where Does Your Love Lie?

Read
1 John 2:12-17

Do not love the world or anything in the world. If anyone loves the world, the love of the Father is not in him. (1 John 2:15)

For many people something that they enjoy doing becomes their hobby. Some may have a particular love for dogs. Others enjoy rugby. Certain people admire antique furniture; others have a passion for films, books, music or gardening. All of these pastimes are relatively harmless as long as we retain our perspective and do not allow them to take up all of our time.

When you love God "with all your heart and with all your soul and with all your mind" (Matt. 22:37), it is hard to imagine developing an obsession about the world or anything in it. But you must be on your guard. The "world" in this sense is neither the physical universe nor the world of people. It is the sum total of all the forces that conspire against the kingly authority of God.

> The wise man carries his possessions within him.
>
> ~ ANONYMOUS

It is the "sinful world" that is ruled by Satan. Greed, lust, power, pride and hate are the signs. Money in particular has the power to enslave you. Your desire for money can become so strong that it takes control of your life, your attitude and your thoughts. Then greed will rule your life. Paul wrote to Timothy about the consequences, "For the love of money is a root of all kinds of evil. Some people, eager for money, have wandered from the faith and pierced themselves with many griefs" (1 Tim. 6:10).

To resist the temptations of the world, you must fill your mind and your heart with the knowledge that God loves you. Let His love rule your heart and nothing else will ever have the power to enslave you.

Lord Jesus, through the help and leading of the Holy Spirit, I subject all my interests to Your authority. Amen.

How great is the love the Father has lavished on us, that we should be called children of God! And that is what we are! (1 John 3:1)

Read
1 John 3:1-10

Most parents love their children very much. Some smother their children with love. They go to extremes, giving their children things that they don't actually need or want. They often deny themselves the privilege of owning something so that they can provide for their children. They give these children everything that money can buy. They lavish them with love, encouragement, support and comfort. Other people complain that these parents are spoiling their children.

God, our Father, does not just love us. He showers us with His love. He does not spare Himself or do a careless job. His love is not sporadic or on-and-off, as ours so often is. It is constant, steady, wise and heartfelt. He gives us everything we need – and more! He never grows tired of loving us; He never takes the day off; He is never irritated by our childishness. He always keeps our welfare and best interests in mind.

> When I have learnt to love God better than my earthly dearest, I shall love my earthly dearest better than I do now.
>
> — C. S. LEWIS

In Jesus Christ, God provided us with an Example, a Model and a Mentor. Through Christ, God proved to us how much He loves us. God's love is personified in Jesus and goes into action through our human experience. Even when we are no longer a part of this world, He will continue to shower us with His love as if there were only one of us.

Thank You, O God of love, that I am also the subject of Your love. I pray today for those who feel that no one loves them. Amen.

We Must Love One Another

This is the message you heard from the beginning: We should love one another. (1 John 3:11)

A young disciple of Jesus Christ was called up for military service. Somewhat nervous, but deeply faithful, he knelt by the bed in prayer. Some of his conscripts were embarrassed and others openly mocked him. But he stayed on his knees, unmoved.

Close by was a man who scorned religion and made sure that everyone knew how militantly anti-Christian he was. He took off his muddy shoes and threw them across the room. One of the shoes hit the praying man on the head. Nothing further was said, but when the mocker woke up the next morning, he found his shoes at the foot of the bed, clean and brightly polished. No one asked because everyone knew who had cleaned the shoes.

Love lies at the heart of the Christian message and its way of life. In a world divided by enmity, fear and suspicion, Christians are called to be witnesses of God's love and present it to others. Today it is needed more than ever in homes devastated by addictions and unfaithfulness. It is essential in the business industry where mistrust and competitiveness are the order of the day.

> Loving others helps them to love God.
> ~ Søren Kierkegaard

From schools and colleges the cries of distress can be heard, because only honest, concerned love can build people up who are being educated.

Hospitals and nursing institutions need love, because love is the foundation of all therapy. Men, women, the elderly and the youth need it. The middle-aged yearn for it. The whole world needs it. It is Christ's medicine for an ill world. You and I can be His agents of healing. We need to love one another!

Lord, bring Your love into a world that is steeped in hate. Amen.

We know that we have passed from death to life, because we love our brothers. Anyone who does not love remains in death. (1 John 3:14)

L ove is not always easy. It does not come naturally. It is, however, natural to love your family members. Some people are easy to love, and others can be more difficult to love.

Something remarkable happened with the disciples of Jesus Christ. In order for them to follow Jesus, they were filled with the Holy Spirit at Pentecost and this brought about a remarkable change in them. Their natural feelings of fear and suspicion for certain people were replaced by a love that they knew could only have come from God.

This was especially clear in their relationships with people from other nations and cultures. Because they had been raised in the Jewish tradition, they had little love for the Gentiles. Now they longed to share the love they had received from God with the same Gentiles they had previously kept at arm's length. God's love was most compassionate and nurturing. It compelled them to care and share with the Gentiles.

> Only love enables humanity to grow, because love engenders life and it is the only form of energy that lasts forever.
> ~ MICHEL QUOIST

This brand-new adventure of love opened up an entirely new dimension in their lives. They discovered that the world was a much bigger place than they had ever known and that there were some amazing people out there. Their lives started when God's love was revealed to them and swept them off their feet. They crossed over from death to life.

Lord, help me to find Your life by loving as You have loved. *Amen.*

Love is Far-Reaching

This is how we know what love is: Jesus Christ laid down His life for us. And we ought to lay down our lives for our brothers. (1 John 3:16)

Much of our human love is a matter of "I'll love you as long as you love me". Even the love between parents and children can reach breaking point.

In the living Christ, God's love reached new heights. Before the time of Jesus, people knew that God loved them and that He required them to obey His commandments. But before Jesus came, they did not know how much God really loved them. Jesus taught the people all about God's love. In the parables of the prodigal son and the unmerciful servant, He mentioned this love. His ministry put God's love to work – the healing of diseases, the feeding of the hungry and His charity to outcasts demonstrated His Father's love.

But it was Jesus' death on the cross that proved that God's love is unlimited. In that one act of sacrifice, God declared before humanity, "This is how much I love you. However unworthy you may be, however rebelliously you have behaved, however weak and faithless you may be, I seek to save you and win your trust with this act of unrequited love. You deserve death, because your sins have alienated you from Me. But I will die in your place. Won't you repent and return to Me in love?"

> To be afraid of the adventure of love is to fear life itself. And whoever is afraid of life is already two-thirds dead.
> ~ BERTRAND RUSSELL

There is nothing sentimental or superficial about God's love. It sets the standard for our love and we must try to live up to it.

Lord Jesus, Savior also of those who are full of hate, grant me a love like Yours. Amen.

Dear children, let us not love with words or tongue but with actions and in truth. (1 John 3:18)

Read
1 John 3:18-24

François Fénelon became the Archbishop of Cambrai in 1695. People quickly realized that he cared about others and was the type of person they could approach with their problems. On one occasion, a number of farmers took refuge in his palace when they were driven out of their houses during a border war.

Fénelon noticed that one man in particular was very upset and when he asked him what the trouble was, the man said that the enemy had stolen his cow. The archbishop replied, "Don't worry, I will buy you another one." But the man could not be comforted: he wanted his own cow back. That night the archbishop and one of his servants went to the village on foot, where the man had indicated that his cow had been taken. Shortly before midnight the archbishop returned – with the man's cow! Fénelon not only preached love - he *acted* it out!

> If any man should ask me what is the first, second and third part of being a Christian, I must answer: "Action!"
> ~ THOMAS BROOKS

One sincere act of love is worth a thousand sermons. Sometimes, we can also love people by the things we say. Encouraging and comforting words can be expressions of love. Often a word of thanks or appreciation can reveal God's love.

There are times in life when words of love are all that are possible for us to give. But a good deed, such as the action of the archbishop, can provide a simple solution in difficult circumstances. Such action can put a struggling person back on his feet. When last did you act in love outside of your immediate family circle?

Merciful Lord Jesus, let my actions always be a witness of Your love. Amen.

Love: Active and Sincere

Read

1 John 3:18-24

Dear children, let us not love with words or tongue but with actions and in truth. (1 John 3:18)

An in-depth study of the life of Jesus Christ reveals one major fact – that He was always practical. Read again about the miracles that He performed – how He demonstrated God's love; how he healed people physically, in addition to the deeply spiritual aspects of His ministry. One event that particularly stands out was the time when he raised a young girl from the dead – and then advised her family to give her something to eat!

True love and concern demand much more than mere words: they call for action. They require you to perform an act as proof of your love and care – even if it is inconvenient. A visit to a patient in hospital or to an elderly person in an old-age home; a card or letter of encouragement to someone who is experiencing difficult times; a phone call to someone who is feeling lonely – these are all examples of the practical expression of God's love. It brings joy and happiness to someone's life – as well as to yours.

> The world is blessed by the people who do things, not by those who just talk.
>
> ~ JAMES OLIVER

When you show your love to others, faithfully follow the example of Jesus the living Christ, because the secret of all of your sincere and loving actions lie in His practical love.

Holy Spirit of God, help me to model myself on Jesus and love others with an active and sincere love. Amen.

This is His command: to believe in the name of His Son, Jesus Christ, and to love one another as He commanded us. (1 John 3:23)

Read
1 John 3:18-24

In the well-known comic strip series *Peanuts* he says to Charlie Brown, "The trouble with you, Charlie, is that you don't love mankind." Charlie replies, "I love mankind; it's people I can't stand!"

Many Christians find this the most difficult part of their Christian faith. It would be so much easier just to love God and serve Jesus Christ. If it were only a matter of loving humanity, that would also be manageable. But it is people who present the real problem for us. If only we could protect ourselves from the unpleasant people, the moody people, the proud and self-centered people, the small-minded people, the childish people, the jealous people, the merrymakers, the strangers, the quick-tempered, the beggars, the idle, the physically challenged and the manipulators – if only we could devote all our attention to loving God.

> When two people deeply love each other, the atmosphere is holier than in a cathedral.
> ~ WILLIAM LYON PHELPS

But God says, "Your neighbor and I are one. You can't have Me if you don't love your brother and your sister." And the problem is that your brother or sister may be among the lazy or manipulating ones. God has joined us together with all of humanity, for better or for worse. And other people find it just as difficult to love us.

Understand this: God is inside the person next to you. If you want to love Him, you will also have to love that person. You need to take the trouble daily to find out where God is hiding.

God of indescribable love, help me to love the difficult people – for Your sake. Amen.

The Origin of Love

Dear friends, let us love one another, for love comes from God. Everyone who loves has been born of God and knows God. (1 John 4:7)

It is not surprising that God's desire is for us to love one another. He Himself is love and He wants us to be just like Him. It was out of love that He gave us His only Son to be our Savior. Jesus overflowed with love and He lived a life of love until the very end. He loved people: He instructed them, cared for them, healed and befriended them. His Kingdom is a kingdom of godly love.

His call to us is not only to reach out in love to others. He wants love to be present within the fellowship of believers. He desires for all His disciples to love one another in Christ. The people of ancient times would look towards the small communities of Christians and say, "Look at their love for one another." We do not have to strive to achieve this. We have accepted that Jesus loves us unconditionally. We have invited Him into our lives and our hearts. He has entered and replaced our hate and fear with His love. In this way He is able to love through us.

> Ask nothing of God other than the gift of love, through the Holy Spirit. Of all of God's gifts there is no other as good, as worthy, as advantageous, as excellent as love. And God is both the Giver and the Gift.
>
> ~ WALTER HILTON

C. H. Dodd, director of the team who translated the *New English Bible*, said, "The energy of love discharges itself along lines which form a triangle, whose points are God, self, and neighbor." God has commanded us to love as He loves us.

I ask You, Father God, for the gift of Your love through the Holy Spirit. Amen.

This is how God showed His love among us: He sent His one and only Son into the world that we might live through Him. (1 John 4:9)

Read
1 John 4:7-21

When you were young, you were probably encouraged to acquire skills and gather knowledge to be able to make the most of life. You probably thought to yourself, "Will I be successful? Will I be happy? Will I be rich?" You simply accepted that these were the things that mattered in life.

The Christian faith suggests something completely different. Success, happiness and wealth are viewed as secondary to life's true purpose. Pursuing them for their own sake will cause you to miss out on what is really important in life: knowing God and serving Him. God's way of life is so crucial to our survival that He sent Jesus to live, suffer and die in order to open up the road to eternal life for us.

God's way of life is true living, as opposed to merely existing. His way revolves around love. Love comes from God and God loves us. This love

> He clothes us in His love, enfolds and embraces us; His tender love surrounds us completely and He will never let us go.
> ~ JULIAN OF NORWICH

is personified in Jesus Christ. We receive His love and share it with others. God's way of life is also a source of joy, worship and wonder to us. He also gives us a way of coping with the dark side of life.

To the guilty He offers forgiveness and salvation. For the sick He gives healing. In the face of suffering He gives the prospect of life after death. In the place of human weakness He gives strength and in the darkest moments of life He sheds light. God's kind of love is sheer grace and joy!

God of love, thank You that You enrich my life with Your love. *Amen.*

The Godly Initiative

This is love: not that we loved God, but that He loved us and sent His Son as an atoning sacrifice for our sins. (1 John 4:10)

We all think we know what love is. Human love is complicated – a mix of admiration, empathy, selfishness, lust, caring and sacrifice. We can experience in our relationships only a glimmer of what God's love is really like.

God's love is always far ahead of ours. He loved us before we loved Him. He loved us even before we were born. He loved our parents before us and He loved the human race long before He called us into being. The human race came into existence *because* God is love. We did not ask Him to love us – God Himself took the initiative. Every other form of love as we know it derives from His love.

Our love for Him and for one another is patterned according to His love. In spite of His great love for us, we hurt Him through disobedience, thereby alienating ourselves from Him. But His only response was to love us even more. He fulfilled His obligation to sacrifice His Son and through that sacrifice we were forgiven.

> Love is the greatest gift that God can give us: for He Himself is love. And our love is the greatest gift we can give to God, because we are giving ourselves to Him and everything we have.
>
> ~ JEREMY TAYLOR

When we accept that He has adopted us – as unworthy as we are – then His love permeates our whole lives. It saves us, heals us, restores us, motivates us and enables us to become like Him. Praise the Lord, for He is good! His love has no beginning and no end!

I thank You, O God, for taking the initiative and loving me first. Amen.

No one has ever seen God; but if we love one another, God lives in us and His love is made complete in us. (1 John 4:12)

Read
1 John 4:7-21

We so often long to be able to see God! Most religions have a physical entity that serves as a focus for the worship of its devotees. We also long to be able to see and hear Jesus and be with Him.

Perhaps this longing is just a weakness on our part. Perhaps He maintains His mystique through being invisible to us. This is how He stays God. We need to use our imaginations and be satisfied with mere glimpses of Him. Perhaps God wants us to see Him in other people.

Our text for today suggests that when we love others, it is a clear indication that God is living in us. He is well-known and can be seen in our love for other people, which makes His love clearly visible to everyone. It has often been said that the best argument for the existence of God is the life of a godly person. It is an astounding

> Nothing binds me more strongly to the Lord than my steadfast belief in His unfailing love.
> ~ CHARLES H. SPURGEON

truth: God's love can be manifest in us, and it can reach perfection if we will practice it.

Has God already begun to love through you? Have you performed a good deed, or made an effort to do someone a service? He wants *you* to manifest His love in its fullness. What an enormous challenge for all His faithful children.

Continue, Lord Jesus, and finish what You have begun in me. *Amen.*

Read
1 John 4:7-21

God is love. Whoever lives in love lives in God, and God in him. (1 John 4:16)

What is love? Someone walks around wearing a T-shirt with a slogan on the front: "I ♥ country music". The word *love* is represented by a heart. Many people claim to love their local rugby team; others love running; others love their country and are willing to die for it; people love their families and take up an entire lifetime doing this; people love their life partners, and they love the Lord.

When the Bible says, "God is love", this means so much more than just, "God loves us." Love is the core quality of His being. All His acts are acts of love. When He judges, He judges in love. When He creates, He creates in love. When He speaks, He speaks in love. When He rules, He rules in love. Everything He does, He does in love. Love is the essential expression of His nature.

> God, who is in need of nothing, brought us, completely useless creatures, into being so that He could love us and perfect us.
> ~ C. S. Lewis

God loves you! He loves you twenty-four-seven. He loves you when you are well and when you are sick. He loves you through all the good times and the bad times. He loves you in joy and in sorrow. He loves you when everyone else has let you down and betrayed you. He loves you when you deserve it and also when you don't.

Are you living in His love – and does His love live in you?

Lord my God, how can I express my gratitude to You for giving me Your love? Amen.

We love because He first loved us. (1 John 4:19)

Read
1 John 4:7-21

Sometimes couples in love jokingly say that the one loved the other one first. There is absolutely no doubt that God Himself took the initiative in the quest for love. He loved us first, in more ways than one.

His love is also the most enduring, because it is steadfast, while ours is fickle. He never slips up in His love for us. His love does not vary in its quality. He bears all our unfaithfulness and deceit. While our love hesitates and fades away, His remains constant. His love is deeper than ours. He spares no effort when it comes to loving us.

The painting of the good shepherd, who went out at night to look for the one lost sheep, is a reliable description of God's desire to save each one of us. His love is more widespread than ours. It reaches people in the depths of their sin and in the stubbornness of their refusal to respond to His love. In addition, His love surpasses ours in that no one is beyond the reach of His saving grace, no one is too evil to be restored to godliness by Him.

> God proved His love on the cross. When Christ hung, and bled, and died, it was God saying to the world, "I love you."
>
> ~ BILLY GRAHAM

Never underestimate the love of God. You can see it in its fullness in Jesus Christ, and its saving power in the lives of the people around you. Feel its impact in your own life and identity. His salvation is freely available to the entire human race. There can be no doubt that your salvation was the greatest event in your life.

Even the angels cannot describe the true depth of Your love, O God. May my life be living evidence of this. Amen.

DECEMBER

"For God so loved the world that He gave His one and only Son, that whoever believes in Him shall not perish but have eternal life."

~ JOHN 3:16

Love

Holy God of unending and undying love,
we praise and thank You for Your greatest gift of love.
This Advent month reminds us once again
of Your unfathomable love for us.
You sent Your Son to show us Your love.
Help us to proclaim Your love worldwide for everyone to hear.
We see little true Christian love these days, O Lord.
Hundreds of people die on our roads.
Rape, crime and murder are the order of the day.
People do not trust each other anymore – even within Your church.
We long to live Your love and hear Your loving voice.
But because we fail to hear Your voice, we perish.
May Christmas be celebrated everywhere on earth.
Also reveal Your love in my life and through everything I do.
Grant us by Your Spirit the strength and faith to witness for Christ;
as messengers of love and peace.
Then the child of Bethlehem will be born again into our world.
Then it will truly be Christmas!
We pray this in the name of the Prince of love and peace,
whose birth we celebrate this month.

Amen.

You will never know that Jesus is all you
need until Jesus is all you've got.
~ MOTHER TERESA

Read
2 Cor. 6:14-7:1

What harmony is there between Christ and Belial? What does a believer have in common with an unbeliever? (2 Cor. 6:15)

There are many disturbing interpretations of the Scriptures. Jesus has been equated with revolution, Marxism and permissiveness. There are those who label Jesus as a politician and others see Him as the advocate for a certain social class or race. These arguments may confuse many people who are doing their utmost to hold on to their faith in Christ in a world that militantly opposes the Christian church.

In these circumstances it is extremely important to understand that God is love, and that the full meaning of Christ's love and teachings arises out of love for God and for each other. Through the centuries Jesus' godly love has penetrated the deepest darkness and overcome the most vicious hatred that the world has ever known.

> It is not when we were reconciled to God through the blood of His Son that God first began to love us, but from before the foundation of the world.
>
> ~ JOHN CALVIN

The Master's love includes loving kindness, tenderness, understanding, tolerance and forgiveness in all circumstances. As John Wesley described it, "Godly love surpasses all other love!" If anyone tries to characterize Jesus in any terms other than love, we can be sure that they are not inspired by the Holy Spirit, but by evil forces. Their doctrines must be rejected as false and blasphemous.

Dear Lord Jesus, in the midst of disagreement and confusion, I confess that You are the personification of God's love. Amen.

To them God has chosen to make known among the Gentiles the glorious riches of this mystery, which is Christ in you, the hope of glory. (Col. 1:27)

Read
Col. 1:24-29

Many Christians think that they must be good in order for God to love them. This is clearly reflected in a mother saying to her child, "If you are naughty, God won't love you anymore." We simply accept that God delights in righteous people and that His Spirit comes into our lives to save us and make us more and more like Him. But the wonder of the Christian gospel is that God loves us even though we are sinners! Without this love we would truly be lost.

Believing in the saving love of God is much more than a theological longing or a discussion topic. It is something that humans react to intuitively. Even while we are aware of our imperfections and sin, we are aware that beyond these things, there is an Almighty God who is continually calling us to a higher and more noble way of life. We also know that we can never attain these heights in our own strength. It is often this realization of the demands that causes us to lose courage and give up striving for an honest spiritual life.

> Our nature forms us, sin deforms us, school informs us, Christ transforms us.
> ~ A. W. TOZER

When you realize your sin and your inability to live life as God requires it to be lived, it becomes absolutely essential for you to allow a willing God to transform you and anoint you with the power of the Holy Spirit, thus enabling you to follow Him and walk in His way.

Loving Master, I am deeply thankful that You have transformed my life according to God's plan and that You have given me the power to co-operate with You in this. *Amen.*

There is a song that asks the questions, "How deep is the ocean? How high is the sky?" No one can give accurate answers to these questions. Likewise, it is impossible for anyone to measure the extent of God's love for us.

But there are times when we feel lonely; when all our hopes have been shattered; when our best-laid plans go wrong and when nothing comes of our biggest dreams. When these things happen, we run the risk of sinking into self-pity, to lose all hope and fall into despair.

Never lose sight of the miracle of God's love. Study the Scriptures and see how He always cares for His people in every possible situation. Just look around you and you will see the evidence of God's grace where you work and live among His children.

> Love is the greatest gift that God can give to us, for He Himself is love; it is also the greatest gift that we can give to Him, because we are also giving ourselves to Him and everything else that we have.
>
> ~ JEREMY TAYLOR

God's endless love for you is proven by the fact that He was willing to sacrifice His own Son for your salvation! There is no greater love than that on earth. Deeper than the deepest ocean; higher than the highest sky; wider than the widest plain – that is the extent of God's love for you.

Thank You, Father God, that Your love for me through Jesus Christ is beyond human understanding. Amen.

Live a life of love, just as Christ loved us and gave Himself up for us as a fragrant offering and sacrifice to God. (Eph. 5:2)

Read
Eph. 5:1-5

There is a world of difference between sentiment and Christian love. Sentiment depends on human feelings or the mood we are in at the time. Christian love is born from the indwelling Holy Spirit who is our Source of eternal life and godly love.

Sentimental feelings vary from person to person. They fluctuate and are easily affected by time, attitudes, special occasions, music and a whole range of other influences. In contrast to this, genuine Christian love is deep-rooted and lasting because it comes from Christ who is always the same, yesterday, today, tomorrow and for eternity.

Christ's love does not depend on circumstances or people's feelings, because it has its foundation in the sacrifice that Jesus made for you and me on the cross: a sacrifice that undoubtedly proved the extent of God's love for us.

> Sentimentality is most definitely not an indication of a warm heart; nothing melts in such a flood as a block of ice.
>
> ~ Anonymous

When you open your heart to the Master and allow Him to live in you and control your life, you will experience the enormous power of Christ's love and it will shine out of you with a special radiance, bringing happiness and joy to the lives of others. In turn they will be able to share the indescribable love of God.

Most loving Source of love, let me never wander away from Your love and give myself over to sentiment. Amen.

Grace and peace to you from God our Father and the Lord Jesus Christ, who gave Himself for our sins to rescue us, according to the will of our God. (Gal. 1:3-4)

The forces of the Evil One seem to be uncontrollable worldwide. Media reports of violence, crime and other barbaric behavior confront us daily and leave people shocked. In the midst of all this trouble many people stand helpless and powerless, wondering what can be done to restore order, peace and stability.

The only way to triumph over the Evil One is to follow Jesus' example. He endured the agony of the crucifixion in obedience to God's will in order to be able to pour out His love on all of humanity.

In this day and age too many of His so-called disciples think that His way is impossible. Their call sounds that violence must be dealt with by violence. History proves, however, that this is by no means the solution. While we are not suggesting that criminals should escape justice, there is a definite need to follow Christ's example and pray in love for these oppressors and their victims.

> Most of the important things in the world have been accomplished by people who have kept on trying when there seemed to be no hope at all.
> ~ DALE CARNEGIE

Just as God transformed a tragic Good Friday into a glorious Easter, so He will transform the current violence and evil into a time when His love will triumph. For this to happen, however, requires our continued obedience to Him. It demands of you and me that we pray for the whole world through the power of Christ's love.

Father God, grant me the grace, as difficult as it may be for me, to follow the example of Jesus and act in love towards all people. Amen.

Though you have not seen Him, you love Him, for you are receiving the goal of your faith, the salvation of your souls. (1 Pet. 1:8-9)

Read
1 Pet. 1:1-9

There are many people who dismiss Christianity as a bunch of stories, while others believe in Christ, live through Him and are even willing to die for Him.

After the outpouring of the Holy Spirit in Jerusalem at Pentecost, Christianity spread through the surrounding areas and eventually reached far-away countries. Many countries adopted the religion and numerous people and cultures embraced it. In fact, one-third of humanity today follows Christ.

Nevertheless, only a handful of people saw Jesus Christ in the flesh 2,000 years ago. Others came to faith in Him by hearing the gospel, or through a personal experience of His love and power in their lives. The people that Peter addresses in today's text lived in the region now known as Turkey. They had not even met Jesus and yet Peter urged them to be willing to die for Him.

Even today Peter is calling us to believe in the living Christ, to love Him, and if necessary, to die for Him. If we do this, we will come to know Him better than many people who saw and knew Him personally. We will be able to live closer to Him, conform to His nature and model our lives according to His.

> A good example is the best sermon.
> ~ ANONYMOUS

We can be among the people through whom Jesus lives again and when others perceive His presence, more and more people will come to know Him, believe in Him and love Him passionately.

Dear God, may the presence of the living Christ be so strong in me that other people will come to know Him, love Him and believe in Him through how I live. Amen.

Read
1 Pet. 1:17-25

Now that you have purified yourselves by obeying the truth so that you have sincere love for your brothers, love one another deeply, from the heart. (1 Pet. 1:22)

It is unnatural to care about and love people we do not know. Fear and resistance are more general reactions.

When Jesus came to earth, the love of God took on human form. Jesus lived a life of pure love. When people came to know Jesus, they discovered that He loved them. His love was so strong that they could not help responding to Him. Their lives and their hearts then became filled with His indwelling love. This love of God deep within them drove out the fear and resistance they had previously felt towards others.

Then they began to act in love towards one another, not because they particularly liked each other but because the living presence of a loving God was at work in them. They came to have an attitude of love. In this way the gospel of Jesus Christ spread to the outposts of the Roman Empire 2,000 years ago.

> Even if you know the whole Bible by heart and the sayings of all the philosophers, what good will it do you without the love and grace of God?
> ~ THOMAS Á KEMPIS

The Gentiles realized that Christ loved them, because they saw the Holy Spirit at work in His disciples, and because Christians loved one another. It was not just a positive attitude, but a strong, deep, powerful and lasting love, because it originated in God Himself.

Christians today are still called to love one another. When Christ lives in you, your heart is filled with His love and you want to love your fellow Christians. Examine yourself and see how deep your love is for other believers, other faiths, other races and other age groups. Make sure that the love of Jesus is at work in your life.

Lord of love, fill my life with love for my fellow disciples. *Amen.*

Strength Lies in Love

I love You, O LORD, my strength. The LORD is my rock, my fortress and my deliverer; my God is my rock, in whom I take refuge. He is my shield. (Ps. 18:1-2)

Read
Ps. 18:1-16

If you are sensible, you will know where your strengths lie. You can find out without being arrogant or proud. Knowing your strengths is an important indication of adulthood. At the same time, it is just as important to find out what your weak points are. Individuals are not the only ones who analyze this: businesses, political parties, sports teams, cultural bodies, and even governments do it. They all work out what and where their strong points are. It has been suggested that one of the secrets of success is to play on your strengths, thereby compensating for your weaknesses – or at least hiding them from the opposition.

> The way to be strong in Christ is to be small of self.
> ~ CHARLES H. SPURGEON

The words of today's text were written by a strong and mighty man – King David. He knew that his strength did not lie in himself, but in God. Many unbelievers today believe that trusting in God is a sign of weakness. They claim that people use religion as a refuge because they need a crutch to support themselves. However, the exact opposite is true. People have faith and strength because they believe in God, because He is mighty and strong. He shares His power and His strength with us.

Paul was a strong person with a huge intellect and a powerful personality. He confessed, "I can do everything through Him who gives me strength" (Phil. 4:13). Whatever your strong points or weaknesses may be, you will be much stronger if Jesus is not only your Savior and your friend, but also your power and your strength.

Savior and mighty Lord, make me strong through Your power and Your grace. Amen.

We always thank God for all of you, mentioning you in our prayers. We continually remember before our God and Father your work produced by faith. (1 Thess. 1:2-3)

It is always a privilege for me to marry a young couple in love. A marriage always gives so much hope. But I never feel happy when I have to bring the couple back down to earth by telling them that their marriage will demand a great deal of hard work.

The love that God generates in our hearts when Jesus comes into our lives and takes possession of us is completely different from romantic love. But Christ will not allow any one of us to sit back and bask in the warmth of those amazing, but selfish, emotions. The love that Christ awakens in us should spur us on to reach out as witnesses to others who do not yet know Him. It should motivate us to care for the lonely; to be sensitive to people involved in conflict; to offer support to those who are experiencing a crisis; and to comfort those in need.

> If you don't want God's kingdom to come, don't pray for it. But if you do, it will require more than prayer alone: you must work for it.
>
> ~ JOHN RUSKIN

A retired Christian businessman became involved in a medical support group in his town. There was clearly a great need for a midwife in the area. The provincial authorities were willing to pay the salary, but the local people would have to supply the accommodation. The businessman went from door to door and collected jam tins. He sold the tins to a jam factory in a neighboring town. He did this repeatedly until there was enough money to build a house for the nurse. What a labor of love! How is the love of Jesus motivating your actions?

Lord Jesus, grant me an abundance of Your love, that I may get to work immediately for You. Amen.

Do not rebuke an older man harshly, but exhort him as if he were your father. (1 Tim. 5:1)

Read
1 Tim. 5:1-8

Times are constantly changing and over the past few decades the pace of these changes has increased phenomenally. Children have exchanged toys for computers; journeys that used to take days can now be completed in a few hours; earlier scholastic achievements are no longer meeting the standards of today's academic world; tried and trusted methods that have stood the test of time are now being cast aside as obsolete.

This state of affairs inevitably leads to frustration and irritation: Frustration on the side of older people who have grown up with the "old" methods, and irritation on the part of younger people who see these "old" methods as obstructions to progress.

If when you're young you only knew, if when you're older you still could.

~ HENRI ESTIENNE

Whether we like to admit it or not, we are living in the world of the young. Retirement age is being reached much earlier and younger people are being promoted to senior positions – often at the expense of older people.

It may be that you find yourself in a position of authority over an older colleague. You will have a better chance of winning his cooperation if you take him into your confidence, show an understanding of his position, discuss forthcoming changes with him and make him feel like a valuable part of your team.

The love of the boy Jesus won the hearts of the teachers of the Law when He spoke with them in the Temple, in spite of the differences in age. Let the love of Christ be clearly visible in all your dealings with your fellow man and work towards mutual respect and trust in this way. God's love will make it possible.

God of love, help me to realize in my dealings with older people that I, too, will be old one day. Amen.

Dynamic Love

Dear children, let us not love with words or tongue but with actions and in truth. (1 John 3:18)

It is often said, "Talk is cheap." It is sad that one of the most beautiful and meaningful words in human language is so often misused, interpreted incorrectly, or misunderstood, to the point that it has become cheap and unimportant in the eyes of so many people. The word I am talking about is "love"! It has been watered down to such an extent that its true meaning has in fact been lost.

Love must come to expression in tangible and visible ways. This may be by financial support, spiritual guidance, emotional consolation, wise advice and many other ways. All of these actions cost the giver something. It could mean spending money or giving up valuable time. True love always demands a sacrifice from the giver.

> I believe in the Scripture that is written: 'I love you as My Father has loved Me,' and we cannot conceive of a higher love.
>
> ~ CHARLES H. SPURGEON

The greatest example of sacrificial love was demonstrated at Golgotha where Jesus took on the burden of our sins and was crucified so that we could receive forgiveness and salvation. Christian love means giving of yourself for the sake of others. It is an action that pleases God. Anything else is only lip-service.

Teach me Your way, dear Lord, that You demonstrated at Golgotha, to serve others through acts of love. Amen.

Your attitude should be the same as that of Christ Jesus. (Phil. 2:5)

Read
Phil. 2:1-11

It is a sad fact that we live in a world where the attitudes and behavior of many people leave much to be desired. Corruption, scandals and violence seem to be the order of the day, and respectable, righteous people are shocked at the lowering of standards and the deterioration of behavior.

We are tempted to hide behind the normal human reaction to the situation: rendering evil for evil by exhibiting the same kind of behavior, or as we say, "fighting fire with fire".

However angry you may feel in your present circumstances – even if you have been a victim – as a Christian you cannot allow yourself to sink to the level of those workers of iniquity who currently reign supreme. It may bring you short-term satisfaction but it will never be a lasting solution for the ills of the world.

> Nothing we do, however virtuous, can be accomplished alone; therefore we are saved by love.
> ~ REINHOLD NIEBUHR

Jesus, the living Christ, has clearly shown us the only way to overcome evil: the way of Christian love! This is not, as some people claim, a sign of weakness. When we acknowledge the courage that Jesus demonstrated on the cross, no one can accuse Him of weakness.

It is the same today as it was back then: only the forgiving love of Christ can triumph over the power of the Evil One.

Holy God, on the cross we see in golden letters the words: God is love! Amen.

Read
1 Cor. 13:1-13

But the greatest of these is love. (1 Cor. 13:13)

In the back streets of London, General Booth of the Salvation Army encountered a character who did not believe in God or in goodness and who, after many skirmishes with the law, remained stubborn and reckless. But one day, after months of patient handling, Booth saw this hard man break down. "Love and kindness," the man sobbed as General Booth's love brought about his conversion.*

Booth realized that it would not help to argue with the man; preaching the Word would make no impact on him. Christ's love broke through this man's hardened soul and touched his heart.

It is most effective for a Christian to put on the armor of love. Any other action amounts to one specific aspect of love, while there are many different ways of putting love into practice. But to be clothed in God's love is the sum total of all the other Christian virtues.

What does love look like? It has the hands to help others. It has the feet to hasten to the poor and needy. It has eyes to see misery and want. It has the ears to hear the sighs and sorrows of men. That is what love looks like.

- ST. AUGUSTINE

Love is the most important because it comes from God. It is the first fruit of the Holy Spirit working in you. In this way the love of Christ becomes a reality in other people's lives. It is the indisputable evidence of the love that Christ has for His faithful followers, whether words are spoken or not.

You can act in love without speaking a word of another person's language. The one who receives your love will know and understand fully. Extending the love of God is the most important thing you can do because it is what Christ would have done in the same situation.

Lord Jesus, fill me daily with Your miraculous love. *Amen.*

---

* Griffith, A. L. *Beneath the Cross of Jesus.*

Over all these virtues put on love, which binds them all together in perfect unity. (Col. 3:14)

Read
Col. 3:5-17

Over a century ago a man by the name of Alexander Mackay went to Uganda as a missionary to bring the gospel of Jesus Christ to the people of the land. He was an extremely practical person: He built roads; constructed water pumps for times of drought; published books, tutored and preached; and translated parts of the Bible into the local language. He had a very strong influence on the life of a young man named Apolo Kivebulaya, who adopted the Christian faith as a consequence of this missionary's ministry. Apolo said of Mackay, "The moment he saw me, I could see God's love shining out of his eyes." Everything Mackay did, he did in love, reflecting the love of the Christ he had come to proclaim.

Love combines all the other gifts and characteristics of a true Christian because it is a dynamic force that comes from the heart. It motivates,

> In the time we have it is surely our duty to do all the good we can to all the people we can in all the ways we can.
>
> ~ WILLIAM BARCLAY

stimulates and coordinates all the other virtues. Without love every other action is empty and ineffectual. Whether it is the driving force behind a missionary in a strange country far from home, or a teacher of the catechism, carefully preparing a lesson, or a counselor supporting someone who is confused and depressed: love is the force at work.

This love is born when you open your heart and life to the work of the Holy Spirit of God. It cannot be made up, dreamt or invented. It must be received from God, who is the only Source of this gift. When He acts in Your life, you will never be the same again.

Gracious Lord, grant me the love that unites, gives and serves. *Amen.*

Read
Col. 2:1-5

My purpose is that they may be encouraged in heart and united in love in order that they may know the mystery of God, namely, Christ. (Col. 2:2)

If you are not growing to spiritual maturity in the way that you desire, it is probably because you are not integrated into a fellowship of believers. You cannot be a disciple of Jesus Christ all on your own. Many people make the mistake of thinking that they can.

Wherever Paul found himself, he proclaimed the gospel of Jesus. Those who came to faith and accepted Christ became members of small, tightly-knit communities. They grew in their faith together with other believers. They taught each other in groups, supported each other, prayed for each other, and took care of one another. They were joined together in a communal love for Christ. They received the love of Christ as one.

Jesus called His disciples together in a group. They did not learn only from Him but also from each other, through experiencing Christ and His love together. You cannot acquire knowledge of God in the same way that you study for an exam. You do not grow in your understanding of Christ by setting yourself apart and trying to achieve things individually.

> Love is not who you are, but who you can become.
> ~ MIGUEL DE CERVANTES

You grow when you give and receive love in a community of believers. In a social context such as this you come to know and understand God better.

If you are not already a member of a Christian group, make sure that you join one as soon as you can, not just to receive, but also to give. You will be amazed at how much you will learn and how quickly you will grow spiritually.

Savior and Redeemer, I ask that You increase my capacity for love and understanding. Amen.

He also told us of your love in the Spirit. (Col. 1:8)

Read
Col. 1:1-8

Selfishness makes Christianity a heavy burden; love makes it sheer joy. Love is the primary ingredient of the Christian life. It is a fact that all the great believers were known for their love. Love is something that is easy to talk about, however, but difficult to put into practice. We are selfish, proud and greedy by nature. But love requires us to be unselfish, humble and generous.

How can we become loving and friendly instead of selfish and hostile? It is not easy; nor does it come through self-discipline – it cannot be artificially awakened. We begin to love in a Christian way when the Holy Spirit comes into our lives. Much has been said about the Holy Spirit empowering Christians with spiritual gifts, like speaking in tongues, healing and other gifts. Much less has been said and taught about the fruits of the Holy Spirit.

> One of the worst things sin did for man was to make him selfish, for selfishness cannot love.
> ~ ANDREW MURRAY

The first fruit of the Holy Spirit in your life is the desire that is awakened in you to overcome your natural selfishness and sincerely love others. When the Holy Spirit takes possession of you He ignites the love in your life – both for God and for your fellow man. This is not sentimental love; it is not a mere inner feeling of goodwill. It is God taking control of your heart and filling it with the kind of love Jesus had for His heavenly Father and for all of humanity.

God of love, fill me daily with powerful, outgoing, caring love. Amen.

As God's chosen people ... bear with each other and forgive whatever grievances you may have against one another. Forgive as the Lord forgave you. (Col. 3:12, 13)

"Your call is receiving our attention. Please be patient." At first it sounds reasonable enough. But after the third and fourth request for your patience you begin to wonder how much it is going to cost you, as you are actually paying for someone else's delay. How patient are you in circumstances like these?

There is much more to the Christian garment of patience than just waiting quietly. The original word was often translated as "suffering". The Christian actively embraces the suffering, problems and trials that come with discipleship. There are Christians who realize that bearing certain setbacks with fortitude can ultimately lead to positive gains. Jeremiah said, "The LORD is good to those whose hope is in Him, to the one who seeks Him; it is good to wait quietly for the salvation of the LORD" (Lam. 3:25-26). Those who are patient find salvation in waiting on the Lord.

Patience also means tolerating the mistakes and weaknesses of others. It deals with those who are hostile to the faith.

> Patience and perseverance have a most miraculous effect, causing difficulties to disappear and obstacles to vanish.
> ~ JOHN QUINCY ADAMS

In London a drunkard came staggering out of a pub while a minister of the Salvation Army was busy preaching on the opposite side of the street. The drunkard crossed the street and knocked the minister down with one punch. The minister stood up, dusted himself off and said to his attacker, "God bless you, brother," and carried on preaching. How much patience would you and I have had in the same situation?

Grant me, O Holy Spirit, the patience to endure until the end. *Amen.*

Over all these virtues put on love, which binds them all together in perfect unity. (Col. 3:14)

Read
Col. 3:5-17

A great musical composition would be completely spoilt if certain instruments were left out of the orchestra when the work was performed. If an author writes a novel, he must decide on a particular theme to give the book meaning. Important elements are essential in the fields of engineering and science. Leaving out any components will affect the entire outcome and turn something which could have been excellent into something awful.

The same principle holds true in life too, and in the area of personal relationships. As people we are comprised of various elements. We enjoy a variety of gifts, abilities and achievements. People differ in race, language and culture. According to our background we receive different educations and inheritances, and differ in our approaches to life.

There is, however, one characteristic that is general and available to everyone who wants to lead a Christian life – and that is love.

> Love means drawing close to another, without self-protection. In love we are vulnerable to hurt, but our faith in the power of love is greater than our fear of rejection. Naturally it hurts to love, but it hurts even more not to.
>
> ~ LARRY CRABB

No matter who you are, you can never be completely fulfilled unless you allow the love of the living God to fill your life and your being, so that it can be reflected in your way of life.

God of love, compel me to love my fellow man, whom You fervently love, as I love myself. *Amen.*

Follow the way of love (1 Cor. 14:1).

It would be interesting to know exactly how much time, effort and money has been spent on trying to find a solution to all the evil and violence in the world. International, national and private organizations have been established, and an enormous amount of money has been donated by well-meaning people in an effort to alleviate all forms of suffering.

As valuable as these attempts may seem, there is really only one solution to all these problems, and that is obedience to the command of Jesus Christ, "As I have loved you, so you must love one another" (John 13:34).

You might feel that this is an oversimplification of a complicated problem, and that it would not be possible to implement on a world scale as a practical solution to the enormous difficulties that are staring society in the face. It is, however, not only possible, but also the only way that peace and stability can be restored in a fragmented and divided world.

> Love for God is the root, love for our neighbors is the fruit of the tree of love. The one cannot exist without the other, but the former is the cause and the latter the effect.
>
> ~ WILLIAM TEMPLE

This campaign must begin with the individual – with you and me. Love must be rooted in personal relationships before it can bear fruit in the international arena. When you show Christian love to your fellow man, it inevitably spreads until the world can be restored to the perfection of God's creation.

Holy Spirit of God, teach me to love, for only then will I see God, who loves me. **Amen.**

He died for all, that those who live should no longer live for themselves but for Him who died for them and was raised again. (2 Cor. 5:15)

Read
2 Cor. 5:11-21

Self-centeredness of any kind has no place in the Christian faith. We often hear of Christian organizations, institutions and communities that are involved in many good works, but they limit these works to their own people.

Adopting an attitude like this means a complete denial of the whole purpose of the birth, life, suffering, death and resurrection of Jesus Christ – disregarding His great command that we should love one another.

As a Christian, your mission is to bring the love of Christ to all people in all circumstances. It was never God's intention that you should operate only within your intimate circle of friends, or your brotherhood. Jesus paid attention to the needs of everyone who came to Him. The Holy Spirit commands us to do the same.

> Love cannot endure indifference. It needs to be wanted. Like a lamp, it needs to be fed out of the oil of another's heart, or its flame burns low.
>
> ~ HENRY WARD BEECHER

To ensure that your witness is effective, you need to put your trust in the Master. He will give you the opportunity and the ability to serve not only those whom you know and feel comfortable with, but all people – no matter what their needs or circumstances may be.

It is your duty, because remember, Jesus died for everyone!

Merciful Lord Jesus, grant that in my service to You, I will never withhold Your love from anyone. Amen.

Read 1 Cor. 12:1-11	Now about spiritual gifts, brothers, I do not want you to be ignorant. (1 Cor. 12:1)

It is a sad fact that as a result of the ignorance, lack of education or insensitivity on the part of others, there are countless numbers of people who are not enjoying an abundant Christian life.

They have been exposed to the ministry of the Holy Spirit in such a way that they have been robbed of the joy of this experience because they feel unworthy; or that they are afraid of the mystery surrounding the Holy Spirit.

It is in large measure the result of the strong emphasis placed on the "notorious" gifts of the Holy Spirit. These include healing, miraculous powers, prophecy, speaking in tongues and their interpretation. While we praise the Lord for such gifts, it is very important to realize that these things do not take any precedence, and that the Christian who is blessed with one or more of these gifts is not entitled to special treatment over his fellow believers.

> Love is never lost.
> If reciprocated, it will flow back and soften and purify the heart.
> ~ WASHINGTON IRVING

Paul makes it very clear: the only gift that is quite easily available to any follower of Christ and supercedes all others, is the gift of love. In comparison, the other gifts can never be as effective.

Therefore, make love your top priority in your quest for these spiritual gifts. God's perfect love will drive out all your feelings of fear about the mysteries of the Holy Spirit.

Holy Spirit, come into my life like a dove and spread Your wings of tranquil love over me. Amen.

I try to please everybody in every way. For I am not seeking my own good but the good of many, so that they may be saved. (1 Cor. 10:33)

Read
1 Cor. 10:23-33

A person with strong convictions often upholds his standpoint, not because he is necessarily right, but because of his pride. It is beneath his dignity to admit when he is wrong and therefore he will defend himself even when he has doubts.

Pride should never stand in the way of honesty, otherwise you are defending lies and being untrue to yourself.

Every person has his own point of view, and to be able to understand it you must listen carefully to what is being said. While you are listening, do not stay on the defensive. You will fail to hear properly because you will just be waiting to counter with a better argument. This kind of attitude prevents opinions being clearly expressed and benefits no one.

> Engrave this upon your heart: there isn't anyone you cannot love once you heard their story.
> ~ MARY LOU KOWNACKI

If you have the interests of your fellow man at heart, you will not be as foolish as to think that you own the truth, but you will listen patiently to what others have to say. This attitude does not mean that you have weak convictions, but will rather lead you to a greater understanding and mutual respect.

What you believe is of extreme importance, but the spirit and attitude with which you uphold that belief will determine whether it is a blessing or a curse for those who live and work with you.

Holy Lord Jesus, help me to uphold my strong convictions in love. Amen.

Read
1 Cor. 13:1-13

Love never fails. But where there are prophecies, they will cease; where there are tongues, they will be stilled; where there is knowledge, it will pass away. (1 Cor. 13:8)

Everyone wants to make a success of life, but how you interpret success is of great importance. Most people think of it as attaining a goal, acquiring riches and gaining social prestige. These gains are commendable, but if they are attained at the expense of true and acceptable values, they mean absolutely nothing.

There are many people who started out in life with high ideals and a clear vision of their goals, but the unexpected pressures of life made them hard and loveless. Reliable connections were broken; families were neglected; love and joy were no longer the hallmarks of their marriage and family relationships. In their foolishness they falsely believed that they have attained success, but they failed to see that they have actually destroyed everything that made life valuable and worthwhile.

> Love is the most universal, forceful and mystical of all the cosmic powers.
>
> ~ PIERRE TEILHARD DE CHARDIN

Whatever the success you attain in life, if it comes at the expense of love, overlooking true beauty and splendor and a lack of respect for the indwelling presence of God, you have failed.

If you have exchanged these priceless treasures for the surface glitter of worldly success and never learnt to love, you have failed miserably.

Attempting to replace the glory of the living Christ with worldly values can never bring true satisfaction. Success at the expense of love equals failure. Godly love never disappoints.

Eternal God, grant me lasting values so that my prosperity will be founded on Your love. Amen.

I ask then: Did God reject His people? By no means!
(Rom. 11:1)

Read
Rom. 11:1-10

Whenever a tragedy strikes, there is always someone who says that it is the direct consequence of God punishing and abandoning those involved. There are many people, ironically enough even those who profess not to believe in God, who are only too eager to blame the Lord for every tragedy that happens.

You only have to look back on the history of the world to discover how wrong this theory really is. Over the centuries people and nations have experienced many tragedies and went through the most dreadful trials imaginable. Barbaric violence and cruelty were responsible for the loss of many lives. Nations have been subjected to oppression and injustice; people have endured bankruptcy; and the lowering of moral standards has been the order of the day. The list of

> I am nothing,
> I have nothing, I covet
> nothing but One.
> ~ WALTER HILTON

tragedies is endless – but the world still exists. And in spite of their own foolishness, people are still living on earth.

If God had indeed rejected His people, the whole world and everything in it would have been completely destroyed a long time ago. But would God, who loves us so much that He sent His only Son to die for us, take such a drastic step?

Christ loves us just as sincerely and eternally today as He did when He walked the earth as a Man. Accept this invaluable truth and live in peace with Jesus Christ, in His love.

Lord Jesus, I come to You trustingly in the knowledge that You will always love and care for me. *Amen.*

God's Gift of Love

Thanks be to God for His indescribable gift! (2 Cor. 9:15)

Christmas! The feast of love! A most blessed Christmas to you and all your loved ones. May Jesus be born once again in your heart today.

You probably know the feeling of searching for the perfect gift for a loved one or friend, only to discover that the price is much too steep to afford. If you then buy something else, you feel that it is a poor replacement for what you really wanted to give. However, it could turn out that the replacement gift is greatly appreciated – perhaps even more so than the one you originally wanted to buy!

The Bible says that God's gift is *indescribable*! Who would dare to put a price on the life of a human being? It is just so ironic that Judas and the religious authorities agreed on thirty pieces of silver for Jesus' life. Even so, a poor woman used up all her savings, paying the equivalent of a year's wages to buy a flask of nard oil to pour out over Jesus.

> Bethlehem and Golgotha, the crib and the cross, the birth and the death of Jesus, must always be viewed together.
>
> ~ J. Sidlow Baxter

God's love for you is so great that He poured out the gift of Jesus Christ for you: a gift of inestimable value and therefore, inexpressibly valuable. He did not do this to buy you, but to save you.

Some gifts enrich the receiver. They offer the means for new endeavors; insight into new fields of knowledge; or a new awareness of how valuable they are. God's gift tells you that you are the most loved human being in the entire universe. This is the true message of Christmas!

Most generous God, teach me by Your Spirit the inestimable value of every gift You give me, especially the indescribable gift of Jesus. *Amen.*

I was young and now I am old, yet I have never seen the righteous forsaken or their children begging bread. (Ps. 37:25)

Read
Ps. 37:16-26

People are often in doubt as to the actual extent of God's love. This is especially true when people are going through difficult times or experiencing adversity. When tragedy strikes, God's love is often questioned. This kind of attitude can easily lead to a situation where our spiritual lives are damaged, doubt fills our minds and the measure of God's love no longer seems reliable.

In such circumstances you will need to draw on all the reserves of your faith that you have in order to establish firmly in your mind that God really does love you. If this were not the case, would Jesus still have died in your place? Study the Scriptures and read about those people who never failed to experience the saving and supporting grace of the God of love – even in the midst of disasters and adversity.

> God gives us His all;
> and His love is palpable –
> a branding of the soul –
> it inspires us to the point
> where we forget ourselves.
> ~ BROTHER RODGER

Spend as much time as you can in the presence of the living Christ and feel His strengthening power start to flow through your entire being, driving out all doubt and fear and replacing them with the trust and assurance that can only be part of a life based on faith, hope, and love for Jesus Christ.

Firmly believe in the all-embracing love of God and you will triumph with Christ.

Thank You, Father God, that You will never leave me nor forsake me. Amen.

Read

Jude 17-25

Keep yourselves in God's love as you wait for the mercy of our Lord Jesus Christ to bring you to eternal life. (Jude 21)

In spite of the fact that the merciful promises of eternal life are Christians' perpetual focus, the death of a loved one is always a shock and leaves a painful emptiness. Although we are able to rejoice in the knowledge that all believers will receive the glorious kingdom of God as their reward, we still wonder what to do with the emptiness and the loneliness in our hearts.

When our Lord Jesus Christ prepared His disciples for His return to the Father, He promised them His peace, and also that He would pour out His Holy Spirit on them so that the all-embracing love of God could fill their lives on earth until Jesus would return for them to join Him in the kingdom of God.

This same peace and love are Christ's gift to you. Trust Him, believe in Him and open your life to Him. Allow Him to guide you in serving in His kingdom on earth; offer your love and compassion to all who cross your path, so that the living Christ in you will be able to work to the advantage of all His children.

> God doesn't love us because we are valuable; we have great value because God loves us.
>
> ~ MARTIN LUTHER

In so doing you will always remain under the protection of the comforting love of God. He will guide you through all the disappointments of this life until you see His glory in the eternal life He has prepared for you.

Loving Lord Jesus, thank You that You never leave me; Your love brings me great peace of mind. **Amen.**

Have you ever stopped to marvel at the miracle of nature that takes place every single day? The gigantic ball of matter that we call earth turns on its axis at a fixed speed every 24 hours. The much larger, burning ball we call the sun, gives off the heat that warms the surface of the earth and radiates just enough light for the human eye to see and the body to function. This all takes place in a predictable form that we humans are able to measure, anticipate and plan for. And every person's life on this planet passes in the time span known as a day.

In a certain sense the rising sun is a manifestation of God's unfailing love. God, who planned and created everything to work with exact precision, expresses His love in His physical Creation. Every new day is a new act of God's love. But His love does not end there. It moves forward and leads the events of history, calling and blessing His people. He is full of love and cares for every individual.

> There is no promise that life won't rain on your parade, but there is a promise that there will be a rainbow afterwards.
> ~ ANONYMOUS

His eternal love is new every morning! It was there yesterday, and also every day before that. It will be there tomorrow and every day after that. It is unchanging, rhythmic and eternal. The message that each new day brings is this, "I love you! I will never stop loving you! I will remain faithful until the end of time!"

Thank You, Father, that in spite of the fact that my emotions change, Your love is always the same. Amen.

Read
Ps. 13:1-6

I trust in Your unfailing love; my heart rejoices in Your salvation. (Ps. 13:5)

We all need something to hold on to when we are faced with life's pressures: a refuge where we can gather strength by remembering all the people who love us and care about us. Some of us look beyond our present difficulties and dream of future peace. Or we keep our past successes in mind and hold on to the best in ourselves. And of course many of us also end up emotionally torn. Some of us only turn to God for help and support in our hour of need.

King David lived through many good and bad times. As a young shepherd he warded off wild animals to protect the sheep. He survived several attempts on his life by King Saul. Through every disturbing sequence of events he always remembered the one unfailing Source of strength – God's love! This carried him through the best and the worst that life threw at him. His own strength failed him. His health deteriorated. His hope faded. Friends deserted him. But the love of God never disappointed him.

> I am washed in the tide of His measureless love – it feels as if I am under the sea and I cannot touch or feel anything except the waters of His love.
>
> ~ St. Catherine of Genoa

You can also trust in God's unfailing love. However deep you may sink into the mire of sin; when adverse circumstances overwhelm you; however lost you feel – you can place your trust in the fact that God loves you! He specializes in helping people overcome crises. Christ, who tasted death, is the perfect personification of God's unfailing love. Whatever you have to go through in life, He has been there before you. He will never disappoint you or let you down. Find Him, and never let Him go!

Loving Father God, I know that I can safely hold on to Your unfailing love. Amen.

Let us fix our eyes on Jesus, the author and perfecter of our faith (Heb. 12:2).

Read
Heb. 12:1-12

In the Christian life there is both power and simplicity. Over the centuries, conflicting doctrines and strange theories concerning the person of Jesus Christ have originated. Today there are literally thousands of interpretations of who He was and what He taught. Countless numbers of people would like to know Him better but are not sure what to believe about Him.

In reality the confusion about who Jesus really is is not as serious as it appears to be, because the great majority of Christians acknowledge the authority of Christ Jesus as the Savior. If they cannot make this simple declaration of faith, they cannot be called Christians. The living Christ is the unifying factor among His followers. People of diverging theological standpoints swear their allegiance and dedication to Him. The tragedy, however, is that so many good people are unable to acknowledge that their love for Him extends beyond their religious convictions.

> Doctrine is the foundation for the Christian life. Everything about the execution of living a life pleasing to the Lord is built upon it. We can't have right living without right doctrine.
>
> ~ S. LEE HOMOKI

Loving Jesus implies that we must also love our fellow man; even those with whom we differ regularly. It is possible to maintain an attitude of love even when you are having a difference of opinion. When the Holy Spirit is at work in our lives, we have a sincere desire to be obedient to God's will and His basic command to love one another. Doctrine and any theological discussion count for nothing if we do not have love.

Grant, loving Master, that Your love will always be the focal point of my faith. Amen.

Persevering in Love

Keep on loving each other as brothers. (Heb. 13:1)

It is one thing to tackle a good business undertaking or project, but quite another to see it through until the end. It is easy to begin a course of action but not so easy to persevere when setbacks, disappointments and failure cross your path.

This applies as much to the walk of a Christian disciple as it does to anything else in life. Jesus said, "No one who puts his hand to the plow and looks back is fit for service in the kingdom of God" (Luke 9:62). We have spent this whole year focusing on faith, hope and love – now it is time to make these virtues a reality in our lives.

The writer of the letter to the Hebrews obviously knew of Christians who were motivated by love. They most likely helped the poor; supported the widows and orphans; assisted slaves in specific ways – there were many in the early church. This love calling could just as easily have been directed to ordinary Christians. They began by extending Christian love, but unfortunately lost their enthusiasm.

> It is not the going out of port, but the coming in, that determines the success of a voyage.
> ~ HENRY WARD BEECHER

Believing, hoping and loving demands perseverance and dedication. To love as Jesus loved is a long-term commitment. On-and-off love just isn't good enough. John said of Jesus, "Having loved His own who were in the world, He now showed them the full extent of His love" (John 13:1).

Let us also persevere in faith, hope and love; let us continue to love our fellow Christians – however difficult this may turn out to be and regardless of lack of response. Let us faithfully follow the example of the Master.

Beloved Master, forgive me when I give up too soon. Grant me Your grace to endure in faith, hope and, above all love – until the end. *Amen.*